Things I've Said,
but Probably Shouldn't Have

· An Unrepentant Memoir ·

BRUCE DERN

with Christopher Fryer
and Robert Crane

John Wiley & Sons, Inc.

Published by John Wiley & Sons, Inc., Hoboken, New Jersey
Published simultaneously in Canada

Photo insert credits: Courtesy Columbia Pictures: page 5 top; Courtesy Bruce Dern: pages 1, 2, 3 top, 5 bottom; Courtesy MGM: pages 3 bottom, 7 bottom; Courtesy Sony Pictures: page 8; Courtesy 20th Century-Fox Film Corp.: page 7 top; Courtesy United Artists/MGM: page 6 botom; Courtesy Universal Studios: pages 4 bottom, 6 top; Courtesy Warner Brothers: page 4 top

Wiley Bicentennial Logo: Richard J. Pacifico

Design and composition by Navta Associates, Inc.

For general information about our other products and services, please contact our Customer Care Department within the United States at (800) 762-2974, outside the United States at (317) 572-3993 or fax (317) 572-4002.

Wiley also publishes its books in a variety of electronic formats. Some content that appears in print may not be available in electronic books. For more information about Wiley products, visit our web site at www.wiley.com.

Library of Congress Cataloging-in-Publication Data:

Dern, Bruce.
 Things I've Said, but Probably Shouldn't Have: An Unrepentant Memoir / Bruce Dern with Christopher Fryer and Robert Crane.
    p. cm.
 Includes index.
 ISBN 978-0-470-10637-2 (cloth)
 1. Dern, Bruce. 2. Motion picture actors and actresses—United States—Biography. I. Fryer, Christopher. II. Crane, Robert David. III. Title.
 PN2287.D44A3 2007
 791.4302'8092—dc22
 [B]

                                                                          2006029348

Printed in the United States of America

10 9 8 7 6 5 4 3 2 1

After the journey of all the remembrances in this book, I could only dedicate it to the person by my side for well over half the trip. My dearest Andrea, without whose honesty, integrity, style, class, beauty and humor, to go with tremendous all around game, I simply would not have endured the journey—
In a word, the woman is quite simply
the Best.

To my daughter, Laura, who has been not only a constant thrill to be the parent and friend of, but her belief and encouragement in me, to always take risks and push the envelope as an actor, has made me absolutely excited to go to work every day with the chance that: We just might do something nobody has ever done before!

Contents

· 1 ·

How Does This Happen, Bruce Dern?

I never dreamed of Hollywood. I never thought of movies. The goal was just to go to New York. I saw movies, but I knew that my way, and any real actor's way, was to go through the theater. The movies were a last resort because they took another skill I hadn't developed yet, which is working in front of a camera. I didn't understand how to do that. But I understood the proscenium. I understood a live audience, communicating in front of people. So I was good enough to go to New York. I would get on the Trailways bus from Philadelphia, where I was living at the time, to New York Tuesday morning and make the rounds Tuesday and Wednesday. The A to M agencies on Tuesday and the N to Z agencies on Wednesday. I had a picture with four different Brucies on it and a bunch of horseshit on the back, which was my résumé. It consisted of scenes that I'd done in class and *Waiting for Godot*. I would leave that picture. The girls trashed it as soon as I left. Maybe some of them kept it, but I doubt it.

The next Tuesday I'd go back to the exact same offices and I'd keep doing it and doing it and doing it, because to me they were intervals, like running track. You just keep repeating, repeating, repeating, and one day you'll get good enough; you'll hit a good race on the right day, and in the half mile you'll start your kick at exactly the right time and be able to sustain it all the way through to the finish. Once I was in New York, I did that May, June, July, August. In September of 1958 I went into the office of Cheryl Crawford, who was one of the three founding members of the Actors Studio, along with Kazan and Strasberg. Cheryl Crawford was a woman who dressed and behaved like a man, but she was fabulous to me. During that summer I realized I had two goals: one was to work for Mr. Kazan and the other was to be a member of the Actors Studio. So Cheryl Crawford's was always the most important place that I stopped at. She had a secretary named Jo who was never particularly fond of me one way or the other.

The very first visit, I said, "Don't trash my résumé, please."

And Jo the secretary said, "Why not?"

I said, "Because I can act."

"Really?"

"Yeah."

"I'll tell Miss Crawford that."

"Tell her I passed my first audition."

"Who judged your first audition?"

I said, "Tell her Mr. Strasberg judged it."

She said, "He doesn't judge first auditions."

"Well, he judged mine. I don't know why."

"It can't have been."

"He was there."

"Okay. I'll tell her."

And then I just forgot about it. Cheryl Crawford went off for the summer. That's the trouble. In June, July, and August they've all gone to Fire Island or Bucks County or wherever the hell they go.

Marie Pierce, my first wife, and I had decided that we were going to move to Flushing, where Marie's grandmother lived. We were going to live with her because she had two bedrooms upstairs and we needed two bedrooms. I had to be in New York all the time. I couldn't keep going back and forth between New York and Philadelphia. Marie would find a job in a bank in New York.

The week after Labor Day, I walked into Cheryl's office and there's a bunch of guys sitting there. All looking exactly like me. All looking like they hadn't had a meal in a year. All looking like Irish terrorists, every last one.

Jo said, "Where the hell have you been?"*

I said, "What are you talking about?"

"Cheryl Crawford has been looking for you since the end of July."

"You told me don't come back because she'd be gone for the summer."

Jo said, "Well, the Actors Studio decided they're going to do this play, *Shadow of a Gunman*, on Broadway, and today is the last day of casting. We're casting for this small part, but it's the key, pivotal part of the play. The bomber. The guy who blows up the building and gets everybody arrested. He's the lead terrorist. It's a Sean O'Casey play, and Mrs. O'Casey is coming over for the opening and Jack Garfein is directing it."

I said, "That's the other guy who judged my audition along with Lee Strasberg. I couldn't remember his name."

"Yes, Bruce. We know all about your audition. We know all about Mr. Garfein and Mr. Strasberg. That's the reason we've been looking for you."

The other guys sitting there are looking at me like, *Who the fuck is this?*

Jo said, "Miss Crawford wants to see you right away. She had no idea where to get hold of you today."

Every one of these guys leans forward in his chair like he's going to get up and say, "Sit the fuck down. I was here before him, and I'm going in there." I see guys who have played lowlifes and junkies on *Naked City* or have been in *A Hatful of Rain*. These guys are all members of the Actors Studio. I'm not. Geoffrey Horne is there and he's

---

*In this conversation, and most of the conversations in this book, you'll notice that everyone sounds a little bit like Bruce Dern. While these represent the gist of the conversations as he recalls them, no one is claiming these are the exact words.

already co-starred in the biggest movie ever made at that point, *Bridge on the River Kwai*. He's the Canadian guy who William Holden screams at, "Kill the Japanese." Jimmy Olson is there. Arthur Storch is there, Stefan Gierasch. They're all in *Threepenny Opera* with Lotte Lenya. They're all sitting there. And I'm going in before them. I walk in the room, and there's Joel Shanker and Jack Garfein and Cheryl. Joel comes over and puts a big hug on me. Jack was famous because he was an Auschwitz death camp kid who got out at nine, went to America, and was adopted by Lee Strasberg. He was married to Carroll Baker, who was *Baby Doll* and had just starred in umpteen big movies and was the biggest movie star around at the time in her age group.

Cheryl said, "Bruce, I'm not going to ask you to read. We found you just in time. Are you available to start rehearsal on a play tomorrow?"

I said, "I've been available all my life to start rehearsal tomorrow. I'll start right now."

"No, you don't need to do that. Do you have an agent?"

I said, "Yes, Edith Van Cleve." Edith Van Cleve was a tremendously big agent at William Morris in New York. I'd never been to California, so I didn't know how big William Morris was or who they were. I knew Edith Van Cleve was big stuff.

Cheryl said, "I'll call Edith and tell her we're giving you ninety-two dollars a week for the run of the play. That's it. You'll have a dressing room that you'll share with another actor. Sign this."

I said, "Sure."

Joel Shanker looks at me and doesn't bat an eye as I sign. All of this is against the rules. Your agent's supposed to negotiate for you, but I don't know that.

Before I could get to a phone, she called Edith and said, "This is what your client accepted and I just wanted you to know that." Edith Van Cleve and Cheryl Crawford go back because they're both in their seventies at this point.

I went right from Cheryl's over to see Edith, who couldn't have hugged me more. She said, "Do you have any idea what you plugged into today? I've been handling actors fifty years. I've never had an actor plug in in one day first time out like what you plugged into today. You plugged into the Actors Studio. Their first play ever on Broadway. With

Cheryl Crawford, Lee Strasberg, and Elia Kazan putting on the play as producers, the only non-Studio member of the play is you. No one knows who you are, how you got here, and they hired you without even reading, based on an audition you did six months ago. How does this happen, Bruce Dern?"

I said, "I have no idea. I was only an hour away from not getting the part."

Edith said, "Cheryl said you made six enemies today."

I said, "I'm sure I made six thousand enemies today."

She said, "No, you just pulled it off. Joel Shanker is in love with you. He said you're so sincere. You showed someone who has been beaten."

I've never forgotten Joel Shanker picked up on that. Later on Kazan told me, "The first thing that ever drew me to you was when I had seen you run a couple of times in Madison Square Garden, and you had that air about you. Whether you won or lost, you could take losing."

We had three previews, and Cheryl didn't take it out of town. The producers didn't have the money to board actors. Since it cost no money to go to the Studio, it's all donations from other members and there's no fund-raisers. The Actors Studio had revenue then only because some of its members had gone on to be stars. The producers exhausted their coffers by putting on this play.

Physically, the Actors Studio was in the 400 block of West 44th Street, between Tenth and Eleventh Avenues, three blocks from the heart of the theater district on the West Side of Manhattan. An old church converted into a big open room with seats and a flat floor, not even a raised stage. Little folding chairs. People do the work onstage, and when it's over you sit there. The moderator asks, "What were you trying to do?" After you tell him what you were working on, he asks the other students what they thought of what they saw. He sums up what we've all said, gives his comments as to what he saw and felt about the work and the progress that the two actors are making in accordance with their careers. He suggests what they should work on in the future and states their strengths and weaknesses. The principle of the Actors Studio is that it's a hospital. What you're working on are not your strengths, but your weaknesses.

To become a member of the Actors Studio, you have two auditions no matter who you are. You audition the first time for three people who judge your audition. They're selected by Mr. Strasberg. In my day, they were selected by Mr. Strasberg, Cheryl Crawford, and Mr. Kazan. If you passed the first audition, you moved on to a final audition of which there were two a year judged by Mr. Strasberg, Miss Crawford, and Gadg*. If you passed that, you were a member of the Actors Studio. They were admitting five or six people a year. Once you're in, you're in for life and it's free.

The producers had to buy the rights to *Shadow of a Gunman* from the O'Casey estate. It was a risk because, in the 1950s, who cared about the 1919 Irish Republican Army? Lee and Gadg walked in at about eleven in the morning on our fifteenth day of rehearsal. We were still sitting at the table reading the play. In twelve nights we were opening on Broadway. The play had not been staged. We were still working on relationships. Lee watched for about five minutes, and we were sent to lunch. We came back knowing nothing.

We sat down at the table, and Lee said, "You, you, you and you, and you, you, you, and you"—and there were nine of us in the cast. "You pick up that table and get it the hell out of my sight. Bruce, I know you can run up and down stairs. Take all this stuff and get it up in the dressing room. Any of you that have to make a phone call go make it now because none of you are going home until this play is staged. And we're going to stage it today."

Bill Smithers, Jerry O'Laughlin, and Susan Strasberg—who was Lee's daughter—were the three stars.

The producers said, "This is hideous and disgraceful. We're shocked and embarrassed to you and for you. But this play's going on. It's going to open October twenty-fifth when it's supposed to open."

Lee turns to his daughter. He says, "You, girl. Over there." She stands where the door would be. "When I count to three you come through that hole." You're in a rehearsal room and there's no door there. "Tall guy, sit down on the box. Other guy . . . older guy." No names.

---

*For most of his career, friends referred to Elia Kazan as Gadg, sometimes spelled Gadge.

Lee said, "Okay, the rest of you, just crouch over there until I call for you." One by one we staged the play. It was the most magnificent afternoon I've been through in my life.

He said, "Runner guy. What's his name? Oh yeah, Bruce. I remember you from *Waiting for Godot*. You're Gordon Phillips's friend or son or something. But you run, right?"

"Well, not anymore."

He said, "Who cares? You're working for me now, right?"

"Right."

"You're Jack's guy, right?"

"Yeah."

"Well, Jack's not here now. I want you and Mr. Reed and Miss Cunningham and Stefan to go up there on the second landing. Suzy, keep talking. Do the lines of the play. You three, I want you to talk about what you read in the paper today. Suzy, speak English for Christ's sake. We're not speaking Hebrew here. Bruce, sports, talk about the Giants. Down here, up there talk."

We were carrying on dialogue because it's a tenement. The principals are in a room down here. We're in other apartments up there. Lee's creating offstage dialogue that will be at the same level as the dialogue onstage to create a tenement atmosphere for the audience. You will never see us, but you'll hear our voices throughout the entire play. The audience is always aware of the pressures around the people in the room who are planning this clandestine overthrow of the Irish government. Well, if this isn't exciting, I don't know what is. This is what I came here for.

I went over to Gadg at the first break and said, "Hey, Bud"—I've called people Bud all my life—"this is it."

He said, "It ain't it, but it's gonna get there."

I said, "I came for this."

Gadg said, "You told me last week you came here to work for me. You ain't working for me yet. You think the rabbi's the only guy who can do this? I'm from Turkey. Wait till you work for a fucking Turk. Imagine if Lee and I were to do something together."

I was so excited and turned on the very first day. That was the beginning of my life.

· 2 ·

Dinner with the Derns

Where I grew up, the houses all have names. It's not 85 Main Street, it's Craig E. Lee. Burke and Craig. Burke and Locke was our house in Glencoe, Illinois. A huge structure with all these bedrooms, and the third floor wasn't even heated because everybody relied on either coal furnaces, which we had, or heating oil, which was rationed. It was pretty grand. My bedroom had a view of Lake Michigan. The property was three acres. There's a picture of it in a historical book.

Down the street there was Andrew MacLeish's house. He was my grandfather's father who founded Carson Pirie Scott department stores. From the time I was born until I was fourteen—my great-grandmother died in 1950—we were there every Friday night until Sunday night. Our own house was two estates and four blocks away. It was Mrs. Andrew MacLeish, then Bruce MacLeish, then Jean MacLeish. Those were the three estates. So it was great-grandmother, grandfather, mother. Even though my father's name was John Dern, they were never the Dern estates. They were always the MacLeish estates.

Bruce was my grandfather. Archibald and Norman were his brothers. Archibald was a Pulitzer Prize winner and is my great-uncle, but I just call him uncle.* He went on and had a big career as a poet, playwright, Librarian of Congress, poet laureate of the United States for several years, and undersecretary of state. Norman was a big guy in Newport society. He was an artist. A writer. Kind of flaky. Bruce stayed home and ran the family business, Carson's.† They all lived to be at least 93. The mother, who owned a house, Mrs. Andrew, lived to be 100 and her husband lived to be 95. My mom only made it to 68 and my dad only made it to 55. My brother's still hanging in there, though he, my sister, and I are all in our 70s now.

Glencoe survives because a large number of wealthy Jewish people moved out of Chicago after the Second World War and started the dominance of the Jewish influence on the North Shore. Glencoe used to be old Chicago money after the fire in the 1870s. People wanted to live where that couldn't happen ever again, so they moved north. My family moved out to the suburbs in the late 1870s, 1880s.

My household was at 94 Mary Street. The houses were on the lake, and where each street ended there was an estate. The estates were next to each other, but they were on different streets. Mr. MacLeish, my mother's father, owned an estate, and the Derns were on the next street. So I grew up next to my mother's father. My father lived next to his father-in-law every day of his life, which seemed not to bother him. As a matter of fact, my parents' best friends were his in-laws. This bothered me a great deal because he seemed to sign off on that without a problem. My father was a hugely successful lawyer, very prominent. His best friend and partner was Adlai Stevenson. My grandfather, George Dern, had been FDR's secretary of war and twice the governor of Utah. One of my sister's godfathers was Edwin Austin, who founded

---

*Actually, he won three Pulitzers, two for poetry, and one for playwrighting, as well as a National Book Award and the Presidential Medal of Freedom.

†Located mostly in Chicago, Carson's was later part of Saks International, and is now part of the Bon-Ton company.

Sidley Austin, which is a law firm that they belonged to. The law firm was started originally by Robert Lincoln, who was Abraham Lincoln's brother. When Lincoln went to Washington, he and his brother split up the partnership because Lincoln couldn't be president and continue in the law firm, so they moved from Springfield to Chicago.

Jackson Burgess was another of my godfathers. He made Burgess Batteries, which looked like prison uniforms. They were black-and-white striped all during the war and after. Louise Dow was my godmother. When my grandmother MacLeish went to college, her roommate for a while was Madame Chiang Kai-Shek. That was rather impressive, although she wasn't Madame Chiang Kai-Shek then, she was just an Asian student. My grandfather's mother was a rather prominent woman in Chicago society, a very well-known educator and philanthropist who started a college for women called Rockford College.

My grandfather, Bruce, traveled around selling items with his buddies, Phil and Frank, from a pushcart on the North Side of Chicago. Bruce had wholesale dry goods and Scotch tartan plaids from Aberdeen and Glasgow. Phil had some licorice candy that he'd give to the people. Frank would sketch their homes for them. They'd go together and spend about twenty minutes in a neighborhood. Bruce and his father, with friends, had the idea for Carson, Pirie, Scott & Co. department stores. Phil ended up being Phil Wrigley, and Frank ended up being Frank Lloyd Wright. Frank moved on to Wisconsin and other places, leaving a good signature around America and the rest of the world. Phil kept us chewing for a hundred years. As for Bruce, there are still Carson's stores in Chicago, but our family is not involved anymore.

I started at South School, where I attended first through fifth grade. For sixth, seventh, and eighth grade, I went to Central School. Most of my teachers were ladies because all the men were in the war. From '41 to '50—my nine years in grade school, counting kindergarten—we had all women. They had a great influence on all the guys and girls I went to high school with because they drove us much more than men to be competitive. Men didn't challenge us in the same way. Female teachers encouraged us from kindergarten to vocalize everything. Nothing was written down. It was all about expressing yourself. We had to have two things: a rug to take your nap on and milk money because it was during the war and you didn't have as much milk at home as you should.

I went to camp every summer. In 1945 I was nine years old, and the camp was on the bottom part of Hudson Bay. Imagine sending a nine-year-old kid to a camp a thousand miles from home? For nine weeks? We took twenty-day canoe trips, three weeks at a time. I was five years younger than any other kid in the camp. The only thing they'd let me do is run on ahead to see how far it was to portage to the next lake because they knew I could run.

We'd eat supper, and if there was a moon, we'd paddle across these lakes at night. It was eerie because the lakes had half-stumps in them. One night, a light came across the lake toward us. We never saw other people. This light got real close, and we realized it was a guy in a canoe by himself. He had a red-and-black plaid Pendleton jacket on. I was in the lead canoe in the middle. As he passed our boat, we grabbed his boat, he grabbed our boat, and he just said, "The war is over." That's the most vivid memory I have in my life.

Though we were lucky as guys not to be hit with the war years, our backgrounds were shaped and formed by them. I'm not bigoted and I'm not prejudiced, but from '39 to '46, you hated the Germans. It was all Nazis. From '41 to '46, you hated the Japs. You never wanted to be the Nazi or Jap at recess. My name was Dern, and that's German.

In grade school, we ran around a lawn on a three-quarter-of-a-mile block. I finished, puked, had a drink of water, sat down, and talked for about a minute with the coach before anybody else finished. I was that much better. He was the first person to think, Wait a second, every week this kid does this and he's been doing it since the third grade. He's not the fastest kid across the football field, he was always second or third at that, but when they stretch it out and go more than 150, 200 yards, he has this ability.

There was a Fourth of July in the big park in Winnetka where Glencoe, Winnetka, and Wilmette kids all got together and ran around the block there too. I won by extraordinary proportions. In a ten-minute run I was at least a minute and a half ahead of anybody else in town that was under twenty years old. And I was ten. It had a lot to do with the fact that from nine to thirteen, I was a gifted speed skater.

My family came to speed-skating meets because a meet was the kind of event where aristocratic families could shine. They were held on frozen lakes in towns. I'm not Catholic, but I raced for the CYO (Catholic Youth Organization) because they recruited me. It's all based on the Silver Skates Program that the *Chicago Tribune* put on. I won all that stuff. I was so dominant that it was almost frightening to my parents. The whole family went in a car, and the grandparents followed, and they set up big picnic tables and sent little Brucie out to beat the shit out of all the rest of these little kids. They sat back in the warm car with the motor running, watching Bruce skate around the lake in this little green CYO uniform.

After the eighth grade at Central School, my parents felt that because I was hanging around with the wrong kind of kids, I should go to a prep school. I didn't get to go to New Trier* my first two years of high school. I was sent to Choate.

I'll never forget *Pinocchio*. Midnight comes and they load all those kids on that big carriage and take them away to the prep school where they all turn into donkeys and are hee-hawing and it's pissing down rain and the carriage master is whipping the horses in the moonlight and the boys' noses are getting long. Being sent to prep school was what that was like for me. And I did tell lies, and I knew what was going to happen. "Oh my God," Walt Disney is saying. "You little bastard. That's where you belong. And that's what's going to happen." These are things that were happening to me before I was ever an actor.

Being sent to Choate was a tremendous violation of my ability to have a normal growth, because I was being pulled away from a shrine. I'd looked forward to New Trier all my life as had every other kid who lived in one of those towns. It's one of the four powerhouse high schools in America that dominate sports and education. New Trier won four national championships in sports in 2003. That was more than any other high school so far in the twenty-first century. We won twelve in the twentieth century.

---

*New Trier High School can reasonably claim to be one of the greatest public schools in the United States. In addition to academic and sporting achievements, for a century it has produced influential graduates in all walks of life, from Rahm Emanuel and Donald Rumsfeld to Scott Turow, Liz Phair, and the band Fall Out Boy.

During the summer before I attended Choate, the school sent three books you had to read: *Moby-Dick*, *Horatio Hornblower*, and *Catcher in the Rye*. At dinnertime, I told this preposterous story that Moby Dick was a venereal disease. It was a horrible story about a disease that Scrooge had contracted that made him so awful and ugly and terrible at Christmas. I had them for about three minutes. My dad liked it because he thought, God, what kind of pills did this kid take to come up with something like that?

Instead of attending New Trier, I'm sent a thousand miles away to Connecticut. If you lived on the side of the tracks that I lived on, on the North Shore, you don't get rebellious because you don't need to be rebellious because you're given a certain kind of spoon. I accepted Choate instead of rebelling.

At Choate, I'm running 880 times that are shocking. There's no freshman track in prep school. You just have a track team. You make it or you don't. I made the track team, and our first meet was against the Wesleyan and Trinity College freshmen. At Trinity, I'm thirteen years old running against a nineteen-year-old college freshman named Lou Thorgison who is the national schoolboy champion the year before in high school. He wins the race, running 1:53.5, which is the best time any kid under twenty years old has ever run. I piddled along, but I ran with him for about 500 meters and then he ran off and left me. I ran 2:03 something, which was the fastest any kid under fourteen had ever run in a prep school.

Lou came over to me after the race and said, "Do you know what you're doing?"

I said, "I don't have a fucking clue what I'm doing. I just stayed with you as long as I could."

He said, "Can I take you over and talk to your coach?"

That was the beginning of my track career, because he told the coach that I had an amazing gift and what he should do with me. He asked the coach in front of me if he knew what he was doing.

Lou said, "You have a boy here who could be an Olympic champion in six years, in 1956, if you know what you're doing. He needs to interval train. He needs to run down the football field, jog back, and do it all day, three days a week in his workouts. Get a book by

Franz Stampfl. Read it and teach the kid how to do that, and I'll send you letters."

I'm a freshman in high school. Two years later, in 1952, Lou made the Olympic team at 800 meters. He was a tremendous influence in my career. Whatever I did was because of him.

I came back and went to New Trier for my last two years. I had a good time but not a great time in high school because I came back as a defeated candidate, so to speak. I had to rediscover, reacquaint myself, and re-friend up with friends I'd had the first twelve years of my life because they didn't accept me when I first came back. They felt I went away because I didn't like them.

The reason I became an actor was that every night at seven we had dinner. At the dinner table were my brother, Jack, who was in high school and was four years older than me; my sister, Jean, who was a year and a half younger than me; and my mother and father. In the house were five other people of the domestic variety including a couple, Florence and Charles: he was a houseman and she was the cook. A lady named Tillie was the laundress. I don't know why we went to the cleaner's twice a week. I always said, "What does Tillie do? Because she appears to be knocking down about eight bucks an hour."

My mother used to say, "Why do you keep track of everything? What does it matter what Tillie does?"

I said, "She's taking up space and she's getting paid to sleep."

She said, "Well, why does that bother you?"

"I don't get an allowance, that's why it bothers me. We have nine bedrooms upstairs that nobody uses. Why does she have to sleep down here with us? She doesn't seem very happy. None of the people seem very happy. You're so shit-faced at five o'clock every day you don't know what goes on anyway."

She said, "Well, why don't you come up to the bathroom and get your mouth washed out with soap again?"

I said, "You couldn't have enough bars stored away for my mouth."

It'd be the same thing. "Wait till your father gets home."

"He ain't going to touch me. He's going to leave it all to you or your dad. Why don't I just hike on over there and see what he's got in store for me this summer when I go to some camp in Afghanistan, Norway, or Iceland?"

I was concerned that the people who made the house run, so to speak, were not my parents.

We're at the table every night, recapping the day, and Jean had very little to say. She wasn't expressive. They didn't ask her to be expressive. They didn't encourage her to be expressive. She wasn't emotionless, but she didn't emotionalize things when she said them, nor did she respond emotionally to things. My brother was a party-liner, saying what they wanted him to say. I wasn't interested, because he was just parroting what the grandfather said or what the father and mother said. It'd come around to me and I had to be more interesting than what I'd heard. So I embroidered. I don't know how many times I said at the dinner table that I wanted to be able to express myself, but they didn't want to hear that. I just wanted to say I believe A, B, C, and D, but I know they would say, "No, you don't believe that. You can't believe that, living in this house."

During my upbringing, there was no discussion of sex. If a woman wanted to get pregnant, you'd squeeze her breasts. That was my sex education. I didn't have a clue until I went to Kankakee.

I lost my virginity in October of 1952 in a whorehouse in Kanka-kee. I was so excited. There were six girls there. I picked out a girl, and she took me into a room. Back then, they brought you over to the sink and washed you off before you could have sex with them. I came in the sink while she was washing me off. I asked her if I could please stay in the room with her for another fifteen minutes so my friends that I went there with would think something had happened. First time, in the sink. I didn't jerk off until after that. That was literally my first orgasm.

The girls were not unattractive. I figured it was a biology lab experiment. I bet on Monday morning I'd be the most popular guy in the biology class. I'd tell them a story they wouldn't believe.

In my next-to-last track meet in high school, the Illinois State meet, a kid spiked me in the mile relay and tore my Achilles tendon. I had to have six stitches in it. Came back the next Saturday in the league meet, which in Illinois follows the state meet. New Trier had a consecutive streak in league championships. I had to win the half mile and the team had to win the mile relay in order for us to win the league championship. My parents had forbidden me to run, as the family doctor had advised them, because I had six stitches in the tendon itself. I was walking on crutches at school.

Saturday morning I left the house. My mother asked, "Where are you going?"

I said, "I'm going to see the meet."

Actually I was dressed, and I ran. I won the half. The stitches started to tear in the last ten strides and it was a photo finish, but I out-leaned him so I won and got the points. We were only two points ahead, so I had to run the mile relay, because if we did not win, the other team would get five and we would lose by a point. I ran the lead-off leg and the tendon tore really bad, but I hung on and gave the lead to the second guy. Our team won the mile relay. It was a very heroic thing, and I got on the front of the *Chicago Tribune*—not just the sports page but the front page of the paper.

I injured myself for a long time, and the lower part of my left leg has always been smaller because of that. Might be why I never achieved quite what I wanted to achieve as a runner.

We don't have a hall of fame at New Trier. 2004 was our class's fifti-eth reunion. Out of 512 people, 357 came back. John Madigan was an officer in our class. He was the president and CEO of the Chicago Tri-bune Corporation, which bought the *L.A. Times*. He was also best man at my first wedding. Dick Segil was treasurer of our class and is married to my sister.

The yearbook they put out every year is called *Echoes*. It's a turn-of-the-century high school, meaning it started around 1902 or 1903. So it's been there over a hundred years. Kids at eighteen are coming up with "Echoes." Already there's arrogance and a historical sense that we'd left something, that we meant something, that our lives were already behind us instead of in front of us. We've already been there and done that. I always had that feeling in the society that I grew up in, Winnetka and Glencoe. There was so much emphasis on achieving that a lot of the people I grew up with felt burnt out at eighteen, nine-teen years old. They had overachieved so much by the time they got out of high school that very few guys who were tremendous athletes in high school ever got a letter in college. They didn't even go out for the sport. They didn't give a shit.

The least-emphasized activity in high school was drama or entertainment. Yet, if you were to make an honor roll, you could start with Ralph Bellamy, Richard Widmark, Hugh O'Brian, Charlton Heston, Rock Hudson, Bruce Dern, Ann-Margret, Jessica Harper, Penny Milford, Elizabeth Perkins, and Virginia Madsen. John Hughes directed two movies there. *The Breakfast Club* originated at New Trier.

My sister has my high school yearbook under lock and key. She would never be allowed to show it to anybody. You read the things that people write where they say what they really think about you. "It was great knowing the greatest bathroom contortionist that ever lived." "The only guy who could look through holes so small and see things so magnificent and weave such tales of grandeur." Things like that!

We had done everything that there is to do by the time we got out of high school. Therefore you get a tremendous drop-off. People don't leave. They stay in Winnetka; they stay in Glencoe; they stay in Wilmette; they stay on the North Shore. They'll go into Dad's law firm. Basically, entertainers, actors, newspaper people, and writers seem to be the only ones who get out of that environment. The gift we got out of New Trier was to run as fast as we could away from it.

· 3 ·

You Can Train All You Want, but the Watch Don't Lie

I went to Penn because I was on a railroad to Penn. My dad went there. My brother, Jack, had just graduated from there. When he left Penn, my brother was a big student campaign manager for Harold Stassen and involved in his career. This pissed me off because Adlai Stevenson was a friend of the family. I wasn't a Republican or a Democrat, but I was certainly for Adlai because he was a bud and he believed what he said. He was what he was. Jack didn't get that because Jack was a follower. Jack was never a dreamer, and Jack was never a leader. I don't know what Jack's agenda was, and I don't know what it is to this day, but he is one of the few quality human beings.

Jack and I are not close like brothers should be, because as he left Central School, I came in. He left New Trier, I came in. He was four years ahead of me. Every time I had a chance to be at the same school with him, he wasn't there. Jack was a runner; I was a runner. Jack was on the track team at New Trier and ran the half mile. I could beat him

18

in the half mile, and I was in the eighth grade. And he got a letter at New Trier.

My sophomore year at Penn I'm running against guys in the Ivy League. In my area, I have the three best half-milers alive, which means I do very well my freshman year. Don't lose any races. In my sophomore year, my first race is in a quadrangular meet—Villanova, Fordham, Pitt, and Penn. It's an indoor race at a convention hall in downtown Philadelphia, where the Warriors played. The first race is a thousand yards, which is the indoor equivalent of an 880, which is seven laps on the boards. I'm a hero on the campus. I finish fourth. I haven't been fourth in a long, long time. I don't cry. I realized who beat me. But nobody else does. I never recovered from that day in front of my friends, in front of the school, because to Madigan, to Segil, to all the friends I grew up with, I was fourth in an eight-man race. All three of the guys ahead of me, the next summer, won medals in the Olympic games, including two gold: Tom Courtney in the 800 meters and Ron Delany in the 1500 meters. From that day on, track didn't mean the same to me. That was the beginning of my disillusionment with running. The extra workouts, the extra mileage, no one trained harder than I did. No one. Not at Penn, not in America, no one in the world trained any harder than I did. I realized I wasn't as good as I thought I was. I wasn't blessed with certain things.

You can train all you want, but you get to a point where the guys get separated, and you're still only this good. The watch doesn't lie. That's the great denominator.

I tried out, but I wasn't good enough to make the Olympic team. I was in an era when America dominated the 800 meters worldwide. In '56, which would have been my year, we had three guys finish first, second, and fifth.

Mal Whitfield, who had won the Olympic gold medal in '48 and '52, was the first alternate at forty years old. Here I am, a sophomore at the University of Pennsylvania, standing on a track next to Mal Whitfield, and when I was in the fourth grade, Mal Whitfield was world champion. When the race started, all I was looking at was his ass. I could never get by him. I pulled even with him. He looked at me and saw this guy running with this little simple "P" on his shirt for

Penn, and went, *What the fuck is this guy doing next to Mal Whitfield?* He decided it's time to slip a gear. He dropped it down one and went *phooo*, and he was gone. I suddenly realized, well, Bruce, that's that. There are those who can move, and there are those who can *really* move. You're not one of them.

I run now every day, and who gives a shit? You are what you are. You're only competing against yourself now anyway. I race myself three or four times a week. Run little time trials. I'll race against guys sixty-five to seventy now. It's fun. I do well in the races in my age group. I can still move. I mean, people think I'm a sloth and I lay around. I'll walk nowhere. I won't stand unless I absolutely have to.

I did a movie, *Believe in Me,* with a bunch of athletic girls who would say to me, "You know, people say that you run. I just don't believe it, Mr. Dern. You look like you can't get out of a car in the morning."* You wouldn't think so except for the twenty minutes I'm out there. I'll get up and motor. Otherwise, it doesn't look like it can happen.

The director Henry Jaglom was in my class at Penn. I don't know what he was doing in school. His father lived in Baltimore, and he was the richest exporter/importer in the United States. I said, "Why aren't you at Wharton?"

Jaglom said, "I'm an auteur."

"What the fuck is an auteur?"

It was just craziness: Henry Jaglom, Bill Link, Dick Levinson, Candy Bergen. Bergen was a little after me, but these other guys were in my classes. Jaglom wearing a scarf even then. When later I ran into him in the movie business, and he was hanging around Jack Nicholson all the time, I said, "Henry, what are you doing here? Why are you making movies for a million dollars? You've got a gazillion dollars."

"I don't ask my family for any money."

Henry's got gifts. He just can't shut up. That's his problem.

I don't know that I ever went to classes I was supposed to go to.

---

*Of course, Bruce was easily fifty years older than these costars in this independent film about a girl's high school basketball team.

After two years, I was out of there. I don't remember whether I got passing grades or not. I took courses like symbolic logic. The only thing I remember from it is the triangle with two dots. I thought that meant "math." Symbolic logic was under psychology, and I thought it was going to be something to help me learn why I'm so screwed up or why other people around me are screwed up. No, it was a math class, and I hated that kind of math—logarithms. When am I going to use that? If it said "ometry"—geometry, trigonometry, elephantometry, or whatever—I was not there.

I had this whim about maybe being a sportswriter or a sportscaster. Very quickly I realized as a journalism student that I couldn't write worth shit. In my first journalism class, my professor was the night editor of the *Philadelphia Daily News*, which was the afternoon paper. Larry Merchant, who still writes there, was around the same time I was. He wasn't a writer yet. He was about the same age I was. There were a lot of hip guys all just starting in Philly when I was there. Dick Clark was starting when I was there. All the singers were coming from South Philly. The Everly Brothers, Bobby Rydell, Tommy Sands, Jimmy Darren, Frankie Avalon. It was a big deal.

There were three papers in Philly, the *Inquirer*, the *Bulletin*, and the *Daily News*. TV killed the evening papers. There are no big evening papers anywhere anymore.

The professor gave us a story about a kid who had a dog that ran across the freeway and got killed. He said, "Put a headline on it."

I wrote the headline for it, handed it in, and the professor wrote, "See me." No grade. So, I went up.

He said, "Mr. Dern, you wrote a twelve-word headline. It's got some passion in it. It's got feeling. But who gives a shit?"

I said, "What do you mean?"

He said, "I can't run this headline."

I said, "Sure you can."

"No, I can't. I don't have space for it. This is a newspaper. Look at the format. I got this, I got this, I got this, and then I got a place for this story. You have got to tell this story in four words and then they'll read it. Your story's not going to be much more than your headline. The headline's very simple: 'Dog Dies, Boy Cries.'"

I said, "C'mon, man."

The professor said, "That's the newspaper business, sir. I suggest to you that maybe you opt out. You can't write. Outside of the editorializing, the storytelling is just pathetic. This is not for you. You have a gift for the language and your version of what you think the language is, which is rather butchered, I might add. I call it Dernsies because I've been listening to you now for about a semester and a half. Everybody in this class and the whole journalism school gets a rather big kick out of you at eighteen years old that you talk this lingoism which nobody can figure out because you invent words off words that do exist but are not quite in the dictionary. You used a word the other day in my class. *Familization*. What is that?"

I said, "Well, it means that when all the people in the Dern family get together and come out with a formal idea that has to do with the family, they familize it. So, I call it familization. It works."

"Yeah, it does work. But it would only work out of your mouth. You have the most colorful use of the language I've heard, but God, don't write that down on a piece of paper, man. Say it. Sneak off with it, but don't put it on paper, because people will look at it and think you're from another area."

I said, "I'm from the D area."

So, the professor encouraged me to give up journalism.

I asked, "What about sportscasting?"

He said, "Well, you've got a high voice, but you know sports. Also, while we're on that, I don't know what you're doing in the back of the class, but all these numbers that you're giving out to people, what's going on back there? These guys come in and give you envelopes every Monday. What is that?"

"We have a little pool, and they come in and they give me notes on how they did on games."

"No, no. They give you green."

"Well, I have little betting pools."

"They give you green with three figures on them. You're a gambler."

I said, "Yeah. Football and baseball."

He said, "There's no baseball in December."

I said, "I like baskets."

He said, "You bet the Warriors last night?"

"Ernie Beck gets sixteen. You've got to bet Ernie Beck."

We talked for a little bit more, and I got to be his friend. He sent me to see a guy named Dr. Charles Lee, who was a teacher and who had an absolutely beautiful wife. Oh my god. She had platinum hair. She wore her hair in ringlets off her shoulders, and she was a weather-woman. He was a dapper, DeLorean-looking guy with silver hair, the head of the English department at the time and a public-speaking teacher.

He asked, "You want to be a sports announcer? Why sports? Why not just on the air? News, sports, whatever, radio."

I said, "I want to see the people. I want to talk to the people."

"Why don't you be a debater?"

"That means arguing."

"No. That means debating."

"Well, that's arguing."

He said, "Wrong."

It was the first time anybody ever gave me something I'd end up using all my career.

In my spare time, I discovered a building on campus that had a sign out front that said, "Moving Pictures." Soon, I became captain of a new team, the Flick Team, where you had to see seven movies a week to qualify. There were three guys: Jerry Sprague, Dan Maltese, who was a runner who later vanished from my life, and myself. No one else ever made it. We would see double features. I remember the first movie I saw was *Sign of the Pagan*, with Jack Palance and Virginia Mayo. Palance always got my attention.

I was particularly touched by movies like the Kazan films and the Stanley Kramer films. *A Tree Grows in Brooklyn*, *Gentlemen's Agreement*, *East of Eden*, *Giant*. I always felt Van Heflin was an enormously underrated actor. *Battle Cry* is a movie I saw several times, and then I remember back, shit, how good he was in *Shane*. Everybody forgets he was even in *Shane*, but when he and Alan Ladd go in that bar, Van Heflin holds his own, and there are some bad motherfuckers in that scene.

Of course, *On the Waterfront*. Paul Newman's movie *Somebody Up There Likes Me*. *Bridge on the River Kwai*. Montgomery Clift's work. *Raintree County* had a big, big effect on me. I remember a lot of death scenes in movies, particularly in that movie.

Lee Marvin has a running race against Montgomery Clift on the Fourth of July in the little town, and he beats Clift in the 100-yard race. Marvin's declared the fastest man in Raintree County. At the end of the movie, they're fighting against each other. Marvin fights for the South and Montgomery Clift fights for the North. Marvin lays dying, and I learned from that that when you have to die, and you're a principal character in a movie, never fail to look at the nobleness in the death, as well as the agony.

Actors always choose the agonized death. That's horseshit. I mean, that's fine if it's a *Gunsmoke* where you're supposed to die as fast as you can because you're the fifth cowboy in the scene. I remember the first *Gunsmoke* I did where Mark Rydell was the director. He said, "Come on, Bruce. I got you out here from the studio. Just die in the scene. What are you trying to do? I mean, it's not Shakespeare."

And I said, "I know. I'm just trying to have people remember."

He says, "Just fucking die. The marshal kills everybody every week. You're not special. You're not dying of cancer. Just die, Bruce. I've got a two-second cut here. Cough and you're out."

I did what he said, but I remember Lee Marvin gets shot and he's dying and he's about five seconds from going out. In his last breath he says, "I guess you think you just killed yourself a reb. Who you killed is the fastest man in Raintree County." Obviously, the running was part of it, but stuff like that touched me, and I thought I could learn to do that. It wasn't that whole thing about being able to touch one person. What a load of shit that is. The point is that it got me. I can't write it, but if I could have said that to my dad, or my mom, or my grandfather, or any of my friends that I grew up with. . . . I always knew it was the fact that there was no communication at home and nobody listened that drove me to the point where I felt I had to do what I did. It wasn't that I wanted to be listened to; I had to be listened to because I couldn't get anybody's attention.

I didn't know what acting was. How did they learn to do that? I started reading about acting beginning with the Russians. I read about Russian history. Teachers/writers like Stanislavsky. It was either Slavskys, Cheskys, or *kovs*; Chekhov, Markov, Brokov. These were revolutionary kind of people. It was 1956. Russians were still the bad guys, and we were the good guys. Then I started reading about the history of the American theater. Theater was the first place to go — New York, Broadway, Actors Studio, Strasberg, and Kazan. They were the teachers. That was the Carnegie Tech of the acting world, and that's where you had to go. I didn't know a thing about movies except that I saw them. It got instilled in me that movies were the secondary place to go.

I wasn't a wanderlust, I had no idea of getting on trains or hitting the road or any of that shit. I wanted to stay in the Four Seasons at night. I wasn't looking to be Jack Kerouac. I didn't know what I wanted to do, but I knew two things. I didn't want to go into the service. There were no wars or anything then, but I didn't want to do that. I didn't want to run competitively anymore. I was burned out.

After six months on the Flick Team, I quit track over an incident about sideburns. I had been competing since I was six years old on ice skates. I was very good as a speed skater, but I quit at twelve to become a runner. I wanted to be an Olympian in both sports. At twenty, I had done everything I wanted to do. I wasn't going to be any better as a runner, I had reached my peak in the 800 meters. Little did I know, I probably had three years left competitively to continue improving at 800 meters. But I didn't have the coaching, nor did Americans have the knowledge that I would have had had I been in Scandinavia, middle Europe, Australia, or New Zealand.

I told my parents I was dropping out of college and going to dramatic school. In the six months of watching these films, the people on the screen touched me, because there was communication going on between them that reached me. When I called my people back home and they said, "You're not going to do this," I had no trouble telling them to get fucked. I was going to do it. It didn't bother me saying that, because I had the strength. If they took the check away from me for the rent, I didn't care. If I had to go with the clothes I had, they couldn't take them away from me. All they could do was stop sending money for me to go to school, and I would find a way. I'd drive a Breyer's ice cream truck, whatever I had to do, I would get through it. I was in the right place at the right time. Wrong city, but it was only ninety minutes away from the right one.

The only thing my upbringing did, in terms of my career, was that when I finally made a decision to do what I wanted to do, I knew I was going to do it for the rest of my life, even though it greatly disturbed my family. The regimen was: when you made up your mind, you stuck to it. There was no question that I wanted to stick to it. In 1956, I made up my mind to be an actor. That's it. No turning back.

I quit Penn on a Friday morning, went straight to Third and Arch Street in Philadelphia to the Bessie V. Hicks School of Acting, next door to the Betsy Ross house where she made the American flag. The Bessie V. Hicks School of Acting has one notable graduate, Charles Bronson.

I enrolled in that school Friday night. There was a Christmas break, and I did go home for that Christmas week. I came back in January. My parents were expecting me to go back to school. I told them I wouldn't. They thought they'd broken me down at Christmas. They hadn't.

I attended dramatic school from the first week of January through the rest of that semester at night because I couldn't get in the day school. In the daytime, I hung around the Penn campus. I couldn't run because I was off the track team and I didn't go to school. My parents didn't pay for my second semester, and I told them not to. I went to movies and I attended any lecture at Penn, or Princeton, or Temple, or La Salle that interested me. I got my formal education as a person and as an actor. Every Thursday a Eugene Ormandy lecture. Once a week a Robert Oppenheimer lecture if I could get to Princeton.

Once, after the lecture, I went up to Dr. Oppenheimer, introduced myself, and threw a few family names out because he wouldn't know who the hell Bruce Dern was, but Archibald MacLeish rang a bell a little bit, and Adlai Stevenson. He said, "Walk me to my class."

So I walked across the campus with him for fifteen minutes, the only fifteen minutes I ever had alone with him in my life. I said, "I've always been fascinated by how you came up with what you said in the bunker upon seeing the bomb explode at Los Alamos."

He asked, "How do you know what I said?"

"Oh, come on, everybody's read it."*

"I don't know. I just know I felt extremely emotional."

One of the things that made me become an actor was that I've always been fascinated with what makes people do what they do, particularly in times of crisis. Why do we behave the way we do under the gun? Why do we make that particular decision? And that's what I'm all about as an actor, and always have been—behavior. In my household, I was always interested in why my father chose to move the way he moved and totally ignore the chaos in his house and not choose to deal with it; why he chose to live next door to his father-in-law all his life and put up with the fact that he lived with a woman who talked to her mother every single morning for an hour before she got out of bed. His and his wife's best friends were her parents. His father was the secretary of war, and he never even went in the service, nor did his kids.

My father had a disability and wouldn't have gone to fight in the Second World War anyway, because he had liver damage and he died at fifty-five to prove it. He just went along with the program. He never disciplined; he never did anything.

Once I was home from college at Christmas. I took my father's Cadillac. I was allowed to use it, and John Madigan, Neele Stearns, and I went downtown, trolling. Madigan and Stearns were successful; I was not. I had the car. The rules of the organization were that the successful people got the use of the group vehicle and the unsuccessful person, even though it was his vehicle for the evening, found another ride home. And the people that were successful would bring the car back the next morning. So, this is what I did. I went home and they went on and did their things with two Jewish girls from Senn High School, who used to hitchhike home from school, neither of whom was Barbara Harris, but I found out when I worked with her twenty

---

*Upon seeing the first atomic explosion, Oppenheimer, the scientific director of the Manhattan Project, made a reference to the appearance of God to Man in the Bhagavad-Gita, saying, "Now, I am become death: the destroyer of worlds."

years later, in a Hitchcock movie, that she went to Senn while I was at New Trier, and she used to hitchhike home from school.

Bill Friedkin* and Phil Kaufman† also went to Senn High School. When the Suez Crisis happened in the mid-fifties, they were the guys who got on the front page of the *Chicago Daily News* because they dressed as Arabs and went out with sheets and towels around their heads picketing the school because they weren't letting Arab students in. They were Jewish kids causing tsuris for their parents all because of their alternative point of view. That's what Friedkin and Kaufman would do. Friedkin used to say, "My name is Abdul Amin. My father is a rug merchant over by Wrigley Field." These kids all went to Senn High School, which is a very progressive left high school. And the girls hitchhiked home.

So anyway, I drove home in another car, and my father came in sometime during the night. He pulled me out of my bed and wailed on me. It was the only time in my life that he ever really looked me in the eye.

"Where is my car? Where is my car? Where is my car?"

I said, "Madigan has it."

I had to call up Madigan and say, "You've got to get the car back here."

Madigan said, "Well, you know, my partner's here. I've got to get her home first."

I said, "I'll tell you what. I'm going to walk down the hall and wake my dad up, and I want you to tell him."

Madigan said, "Oh, God, no, man. I'm not talking to John Dern. He beats my dad in court. He beat my dad in the Supreme Court. Christ, I can't talk to your father. Can you get over here?"

I said, "You asshole, you have my dad's car. You come over here, you pick me up, and I'll drive you and we'll take these whores home. Get over here. I have to go to my dad's room and tell him that I'm getting the car. There's no ifs, ands, or buts."

---

*The director of *The Exorcist* and *The French Connection*.

†The director of *The Right Stuff*, *The Unbearable Lightness of Being*, and *Henry and June*.

We worked it out, and I got the car. But it's the only time my dad ever really paid attention to me, because his car was missing and it'd been given to me under strict orders of return.

Starting that September, I went to the day acting school until the following May, when the school closed and never operated again.

In one of my classes, I did a scene with a girl named Betty Hauck, and she had two roommates. One of the roommates was Marie Pierce. I went to work on the scene at their house, and Marie ended up being my first wife. She worked in a bank. The goal of the dramatic school was to make me feel that I was a good enough actor that I could go to New York. Anybody's career consists of little steps. The rules of the game are you've got to learn how to do what the people are doing and you have to dare to think that you're good enough to risk.

There were two things I didn't want to do. I didn't ever want to be in a community theater play, and I didn't want to be in an experimental film, an industrial film, or a commercial because I knew that exposure in the wrong medium could sell you down the drain. Your introduction to people through the wrong kind of exposure would slot you forever.

My goal was to get good enough in the dramatic school to be in the play at the end of the year. I was good enough to be one of the five guys in the play. Also, my teacher told me I was good enough to go to New York and look for work as an actor. I had the courage to hit the pavement and leave pictures and résumés. Well, I didn't have a résumé. I learned very early on in my household, when I was six or seven years old, that the fact that you don't have a résumé doesn't mean shit. First of all, they're not going to check on what you've done. Second of all, you've got to be very creative in what you've done and not list credits that casting directors can check on. And third, don't oversell yourself so that if you put a credit down you can't back it up. If they say, "Oh, you were in *Hamlet*. Why don't you do a little something from that for me right now?" You've got to be able to do it right there if they ask you, even if you're waiting in line to get a shoe shine or collecting your sixty-five at the unemployment.

Our final production in May 1958 was *Waiting for Godot* at the Academy of Music in Philadelphia. We sold it out every night for two weeks in front of fourteen hundred people and we weren't even in Equity. We got paid a hundred dollars a week. The owners of the school skipped, closed the school, took all the tuition money, and formed some musical theater somewhere and did pretty well. My acting teacher, Gordon Phillips, who was the head of the school and a member of the Actors Studio, took me to New York, and we did a scene as an audition for the Actors Studio.

The year I got in the Actors Studio, Dennis Hopper was back in New York trying to become a better actor despite the fact he'd already been in *Giant*, *Rebel Without a Cause*, and a bunch of other movies. There were six or seven actors or actresses like Dennis back there at the time: Lee Grant, who'd been in movies as a young girl; Anne Bancroft, who had been in Hollywood using another name, got her brains kicked out for seven years and went back to New York, changed her name to Bancroft, learned how to act at the Studio, and was starring in *Two for the Seesaw* with Henry Fonda on Broadway, then came *Miracle Worker*, which turned her career; Julie Harris, who was a Broadway star for years and years, starting as a kid, and never got any recognition in films until Gadg said, "Look, I want you to play Jimmy Dean's girlfriend in *East of Eden*." After *East of Eden*, everybody wanted her. They said, "Who is this girl? She's a gem."

Another one was Lois Smith, who's also in *East of Eden*. The next time you would remember her is as Jack Nicholson's sister in *Five Easy Pieces*. Where's Lois Smith in between? It's a sixteen-, seventeen-year difference. She was always there.

When I came into the studio, the women were the most prominent actors. The women dominated because they were the most impressive. The guys, upon getting some initial Broadway success, went to Hollywood immediately after one hit play. For the actresses, it wasn't the same.

Actors Studio never gained legitimacy in Hollywood. It has gained it far more on Broadway and in regional theater around America than it ever has in the movie business even though a great many movie stars of the fifties, sixties, and seventies come from the private classroom of Lee Strasberg, as well as the Actors Studio. Mr. Strasberg passed away before he could teach the kids in the eighties and nineties. Laura Dern

YOU CAN TRAIN ALL YOU WANT, BUT THE WATCH DON'T LIE   31

studied with Mr. Strasberg when she was twelve, thirteen, and fourteen, and she was one of the last people to ever study with him.

When I came to the studio, I had all these women who were not
beautiful, young ingénues, but actresses who were in their late twenties or thirties, because Mr. Strasberg and Mr. Kazan and Miss Crawford were not enamored of ingénues. You can't teach people the
Method if they don't have a good amount of life experience. They're
not old enough. Later, I taught for Lee Strasberg at the Strasberg
Institute in L.A., and I moderated at the Actors Studio.

The reason Kazan and Strasberg are who they are is they both put
their money where their mouths are. Strasberg taught during the
1930s, '40s, '50s, '60s, '70s, and '80s. That's six generations of producing actors who continually went from Broadway to stardom to California in the movies to international stardom. He made actors who came
from the opera and musical theater into movie stars. He taught people
from every facet of life. At the Studio, I would see people from
Marilyn Monroe to George Gaines, who made his reputation in the
Police Academy movies.

Lest anybody doubt that Lee, himself, could do it, let's take a look
at *Godfather II*. How good was he in that? He's lying on the bed, and
he says the most deadly line anybody's had in a movie. Forget "Make
my day," which is good. Lee said, "I'm going in to take a nap. I'll leave
the suitcase here. When I come out, I'll open it up. If there's two
million dollars in it, I know I have a partner. If there isn't, then I know
I don't."

Sadly or ironically, most people now know the Actors Studio only
through the James Lipton show on Bravo. James Lipton has never
asked me to appear on his Actors Studio series. How about the fact that
I'm an Actors Studio member, of whom they've only used eleven since
the show started? He's had Courtney Love and Barbara Walters. These
people aren't in the Actors Studio. I'm in the Actors Studio.

When Lee Strasberg died, Anna, his wife, was left the Actors Studio. She sold the Actors Studio name to James Lipton. She didn't realize what he was up to, which was a show where he used the Actors
Studio name and proposed to have prominent members of the Actors
Studio come on and talk about their careers and working at the studio.

He's had DeNiro and Al Pacino on and a few others, but I haven't seen an Actors Studio member on in a long, long time. He had Charlize Theron on. He asked her if she had worked with any members of the Actors Studio, and she said, "I've worked with one. Wasn't Bruce Dern a member of the Actors Studio?" He said, "Let's not get into that."

I don't know what the fuck he meant. I've never met Lipton.

· 4 ·

The Name Is Stern,
Bruce Stern

Shadow of a Gunman opens and there are two reviewers in New York that mean something: Walter Kerr of the *New York Herald Tribune* and Brooks Atkinson at the *New York Times*. These are esteemed theater critics who have never been equaled in the history of the theater since then. Brooks Atkinson wrote a review that said it's not the best play O'Casey wrote, but it's damn good. It's not the best interpretation ever directed or acted that's been on Broadway, but it's the Actors Studio. It has tremendous performances. It's the greatest collective piece of work you're going to see in the theater certainly this season or for many seasons to come because of the interaction of the actors, the Stanislavsky theory of acting at work. I'm not saying hurry to it, but don't miss it before it's gone. That's the white lie theory. What he's saying is, make sure you see it, but you don't have to make it the first thing you see. He was kind, but he didn't say surefire. Brooks Atkinson singled me out in saying that one of the most illustrious moments that Broadway has seen in quite some time is an indelible rookie performance by an actor I'm sure we will hear a great deal more from in the coming years, Bruce Dern, who stands the audience on its ear with his brief, memorable performance. Walter Kerr's review said aha, the Actors Studio is creating Frankensteins in its basement once again. This time, they're charging us money to watch them make disasters. He hated it. The last paragraph of Walter Kerr's review said the one saving grace of the Actors Studio's gravely mistaken venture into the Broadway theater as a producing company is the individual performance of a heretofore unknown actor named B-R-U-C-E S-T-E-R-N and the play's only honest moment. This actor appears for only fifty-two seconds in which he absolutely not only paralyzes the audience that he performs in front of, but paralyzes the American theater. You cannot breathe while this man is onstage. He is that good. That's the end of the review.

The next morning I get a phone call from Mrs. John Dern. She calls me up, and she says, "I read the most disturbing thing in today's *Herald*, Chicago edition, that I have ever read in my life. Your grandfather called me this morning from his office. He will never speak to you again as long as you live, nor will I. Consider yourself persona non grata at ninety-four and eighty-five. You are done. I will see to it that this will be taken care of legally. Mark my words and make no mistake about who it is that's telling you this, Bruce. This is not some rickety person from your past. This is me. You have ceased and desisted in this family because you chose to change your name to the other side."

They thought I had changed my name to be accepted in the community of the theater. To get a job. It didn't matter what the man said about me. It didn't matter where I was or what I was doing. At the same time, in the same theater district, I have an uncle (Archibald MacLeish) who had his Pulitzer Prize–winning play *JB*, directed by one of my producers, Mr. Kazan. I should have included my middle name, Bruce MacLeish Stern, and I'd have been fine.

The only training I ever had was what I got in Philadelphia with Gordon Phillips and Morgan Smedley, who were the two acting teachers I had. Both were internal teachers, from the inside, emotions out. The British, for example, train from the outside in. The British will read a line in a script twenty different ways until it sounds right for their character to say. Then they'll do it that way. I can't work like that. I have to find the character first and build from my insides, from my life experience, from what I feel the character is into using the five senses, through emotional memory and sensory memory. The ability to learn to act is having the ability to be publicly private. If you can do that, you can act. If you can't, be Alex Trebek and get the fuck out of my way. If you're not willing to expose your heart and your soul and your raw nerves, this is not the business to get in. Is it an art form? If open psychiatry is an art form, then that's what I do.

I have always been enormously overwhelmed by the spectacle of opera, except in the building where it says opera. I can't get through an opera. The opening of the Olympic games and the next seventeen days to me is opera. The Tour de France is opera. When everybody stands up and sings the anthem to any outdoor event where you have a hundred thousand people is opera. The World Cup is massive opera to me. You lose; you go home. We're talking countries. We're not talking Oxy versus Cal Pomona. In certain countries, if you lose and go home, you don't know if you're going to wake up the next day.

When I was in *Shadow of a Gunman*, our theater was next to the Music Box Theater, where there was a play called *The Visit*. Our curtain was at seven thirty and the people next to us had an eight o'clock curtain. Every night at about seven twenty, ten minutes before our show began — and I wasn't on until well into the first act — a big limousine would drive up to the alley entrance of the Music Box Theater. A tiny, frail lady, maybe five feet two, would get out of the car with a poodle in each arm and walk into the theater. The chauffeur would then open the other door, and this huge man about six feet seven, white hair around the sides but bald around the top, would get out. He had a poodle in each arm, and he would walk in behind the lady. It was quite a show to me.

One night, Gadg came by to see the play. He said, "What are you doing out here?"

I said, "It's opera, man. It's opera."

He said, "What's opera?"

I said, "Come tomorrow night at seven fifteen."

"Yeah, sure, because you ask me to come I'm going to come at seven fifteen when the play doesn't start until seven thirty. I really want to spend fifteen minutes watching traffic go by. Are you going to run an 880 that will be over in a minute and fifty seconds? What am I going to see?"

"You're going to see opera."

"Well, coming from you, I'll be here."

The next night Gadg is there at about seven twenty. Five minutes late. I said, "It hasn't happened yet, but trust me it'll happen because the theater lights are on and people are standing outside."

All of a sudden, there's headlights and the big limo pulls up. I said, "Don't say a word. Just watch it."

We watched the whole opera. It took about two minutes. The little lady got out. The big guy got out. Went in. I asked, "What did you just see?"

He put his arm around me, squeezed me real tight, and said, "Yes, sir, that's opera. It don't get any better than that."

What we watched was the Lunts go into the theater to do *The Visit*. That's how they arrived each night. Even though he was a Jewish immigrant from Turkey who had risen to the top of his game, whose roots were really in the theater, Mr. Kazan knew that was the American theater. Alfred Lunt and Lynn Fontanne. It didn't get any better than that. And I loved it. That's what the Actors Studio never achieved, never could achieve, and never will achieve.

The American musical theater is revered here. The Actors Studio, the Group Theater, even the Mercury Players will never be revered here, and the Mercury Players was Orson Welles, Joseph Cotten, Agnes Moorehead, all the *Citizen Kane* people, *The Magnificent Ambersons* people. All the great plays they did on Broadway. *The War of the Worlds* radio stuff.

In 1999, a television movie called *RKO 281* was made with Pig's Dad in it. James Cromwell.* I call him Pig's Dad because I could never remember his name. *RKO 281* mesmerized me because I'm a devotee of the Hearst family; that whole family is big, big stuff. In the

---

*Cromwell may be best known for his role as Farmer Arthur Hoggett in both *Babe* movies, a departure from his normal array of judges, officers, and elected officials.

movie, Melanie Griffith's character, Marion Davies, is ragging on William Randolph Hearst after seeing *Citizen Kane* at their own house. If Hearst is a big deal, he could have stopped it from being made or distributed so no one could ever see it because they made fun of him and made her into a joke. Hearst says, "I've done my best. I can't do anything more. I'm not going to be able to stop it. I'm not God." Davies says, "Not only aren't you God, you're not even a great man." Then he says the most devastating line I've ever heard anybody say in a film in my life. He says, "There is nothing to understand. Only this: I am a man who could have been great, but was not." That just gets me.

Shadow of a Gunman closed at the end of December 1958, and in January 1959 I went into rehearsal for *Sweet Bird of Youth* for Kazan, which took me to September of 1959.

In March of 1959, I got called to Paterson, New Jersey, to have a physical for the army. I had to do the play that night. I had a doctor's letter that said I had a hernia potential on both sides since birth. I don't know technically how you describe it except that you're supposed to have webbing on either side of the scrotum. I don't have that webbing. The hernia's never come down, but in order to be in the service, before they'll let you go through basic training, that webbing has to be reconstructed. The doctor had told me way back in high school that in order for me to be drafted I would have to have that repaired. He said, "Unless you want to be in the service, don't have that repaired, and make sure you keep this letter with you when you go for your draft thing. Show them the letter, but don't give it to the sergeant no matter what abuse he gives you verbally or how many times they laugh at you. When he says, 'Go over there and stand with the queers,' go over and stand with the queers because then you'll get to see an army M.D. and show him the letter when he examines you. Don't give it to the guy who says, 'Cough' because he'll say, 'You're fine, give me the letter,' and you'll never see the letter again." I had absolutely no pull, even though my grandfather had been secretary of war. He died the week I was born in 1936. This was twenty-three years later. So, I went to Paterson, New Jersey, and all morning long I took written tests. I was scared to death that I was going to go into the army the afternoon after the test. We'd just opened *Sweet Bird of Youth* about three weeks earlier. It came to the physical, which was after the break at lunchtime. I got in line. You get undressed and you stand there and the guy comes down the line, cough, cough, cough, cough, cough. He came to me, and he said, "Cough. You're fine."

And I said, "Well, actually I'm not."

He said, "What do you mean?"

I said, "I have a hernia potential."

"I just checked it. You're fine."

"This letter says I'm not."

"Let me see the letter."

"It's right here," and I held it away from him. It was two paragraphs long.

He said, "I don't need to read that shit. You're fine. I just checked it. I'll check it again. Turn your head and cough. You're fine. What does the letter say?"

"The letter says I'm not fine."

He said, "What are you, some kind of an asshole? Get over there with the rest of the faggots," which was exactly what the doctor had told me in Illinois five years earlier.

I said, "Okay. I'm not a faggot."

He said, "Get over there."

So, I got over there. The rest of the guys finish their physicals. There's about twenty-five guys, now dressed, who are walked down the hall to sit in chairs outside of an office. It's now four o'clock in the afternoon. All the other guys have been sent home. They're done. They'll get a letter in the mail. I go into this waiting room. One by one the guys go in. I'm the last guy. It's now ten of six. I'm in Paterson, New Jersey. I ride a souped-up motorcycle. My house is probably eighteen minutes away, because we live in New Jersey, but the theater's probably forty minutes away. I can't go home, but with traffic coming toward me from New York City, I can make it to the theater. The curtain's at seven thirty. I'm sweating it. It's now six o'clock. I go in and there's a colonel sitting behind a desk. I stand in front of him. He looks up at me. He's got Italian tinted glasses on. The only time I'd ever seen glasses like that before or since then was a year later in the Italian

Olympics in 1960. The guy who won the 200 meters was from Italy, Livio Berrutti, and he had those tinted, orange, Italian sunglasses that are so fabulous. We never get them right here. They're just great-looking. Mastroianni used to wear them. And this colonel had them on. I'm just standing there. He says, "What's your problem, soldier? You don't want to be in the service, do you?"

"No, sir, I don't."

"I know you."

"No, sir, I don't think so."

"Yeah, I do. I'm going to make a deal with you. You're going to do something for me and I'm going to do something for you. What are you in here for?"

"I'm in here because the sergeant said that I didn't have a hernia. And I don't have a hernia, but I got a letter here that says I got potential for one."

He says, "Can I see the letter?"

And I say, "Yeah, if you're a doctor."

"Can I feel?"

"Yeah."

He gets up, comes around the desk. He says, "Cough."

I just cough right out.

"Mr. Dern, please turn your head."

So I turn my head and cough.

He says, "Yeah, we would have to do surgery on both sides to sew this up. Obviously this has been something at birth or in the first year of your life where your tissue never connected. In your file here it says that you ran in college. But you don't run now, do you?"

"No, sir, I don't."

"You do something else now, don't you?"

"Yes, sir."

"I know. Here's the deal we're going to make: see this box here on this form? I'm going to put a 2-A in that box. You know what that means?"

"No, sir."

"That means you're not eligible to be drafted by the United States Army ever."

"I thought a 4-F was supposed to go in that box."

He says, "No. 2-A means you are ineligible permanently for the draft. Isn't that what you want?"

I say, "Yes sir. That would be very nice."

So he puts a 2-A in the box, then sits back and says, "Now what are you going to do for me, Mr. Bruce Dern, who replaced Mr. Rip Torn last Friday night in *Sweet Bird of Youth* and gave as good a debut performance as I've ever seen an actor give?"

I say, "Well, I have a feeling you're going to tell me."

He says, "You're going to give me and my wife and my commanding officer and his wife the four best seats in the orchestra for this Saturday's evening performance of Mr. Newman and Miss Page and I gather Mr. Torn will be back so I won't see you play his role. I'll see you play the bartender or whatever little part you play in Mr. Kazan's production of *Sweet Bird of Youth*. And I expect to have you join us for dinner after the play, and if you could have Mr. Newman come by and sit down and talk to the two wives for just five minutes, which I would suggest you try hard to accomplish, I would feel that we've made a fair swap, wouldn't you?"

I say, "I'd consider it done, sir, except the Mr. Newman thing I can't vouch for because I'm not that kind of an acquaintance of his yet."

He says, "Well, I'd take it under advisement to get it done."

He stood up and shook my hand. And from 1959 until 1989 I got a letter from that man every Christmas with a list of everything he'd seen of mine every year. After *Black Sunday*, he started critiquing the performances. Then, after *Tattoo*, he started grading the films. With *Coming Home* he gave me emeritus status for the rest of my career. He thought it was one of the superb efforts in the history of moviemaking. He was a colonel, but he was also a psychiatrist. Most of the guys that washed out that day were psychiatric cases. I never went in the service, and I never saw him again.

One of the first things I learned at the Actors Studio was sense memory and emotional memory. And one of the things you always do is deal with the skeletons you have in your closet or the happy, sad, frightened, terrifying, up moments and bad moments in your life. To this day, I still carry my draft card because I'm absolutely terrified that they're going to call me.

On the first of October 1959, Kazan pulled me out of the play and took me to Tennessee to do *Wild River*. I did not come to Hollywood. The whole movie was shot in Cleveland, Tennessee. We shot there in October and November into early December. I finish off the 1950s with *Wild River*.

In *Wild River*, I would say I have a part equivalent in size to one-half of Fredo's part in *The Godfather*. Not as important to the story, but I'm in about seven or eight scenes, onscreen maybe twelve minutes, two or three sentences in each scene. They leave my name off the screen. There's no credit. It's not a "fuck you," but it's an oversight by Gadg. He didn't pay attention to it. This pissed me off. I sent a lot of people to see it. I'm on the screen, not a word of mine cut. But they don't give me a credit. For the people I grew up with, I'm not in *Wild River*. They're not going to see the movie anyway. The last thing they do is see movies. They just want proof.

After *Wild River*, Marie and I split up. The producers of a Tennessee Williams play, *Orpheus Descending*, which has already been running a few months off-Broadway, hire me on a Thursday, and I have to go in Saturday night. I have to learn this whole play in two days.

The lead girl is Diane Ladd.

A few months later, Diane and I get married, and that fall we have a baby, Diane Elizabeth, and I start driving a cab. Mr. Kazan is preparing *Splendor in the Grass*, which is all about guys in college. He refuses to give me a part because of my railing him about not giving me a credit in *Wild River*. If I hadn't quit college, I would have graduated in '58 so I'm in the right age group.

I'm still in New York. I'd been held back by Mr. Strasberg and Mr. Kazan, who said I was not ready to go to California yet. I was moving along at a rapid pace, but upon examining the competition, I was behind because guys who in '58 were at the Studio, had already come to California, and been in the movies. I was still in New York. I was not on my way to Hollywood and hadn't received permission, so to speak, from my leaders to go to Hollywood. I had no ticket to go. That was a big, big wake-up call for me. After the end of *Orpheus Descending*, I did an episode of *Naked City* and a *Route 66*. That was it. I went eighteen months without a job.

I was playing in a baseball game on the Sunday before Memorial Day in Central Park, and Johnny Strasberg, who was Susan's younger brother and Lee's son, was my right fielder. He was left-handed and he hit good, and his dad used to come to the park because Lee was a dad. He was a big sports fan, a big Giants fan. We were playing for money then in the park, and we had the best team. We were just actors, and we took on all comers on Saturdays and Sundays on diamond number three. The park rats would come play us. George C. Scott was our pitcher, and Charlie Dierkop and Bob Loggia were on the team. Bob was a very, very good player. Newman was on the team. He could hit. We'd win a game, and we'd just hold the diamond and keep playing. Each game was for a hundred dollars, so each one of us won eleven dollars. We'd start at nine thirty in the morning. We played quick nine-inning games. Lob ball. The scores weren't big because we could field. No one hit a ball over our heads because we'd catch everything. It was May, so you played until almost nine at night.

I went up and sat with Lee. He said, "Why didn't you hit away when Johnny was on third base in that last inning? You almost lost because of that."

I said, "I don't know. I was tired, I guess. I haven't eaten anything."

He said, "What are you going to do for Memorial Day? Are you going to play ten games like you did last weekend?"

I said, "Shit, I don't know. I don't even know why I'm still here."

He said, "Why don't you go to California?"

I looked at him and said, "What do you mean? I thought you didn't want me to go yet."

"No, you've been ready to go for about six months. I thought you had issues with the baby."

"No, the baby's in Mississippi. Diane's on the road with *The Fantasticks*, and I'm here by myself driving my pathetic little cab."

"Go to California. Make a living. Nothing's happening for you here. You're not going to get a good job in the theater."

"Am I prepared to get work there?"

He said, "I don't know. Nobody's going to know who you are until you're sixty years old anyway."

I said, "Come on, bud. That's thirty-five years from now."

He said, "Bruce . . ." I faced him and really looked at him. "You will be underappreciated until you're in your sixties."

I said, "Why is that?"

"You have a unique ability. You have the ability to make people believe you are who you play. You have this personality that is kind of chameleonesque, you dissolve into the characters, even though you have a stronger personality than the personalities that become movie stars. You are not a personality movie star. Therefore you are unidentifiable as a movie star until you have thirty to forty years of an indelible image on an audience. Then they will embrace you and make you what you're going to be in the movie industry. As far as the theater goes, after about thirty years, they'll bring you back doing whatever you want to do because of that. Your durability because of your athletics and running will enable you to work well into your early eighties and be an entity in your seventies, better than anyone in your generation."

"You mean it's like a marathon. Everybody does the first sixteen miles, then we think about racing."

Lee said, "I couldn't have said it better. That's exactly what it is. Put in your sixteen. Then, look around, see who's there, and start to race. I guarantee you you'll be there after the twenty-third or twenty-fourth mile. You'll move up to wherever you want to go."

That's basically the credo I've always had. I'm definitely beyond sixteen.

· 5 ·

Sick Brucie

Lee Strasberg told me to get on a plane the next day. Mike Gruskoff, my first Hollywood agent, met me at the airport and told me I was going to have a reading for a TV show called *Surfside Six* that afternoon. Gruskoff drove me over to Warner Bros. I auditioned, went out, and sat in the car. Gruskoff went back inside and came out later and said, "You got the work. You report seven thirty tomorrow morning, but now you've got to go over to wardrobe." He drove me. I had no car. My wife was in San Francisco. The baby was in Mississippi. I knew nobody in California except Paul Newman, who had told me, "If you ever come to California you call this number. If you ever need anything, call me." I've never called him to this day. I never will. It was a princely and gentlemanly thing to do, but did he really mean it? I learned a lesson from him. You better not say that unless you mean it, because most people are going to call you. So I don't say it.

I went to work the next day and worked a week. Gruskoff said, "Take the rest of this week off, and starting on Monday, I'm going to introduce you to every casting director in Hollywood. Then basically I'm done with you. I sit back and wait for the phone to ring. I'll call you when there's something I want you to do, and you'll go meet people and that's it."

In 1962, Universal alone had fourteen hours a week of westerns on television. Now nobody makes a western, but then you had fourteen weeks of work just at Universal if you were a layman actor like I was. You did a *Virginian*, you did a *Wagon Train*, you did a *Laramie*. Then there were all the other shows like *Sugarfoot, Bonanza, Daniel Boone*, and *Billy the Kid*. You didn't stop working if you could do westerns. After *Stoney Burke*, everybody said, "He can do westerns. He can ride." Shit, I never rode. The Actors Studio never taught me to ride. You've got to walk a long way to see Gadg Kazan or Lee Strasberg get on a pony.

In May of 1962, we lost our eighteen-month-old daughter, Diane Elizabeth. It impacted our marriage in two ways: First, it went into a state of nonrepair. It was difficult for Miss Diane and me to go on after that because the marriage wasn't in good shape before. It wasn't the crowning blow, but it was something we as a couple would never get over. Diane chose not to deal with it. That was a mistake. Number two, because of one tremendous person I hardly knew and some unforeseen circumstances, we were helped through the immediate period.

The child accidentally drowned on a Friday night. My godmother, Louise Dow, came out and took over our house for three days—answering the phone, cooking, getting us through the weekend, helping me do the funeral stuff, getting the child to Chicago, and having her buried with the family. We had a ceremony in L.A. I wasn't up to accompanying a little casket to Chicago and putting it in the ground. I felt I'd done that. We sent her back and had her buried. On Monday morning, at about seven thirty, my phone rang.

"Bruce, this is James Whitmore. You remember me?"

"Yes, sir, I remember you very well. Every time I've seen you on screen, you've been fabulous. You never get enough credit."

"Well, that's not what's important right now. I'm at the Four Star Studios in Studio City. Do you know where that is?"

"Yes, I do. It's about six and a half minutes from where I live by foot."

"Could you be here by ten of eight?"

I looked at the clock. "Yeah, I can be there by ten of eight."

"Why don't you get over here as fast as you can? I have a TV series called *The Law and Mr. Jones* that I'm the star of and I'd like you to play the lead in this week's episode. You can be in front of the camera by nine and you've got quite a bit of dialogue to do. We're not going to give you any heavy stuff this morning, but we will by this afternoon. You've got a scene to shoot with me in a courtroom. So get your ass over here."

I said, "Okay, sir."

They put me in wardrobe. Mr. Whitmore came in and saw me when I was in makeup. I'd met him once at a function at his house off Sunset in Rustic Canyon. Some political kind of thing that I didn't know was a political thing. I didn't know anything about James Whitmore's politics. He was a class act, what he did for me that day. Sydney Pollack was the director. Hugh Marlowe, the lead, was not kind to me and didn't understand why I was there. I understood, but I wasn't going to say anything. Nobody said, "I'm sorry that your child died two nights ago." But clearly that's what Mr. Whitmore had done for me. I thanked him within five minutes. I said, "I want you to know that I get why I'm here." I put my arm around him, and I gave him a big hug, and I said, "Forever I will appreciate you for this."

He said, "If you ever bring it up again, I'll kick your ass. What happened to you this weekend has nothing to do with it. You're a terrific actor and you've never had a chance to play a leading role and this is it. Let's kick some ass together." He never wanted a thank-you. It was big, big stuff.

After that, I had a recurring part on *Stoney Burke*. The series ran a year. I left after the seventeenth episode. The only person I could have hated in Hollywood was Jack Lord, who played the title character, and he wound up in Hawaii. I didn't hate him, but I thought he was arrogant and pretentious. He wanted me out of *Stoney Burke*, and I finally did get out. I wasn't fired, but he would've fired me, I'm sure, if he had had the chance. For seventeen weeks, I played E. J. Stocker, and every week I said, "Stay with 'em, Stoney." That was my one line, but he still made it uncomfortable for me. He thought both Warren Oates and I were hogging the camera.

Leslie Stevens directed the first eight episodes, then other directors like William Graham and Tommy Gries started coming in. Gries was a big influence on my career because he directed me in two movies in the 1960s: *Number One*, with Charlton Heston and Jessica Walter, and *Will Penny*, also with Heston and one of the classiest women I ever knew, Joan Hackett, a saint. Oddly enough, Heston never knew I went to New Trier until I told him one day on *Will Penny*. He told me about the people who were at New Trier when he was there. Hugh O'Brian, Rock Hudson, and Heston were all in the same class, and none of them knew each other until they came to Hollywood.

I stopped running when I quit college. In September 1962, I started running again, day by day, consistently. So basically, from '58 to '62 is the only time in my life since I was nine years old that I wasn't running or speed skating daily. During *Stoney Burke*, I started having time on my hands because I had to be there every day, but I didn't have anything to say or act. I didn't want to ride horses and shit like that, and I didn't have to. That wasn't going to be my hobby. I wasn't going to turn into a shit kicker. So I started running. I'm twenty-six years old and I'm still at a point where I could really be progressing and training and running. I was not that good anyway, so why not try and be better at it? So I just started running, thinking, well, let's see how far I can run. While filming a show, whether it was a *Fugitive* or whatever, I would run. Run to work, run home. I started building up a reputation where people would say, God, I remember Dern. He'd run from his house in North Hollywood to Fox, and then he'd run home. Or I'd run into Hollywood. I just ran everywhere. Or I'd run one way. If they took me to work in Malibu, I'd run home from Malibu to North Hollywood. I'd work all day and run eighteen miles home. I started building up this reputation as a long-distance runner and then started running incredibly long distances, like from Santa Monica to the *Queen Mary* (in Long Beach) and back. Two Saturday mornings a month I'd run forty-five to fifty miles. I started doing things like running the John Muir trail or running around Lake Tahoe and running to Ventura, running the California missions, forty-four of them, and each one's about forty-four miles apart. So I'd run from one mission to the next in a day. I was good at it. I was getting from A to B on my own.

If the plane went down, somebody had to get out, I could get out. If I survived the crash, somebody had to go for help—I could at least go and tell people that we're out here.

After *Stoney Burke* was over, I was thrown into the open market of episodic television. In 1963, I have no game plan, no image. I don't understand how it's supposed to work. I'm getting restless and impatient because guys are emerging with good roles in movies and I'm not. I'm bogged down in television. Jimmy Caan's getting leading roles. George Segal's getting leading roles. The ship has sailed for Beatty, Eastwood, Redford, Richard Beymer,* George Hamilton. Those guys are out of the gate and on their way. Charlie Robinson. Gary Lockwood. Ben Piazza. Keir Dullea. Not Brucie. Not Jack Nicholson. So Jack does his own movies, *The Shooting* and *Ride the Whirlwind*. Warren Oates is working. Vic Morrow's out there, but Vic Morrow's had ten years. He did *Blackboard Jungle* in the 1950s. Dennis Hopper is out there. Peter Fonda's already emerging, even though he just got out of college. I've done some time. I started with Mr. Kazan. So where am I? Did I stay too long in New York? Did I listen to the wrong people? Am I being sold wrong? Am I being put up for the wrong roles? Am I not good enough? Am I not ready?

Back in our early TV days, Harry Dean Stanton, Warren Oates, Jack Nicholson, Dick Bradford, and I had a deal. I got to know Jack periphery wise. I knew Harry Dean because I worked with him on a *Gunsmoke*. I knew Warren Oates because of *Stoney Burke*. Dick Bradford, who was more successful than we were at the time, was a very good friend of Jack's. We worked four studios: Universal, where they had all those hours of TV; Warner's; Fox; and Columbia. We couldn't hack Walt Disney. We weren't going to get on the family hour. That was Dean Jones or Don Knotts. Paramount didn't do much television.

The deal was, if one of us got a job at one of those studios, he would leave a pass for the other four guys to have lunch with him, at which they were never to show up. The four guys could not come visit

---

*Beymer's ship may have sailed, but it soon ran ashore. Beyond playing Tony in *West Side Story* and a good part in *The Longest Day*, he never became the star many people thought he would be.

you on your set. By leaving a pass, we got to know all the secretaries in all the offices of all the shows. They would slip you the script for next week's episode. You would walk around the lot or get in your car and read as fast as you could. You'd look for a part that you could play. It couldn't be the lead. It had to be a numbskull part. You'd write it down, give it back to her, then go to the *Laramie* office, the *Wagon Train* office, the *Shenandoah* office, and the *Virginian* office, and go to all four studios like that. Monday through Thursday. We didn't work Fridays. If the guy wasn't working, we had to find a way to bull-shit ourselves onto the lot.

When we left the studio, we'd find a gas station and call our agent. If he was out, we'd tell the secretary, "The part of Dave in the *Virginian* episode 'The Prey' starts shooting next Tuesday. Works a day or two, it doesn't matter, but Bruce is right for the part of Dave, and tell Jerry Hinshaw that he's right for it."

Anyway, we started this little network, and the greatest recipients were Harry Dean Stanton and Bruce Dern. It didn't get us better roles, but it helped us make a living. We did that for two years. I got the most work at Universal. I couldn't crack the contract players, though. That was the tough thing. You didn't get the leading roles because there were so many characters in each series every week they had to pay off a character with dialogue. There weren't enough lines left over to have guest stars.

When I would get a *Gunsmoke*, the directors were guys who I'd worked with at the Actors Studio, like Sean Penn's dad, Leo, or Mark Rydell or Sydney Pollack. We had started together and left New York at about the same time. Sydney Pollack was John Frankenheimer's assistant. Mark Rydell was a terrific soap opera star as an actor, then came to L.A. and was an assistant for a while, then got to direct television and eventually movies. Leo Penn was a fabulous actor. I don't know that his kids ever got to see him act, but goddammit he was good on Broadway. He never got a shot as an actor. He wanted to direct, and he was a wonderful guy to work for as a director. God, he was wonderful.

You're working at the studio, but you're not working at the studio. In other words, you're doing TV at the studio while Charlton Heston is walking past you, while guys your age are starring in movies. There's

Warren Beatty going to work with Vivien Leigh on *The Roman Spring of Mrs. Stone,* and having sex with every starlet or star, including Vivien Leigh. He's your age, and he's had not only your wife, but everybody else's wife on the lot. He's eating lunch in the commissary at the big table with Mr. Wasserman and you're there with Harry Dean Stanton picking over one piece of chicken that you're sharing because you only have twelve cents.

Neville Brand's the baddest guy I've ever met in the business. Second-baddest was Audie Murphy. But in reverse, they were the number-one and number-two war heroes in American history, particularly in the Second World War. Audie Murphy not only got every award you can get, but then they did the life story of him as a movie. I mean he ripped the heads off Nazis while he was dying. They left him for dead. But he lived. He said, "I'm all right." Holding his own blood bags, he went and killed bad guys, and then he went to the Pacific and did it again. Neville Brand was right behind him in accomplishments.*

Forty years ago, five gangbangers pulled Audie Murphy's car over in front of the Beverly Hills Hotel, not knowing who they were dealing with. They wedged his car into a curb. He got out of his car and said, "You gonna use a bullet? Kill me. Because you've got one shot." A guy gets out with some kind of machine gun. And before the guy could fire the first round, two guys were dead. Dead. When the cops were arriving, the fifth guy was lying on the ground begging for his life. Audie turned around, looked at the arresting Beverly Hills cop, winked at him, went clap clap clap, got in his Porsche and drove away. The police said, "I think that was Audie Murphy." They never charged him.

Now I get on the set with this man, and my scene is, I come up to him and confront him because he's the leader of the wagon train. He eventually tells me to get back with my wagon and my family.

R. G. Springstein's the director, a very soft man. So, we have rehearsal, and I go to Audie Murphy and say, "You know, I don't think

---

*Audie Murphy really was the most decorated combat soldier in World War II, and Hollywood put him in movies to capitalize on that fame. While Neville Brand was also a war hero, he often decried the attention Hollywood put on his war record as just public relations.

you're doing well with the way you're leading this train. We're not making any time."

He says, "Get back to your wagon."

And I say, "I don't think so." He's supposed to point his gun at me and scare me enough to get back to my wagon because I pull my gun on him.

The director asks, "You ready to shoot one?"

Audie Murphy says, "Yeah."

He goes back to the front wagon, getting ready to shoot. Most relaxed, nicest guy in the world. I go up to R. G. Springstein and say, "You know, I studied at the Actors Studio and he's not scaring me. Don't you think he should at least look like he scares me? Because I've got to pull my gun out and point it at him."

The director says, "Well, on your close-up you can pretend like you're really scared. Don't worry about it. We'll cut it in such a way that the audience will never know that you're not scared."

He yells "Action," and I walk up to Audie Murphy and put an edge on it. I say, "Hey. You. You're doing a piss-poor job with this wagon train. Get it up the gulch."

"What'd you say?"

"I said you're doing a piss-poor job with this wagon train."

He says in a way that just chilled me, "You're looking to die. Get back to your wagon. You've got two seconds. One . . ."

I turned around and walked away.

"Cut. That was a good one, Audie. We're ready for your close-up now."

So Audie goes back to the start for the close-up. And I walk back by Mr. Springstein, and he said, "Scary enough for you?"

"He wasn't acting, bud. Man, oh man, where did that come from?"

"He was just playing with you. Imagine if he'd got mad."

"Was that for real?"

"After he does his close-up, ask him that."

We do the close-up. He does the exact same fucking thing only even more frightening. He goes, "You got one second. One . . ." and cocks his rifle. I turn and go back.

"Cut. That was great, Audie."

"Thanks, R. G."

Audie looks at me and goes, "Question?"

I say, "That was pretty goddamn good, sir."

He goes, "I hope so." Cocks the gun again, and two live shells come out on the ground. "Imagine if I'd pulled it. You wouldn't have been able to do your close-up, would you?"

I said, "Are you shittin' me?"

He said, "You worked for Kazan. He liked to take a look at the elephant. Pick those up and send them to him in a fucking envelope and ask where he was from '41 to '45."

I told Gadg that story because he loved Audie Murphy. He always wanted to put him in a movie. Audie Murphy never worked for him.

I worked for Neville Brand once in a regular TV show, and then in his series where they were Texas Rangers. Whoo, man.

In 1965, I did an episode of *Alfred Hitchcock Presents* with Teresa Wright and Pat Buttram. It was probably the one single show that I ever did in my career that turned the tide, filmwise. I play a laborer who helps them pick peaches before the frost comes. They give me a place to stay in a shack out back for the two days they've hired me. I'm a lurker. It's the first time I am bad Brucie. Sick Brucie. I'm trying to get Teresa Wright's character's attention because I'd like a little piece of her. Teresa Wright has won an Oscar (for *Mrs. Miniver*). Miss Wright is a Kazanite and one of the revered ladies of film.

I'm walking on eggshells. I'm also there with a mission: nobody's ever going to forget me because I've never done a *Hitchcock*, and it is a big guest-starring role in terms of being the bad guy. There are only three of us in the show, plus her pet squirrel. I'm supposed to scare Miss Wright's character to death to make the show work. I kill the little squirrel so she can cook it for stew. She was going to do it anyway. I rushed the death a little bit to piss her off and scare her. We shot it, and the crew enjoyed me. It was the first time I saw a response like I'd had in the theater where I had a beginning, a middle, and an end, and I moved from this point to this point to this point. A couple of times we had to do it over because Miss Wright broke up and laughed out loud. She'd start laughing because the way I'd behave and put words together was so strange. I said, "That make you laugh, ma'am?"

She said, "I know I'm not supposed to laugh."

I said, "Who told you you can't laugh? Somebody in your life got inside and told you you're not supposed to laugh? Maybe I should blow in and cut his tongue out and sew it on his face, and that way we could watch when his tongue starts flapping."

The director, Harvey Hart, left it all in the show. Miss Wright came over to me and said, "Where do you feel that you have the right to do that? It's the most magnificent gift I've ever seen. Have you been doing that all your career?"

I said, "All what career? This is my first day in the business."

"But you were on Broadway. I saw you in *Sweet Bird of Youth*. I remember Mr. Kazan talking about you one day at the Actors Studio."

"Well, that was very nice, but that was eight years ago. What about now?"

She said, "Well, I always wondered. . . . Haven't you been working?"

I said, "Yeah, but I never had a chance to do anything like today."

She said, "This is amazing, that you could take my breaking up, which I would have thought would have killed the scene, and turn it around and make it work for the scene. Mr. Hart kept it going because he trusted you. Where did you get that ability? I see now what Gadg was talking about—this ability to take anything that's happening in the present and make it work for the material and transfer it into your character."

I said, "That's where it's at for me. That's what it has to be."

"Don't ever stop doing that. Don't ever think you don't have the right to do it. Don't ever let any actor intimidate you."

Miss Wright was a wonderful partner. The third day of shooting— you shot them in six days—I found out that Teresa Wright had a clause in her contract, and I've never heard of it before or since, that she doesn't have to loop. She refuses to loop. Which means if her voice is too low, that's too bad. She's not looping it.

One day before our scene, we were standing around talking, and I said, "You don't loop."

"Never."

"How do you get away with that?"

"I don't loop."

I put my arm around her and I kissed her on the cheek and I said, "I love that."

She said, "I can't do it unless the people are in front of me. They're not going to call the people in at twenty-eight hundred dollars an hour. So I can't do it. They know that going in or they get somebody else to do the role."

I said, "Madam, you have inspired me."

She said, "You'll never get it in your contract because no one ever gets it. A lot of times Julie Harris* plays my roles because I don't get it. But for this, I got it."

I said, "That means we have to get it perfect every time."

She said, "No, it only means I have to get it perfect every time. Sometimes my performances are awful, Bruce, but it's good for sound."

We have one day left to shoot, which is going to be on Monday. Friday afternoon about four, in walks the Penguin. Everybody stops because Mr. Hitchcock is on set. I turned to Teresa Wright, and she said, "He looks funny, doesn't he?"

I said, "He's a penguin."

"You dare to call him a penguin?"

"That's what he is."

"By God, you're right. He walks like a penguin. But he's huge."

"Does that surprise you? Imagine if he stood straight how big he'd be."

"That's the point."

If Mr. Hitchcock stood straight, he was about six feet one and weighed about 280. You never got an idea of how big he was. The son of a bitch walked straight up to me. And what nobody understood is I'd worked for Alfred Hitchcock two years earlier on *Marnie*, where I never saw the main crew. It was just me. But I saw Hitch, who would motor over from the main set for hours because he was much more excited about what we were doing because of an unusual lens and my

---

*Another Actors Studio member, with the most Tony nominations and wins in history, Julie Harris may be best remembered as Lilimae Clements on the soap opera *Knots Landing*.

work, I hope, but I think it was the former. Hitch doesn't go to the director, doesn't go to Miss Wright. He walks straight at me and says, "It's so nice to see you, Bruce. You're one entertaining soul, you are. I have a feeling you might be up to having a career."

I said, "Well, if I could work for you, I probably would have a career because you have great material for me."

He said, "Somehow I think this might be the tip of the iceberg for you."

"From your mouth to God's ears."

Hitchcock then turned to Teresa Wright and said, "You, madam, are quite exquisite in what you do. But this young man . . . ," and she finished the sentence, "Is extraordinary. Is he not?"

Mr. Hitchcock said, "That's a strange word. Extraordinary. Would that mean we would have to single him out as one of a kind?"

The next Monday I finished shooting the episode, and I didn't hear from Hitchcock for eleven years, until *Family Plot*.

In January of 1966, I lost an opportunity to do five or six things that could have propelled me into the mainstream of moviemaking. I couldn't get into the last class of contract players at Columbia. Who was the last actor to be put under contract in the history of Hollywood? Harrison Ford, at Columbia, in late '65, early '66. I couldn't get a reading on *Cool Hand Luke*. Harry Dean Stanton was in it. Lou Antonio was in it. Every young guy in Hollywood was in it. I wasn't in it. I started getting jittery because I thought, hey, wait a second, these people don't know who I am. They obviously don't watch television. There were several movies like *Sand Pebbles* in which there were big castings of guys in my age group. I was never even offered an opportunity to read. It wasn't happening. Some of those people know me because I worked for them in television. But now as they're starting to get movie jobs, they're not hiring me. I always thought they're not going to hire me until they get bigger britches. They have to hire people that the producers they're working for want them to hire in order to ensure their place in the business. They're not going to hire the actors they want to hire. Or is it that they don't want to hire me because they were bluffing me all along? The position you get yourself in the rest of your career is: Are people saying they like you because they like you, or are people saying they like you because they want to get out of there as quickly as they can rather than critiquing you honestly? That's why it's very tough to go to premieres and industry screenings. What are people going to do, come up and say, "It wasn't your best work, just not there this time"?

As I've gotten older in the business, I've realized you have to have a tremendous built-in shit detector for yourself, and you've got to learn how to take a compliment and how to take criticism. Because of what I considered an inordinate amount of dues paying, I learned to take criticism too well early on and never learned to take compliments honestly. I was suspect of any compliment I ever got and only read bad reviews. I never believed good reviews, especially when they were verbal reviews from critics or friends face-to-face.

· 6 ·

I'm Having Bill Smithers's Career

In January and February, I started to panic. It wasn't actual panic, it was just worry: how do I get off the television train and get onto the movie train where I had had a taste of major motion pictures? In March, I got a phone call to meet a guy named Roger Corman at his house. I didn't know him, but I'd seen his movies, and I was very struck by *The Pit and the Pendulum*, because it looked like a $10 million movie to me. I didn't know it wasn't until I got to know him. Roger said, "I'm doing a motorcycle movie called *The Wild Angels* and we're doing it in about ten days. There's a part in there I want you to play."*

---

*In this financially successful B movie, Dern's character is called the Loser, and his wife, Gaysh, is played by Diane Ladd. The movie is primarily famous today for Peter Fonda's eulogy to Dern's character, where he utters the immortal lines, "We want to be free! We want to be free to do what we want to do! We want to be free to ride. And we want to be free to ride our machines without being hassled by The Man. And we want to get loaded. And we want to have a good time! And that's what we're gonna do. We're gonna have a good time. We're gonna have a party!"

Diane was in the other room. He said, "I've seen your work. I like your work. The reason you're here is because I was in New York about eight years ago and I went to see *Shadow of a Gunman*. I will never forget how fabulous you were. You took over that play, and I was mesmerized by your work. It was so wonderful. I don't think I'd seen work in the theater like that. I was so astounded that nothing really happened with your career. You seem to be the essence of what the Actors Studio is all about. After this film is over, could I talk to you about going to the Actors Studio as an observer? I love the work of Actors Studio actors."

I never dared approach Roger with this, but I think he was talking about Bill Smithers, who was the star of *Shadow of a Gunman*. I was on stage fifty-two seconds. Bill Smithers never had much of a movie career, but he starred opposite Jack Palance in *Attack*, directed by Bob Aldrich, in which Palance was great and Smithers had the lead. Smithers then starred in a television series called *Executive Suite* at Metro in the late seventies. They did something with his billing. He sued Metro, and from the day he filed his suit, he never worked much in Hollywood again.

Corman told me Peter Fonda and Nancy Sinatra were going to be in it, and he mentioned some other actors he was trying to get to work with. He wanted to change and upgrade the acting of his people.

I said, "There's nothing wrong with Vincent Price and John Kerr and the other people you're working with."

He said, "No, I need hoodlums. I need guys who can pull it off and be sympathetic. Do you ride a motorcycle?"

I said, "Yes, I ride a motorcycle."

He knew a bit about my family background. He said, "Where does somebody from your background learn to ride a motorcycle? Or where does somebody learn to terrify a woman with a squirrel?"

The most interesting thing about *Wild Angels* was learning about the Hell's Angels and meeting Earl Finn, who became a lifelong friend of mine and was a bona fide outlaw biker one percenter.*

---

*The head of the American Motorcyclist Association once said that 99 percent of all riders are good, law-abiding citizens. Outlaw bikers like the Hell's Angels proudly proclaim to be part of that other 1 percent.

From '66 to today, nobody has bothered to make a biker movie that was a major motion picture. Nobody sat down and said, "Let's make a fucking movie and spend some money." It was always the drive-in theory of biker movies. John Cassavetes tried to make one, but it was lame (*Devil's Angels*). He should have been ashamed of himself. He loafed through it. He took a check and didn't get behind it. He was at the height of his directing ability, and he signed off on it. That was too bad, because he could have thrust it into the forefront; he was that good and that creative.

At the end of 1966, a couple of things happened simultaneously. Mr. Strasberg decided that it was time to open a West Coast version of the Actors Studio. Carroll Baker and Jack Garfein, who were a couple, Mark Rydell, Sydney Pollack, myself, Lee Grant, and Martin Landau were involved. They didn't realize the trap of a West Coast Actors Studio. I was the only one who did, and I brought up the danger. I lost in my caution, because they convinced me it could be overcome. It never worked to the satisfaction of Lee, and it has never worked to my satisfaction, the danger being that in Hollywood you cannot have a workshop where the emphasis is on actors dealing with weaknesses or works in progress when you have the buyers in the workshop. It's impossible. Actors lose work because of that. You cannot go up and work on your weaknesses in a class where your observers, writers, directors or producers, who are not members of the studio, are buying actors daily. It doesn't work. I've seen it happen to many, many people: Jack Nicholson, myself, Geraldine Page, Kim Stanley, Barbara Bain, Martin Landau, Peter Falk. Directors would walk out and say, "God, that's great," and the next day the actor's name is crossed out because the work wasn't at the level they had the night before. In New York, it's understandable, because you're talking about the theater and everything is a work in progress. The Schubert people are not in the workshop. In L.A., producers are directors. Directors are writers. Casting directors are allowed to sit in and watch actors work, which should never have been allowed in the first place. When you get a Charlton Heston who asks, can he be an observing member of the studio, or a Jack Warner, or a John Frankenheimer or a George Stevens, are you going to turn them down and say they can't observe?

I got Roger Corman in to observe, and that was the best thing that ever happened to him, because he learned about the acting process. He knew nothing. He was bright enough to know he wanted all Actors Studio actors in his movies because they can dance and invent on their feet.

Mr. Hitchcock said to me, "Bruce, Barbara Harris asked me, 'Would I like to come by the Actors Studio.' I said, 'What do they serve?' She said, 'Nothing.' I said, 'You mean there's not a menu? What a shame.' She said, 'It's a place where actors go to work on their craft.' How come I never see those actors in films?"

I said, "Because you never go to a fucking film. You don't even go to your own films."

He said, "Well, this is true. Could *you* sit through one of my films?"

We opened the Actors Studio West. Lee came out for two weeks at the end of 1966 during the Christmas holidays. The plan was he would come out in May when the New York studio closed and be in L.A. during the summer and go back in the fall to run the New York studio. It was a big success, because it juiced the community. The trouble was there were more observers who were not members than who were members. A lot of the members didn't want to risk working in front of directors who were casting. Therefore, you didn't get the quality of work. You didn't get the people who deserved to work. That was the failure of it, but the pluses of it far outweighed the failures. The quality of the work never lived up to what it did in New York, but the idea of having it in L.A. was better. People got in who shouldn't have gotten in because they were in *Charlie's Angels*.

There was an actress (Tanya Roberts) who was in *Charlie's Angels* and became a member of the Actors Studio. She auditioned both times and passed. There were six of us who judged and taught, and Mr. Strasberg would come out, and occasionally Gadg would come over and look at the work. While he was filming *The Last Tycoon* was probably the last time he was interested in it. About the time I went to do *Gatsby* is the last time I'd been to the Studio, and that was over thirty years ago.

At the end of '66, Diane was pregnant. Marty Cohen, our manager, decided he wanted to make a movie that would be a vehicle for us, a motorcycle movie. What else? *Rebel Rousers*.

He said, "I'll direct it." This is a manager.

We said, "You get the money, you can direct it."

"I've got a script. We'll do it in fourteen days. It'll be a motorcycle movie in which you run this one percent outlaw gang, and Diane's your old lady."

I said, "No, that's not going to work. I'm not on a motorcycle, and I've got a woman that's pregnant."

Cohen said, "I need a star. I have a relationship with Cameron Mitchell. You and Diane will be the stars with him. But he has to be first above the title."

That's fine. We don't belong up with Cameron Mitchell, who should've been nominated for an Academy Award for a great Kazan movie nobody ever talks about called *Man on a Tightrope*, about a circus that travels through the Alps just after the Second World War, and there's a lot of Jewish and Austrian people in the circus who are trying to get out of Europe forever. Cameron Mitchell finds out they might still be wanted; the tightrope being, which side were they really on?

I cast six guys in *Rebel Rousers*: Jack Nicholson; Harry Dean Stanton; Earl Finn, a one-percent biker in real life; Lou Procopio; Phil Carey, who ended up being a prison guard in Susanville; and Neil Nephew, who had just married a girl in my acting class. He was a big friend of Curly Bob Rafelson. He'd been around Hollywood a long time. Neil Nephew was married to Ellen McCrea, who was the costar of a TV series called *Iron Horse*, starring Dale Robertson. In 1967, Neil changed his name to Neil Burstyn and Ellen McCrea became Ellen Burstyn. She was a student in my acting class with Billy "Green" Bush, who later became famous because his twins were the two girls on *Little House on the Prairie*. He was Jack's friend in *Five Easy Pieces*, and he's in *The Culpepper Cattle Company* and *Alice Doesn't Live Here Anymore*, playing Ellen's husband at the beginning of the movie.

There was another guy in my class who I helped on one specific role, and I probably did him a great disservice instead of a great service. We prepared extensively for his first role in movies, which may have hurt him because he was so good in the movie. Nobody was more authentic than he was. He can't live it down to this day. Another actor who was in the movie with him still has to get up and leave the room if he walks in. He's absolutely terrified of him. I worked with this actor, and if you think *I* got pigeonholed, this guy *really* got pigeonholed and it's my fault. I coaxed him to go with it one hundred percent. The actor's name is Bill McKinney. He was the guy who fucked Ned Beatty in *Deliverance*. How real was he? He never let up from the day he arrived until the day he left, not just on the screen but offscreen. He'd walk by Ned Beatty and go, "Not only are you going to squeal for me, but when I come by your room tonight you're going to keep your eyes open the rest of your life." He wasn't like that at all. Burt Reynolds was the only guy who knew about it because he'd been tipped to keep everybody relaxed so they didn't assassinate him.

So in '67, we do this little motorcycle movie, Cameron Mitchell, the group of six, plus Miss Diane. We've got a little swagger under our belts. We've got *The Wild Angels*, which did okay. Jack has already done almost a decade of independent movies on his own, plus working for Roger. I'd been around almost a decade now. I'm a Kazanite, and so is Cameron Mitchell. We're doing Roger without Roger. Marty Cohen doesn't have a clue. There are some paying problems on this movie, but I'm standing by because my manager is producing it along with his friend Rex Carlton, who was dubious at best. At the end of the first ten days of shooting, they don't have money for my actors. I'm going to get my money because my manager is the producer and director. That's not right.

I said, "Marty, we can't finish this movie today unless my guys are paid."

He said, "Rex is coming with the money."

"No. You're not getting your last two big scenes without the guys being paid."

"Come on, Bruce, you've got to finish so we can get it in the can."

"We're stuck until Rex comes with the money for my people."

So we stopped. Rex came, and he didn't have enough money.

I said, "We'll finish, but Jack, Harry Dean, Neil, and Lou are going to Rex's house and they're going to haul out three or four of his paintings and take them home and sell them tomorrow so they get their money."

Marty said, "Then I'll have the police call on them. They're going to go to jail over a few grand?"

I said, "Yeah. You're talking about one percenters. Rex has just volunteered to be a one percenter himself."

"Well, he doesn't have the cash."

"That's too bad. Just give us the keys to his car and we'll go sell it because we are going to get our money."

That's what we had to do. My manager wasn't in on it—his partner crossed him. Said he had something he didn't have. Then Rex was gone. Gone. But everybody got their money at the end.

I was the peacemaker. It was out of necessity for three factors: One, Cameron Mitchell's wife in the movie, Karen, was having a baby. Karen fell for me, and I was willing to take on the responsibility of having a girlfriend who was having another guy's baby who was the star of the movie. Number two, Karen was played by Diane, my wife in real life, and it really was my baby. Third, it was my ass on the line, because I hired a bunch of guys that I find out halfway through the movie weren't going to be paid. I felt responsible to them, and I was being screwed by the guys I was working for, who were also ripping off the guys I was working with. I was caught in a horrible dilemma, which I knew nothing about going in. We were trying to make a movie in which all the work was going to be totally honest and real. We were going to get some chances to act. There is some pretty goddamn good acting going on where things are flying around and people are into moment-to-moment behavior and everybody's getting chances to do things with a beginning, a middle, and an end to each character in each scene, and nobody's getting away with anything. There are no star trips going on. Each one of us threw ego out the window and tried to make a movie that made sense. Out of that came a sense of dignity from me and my character just trying to keep from drowning, holding it all together in front of and behind the camera. It was pretty exciting work when you consider it was total chaos.

We also had László Kovács as our cameraman, doing a fabulous job on one of his earliest movies after coming from Hungary. I didn't know anything about him. He was working with an eight-man crew. And Bud Cardos was the production manager, producer, line producer, assistant director, doing a hundred jobs at once. Everybody pulled two oars instead of one. It was working.

I would walk down the beach when we were shooting at Paradise Cove. Sitting between two huge rocks, frustrated, very touchy, down, sad, and angry, was Jack. Tearful some days. Depressed most days. He was going through a divorce from his wife, Sandra, who was the mother of their daughter, Jennifer, who couldn't have been more than a year and a half old. Jack could still rise above it all, even though he was terribly wounded. I had a love for him from that time on and would do anything to help him out. He was writing a script, *The Trip*, with a part that he intended to play himself. We were going to shoot it a month later. He knew it, but I didn't know it. The first two pages of *The Trip* script were a description of the wall in Peter Fonda's character's room—a memorabilia room. On it was a photograph of every single person that was synonymous with the years 1936 to 1966 in my world or Jack's world: Ravi Shankar to Krishnamurti to Bill Russell to the big-name writers. Each one was described in as much detail as possible. In the movie you see that wall with all the pictures.

I'll never forget that day, when I saw a wreck of a guy writing that script because of the circumstances in his own life, the emotional grips that were on him, the frailty of the human being. I fell in love with Jack, and I realized what an amazing guy he was. My heart went out to him. Then we turned the switch on ten minutes later, and he was there, take after take after take, rising above his own problems.

Rebel Rousers ended about January 25, and I went to Bishop, California, on the twenty-seventh to start *Will Penny*. I played one of three sons of Donald Pleasance, who was the bad guy. Charlton Heston was the star, Joan Hackett was his wife, and director Tommy Gries's son, John Francis, was their little kid. All Heston's line hands were running his winter herd with him because he wasn't an owner or a rich man, he was just a cowboy. Heston is very good in that movie. Slim Pickens, Ben Johnson, and Roy Jensen, who played with the Washington Redskins, are in the movie with a bunch of real cowboys.

I got word on a Thursday night that Diane had gone into the

hospital, and I got a plane down to Santa Monica, so I was there when Laura was born. The next morning I flew back in time to go to work by eleven. Four days later, Diane got out of the hospital, and we wrapped Laura up at five days old and drove to Bishop and stayed three days before I had a day off. Laura slept in a drawer in a motel room while I worked.

We're finishing *Will Penny* the last week of February, and I get a call from Roger, who asks, "You ready to go to work? We're going to do a movie called *The Trip* that Jack Nicholson's just finished writing."

"I know. I just finished a movie with him." I told him about *Rebel Rousers*.

"Wow, he never mentioned a word to me about it."

I said it was a Roger Corman production, ten days, a little motor-cycle movie. It's as good an avant-garde work as you'll ever see. The movie's terrible, the writing is good, and you won't see better work in terms of an acting ensemble.

I go to do *The Trip*, and there are the usual suspects: Peter Fonda, Susan Strasberg, Dennis Hopper. I didn't know Dennis at all until that movie. I got to know him well. Dennis isn't really in the movie. He shot the second unit because it was an acid trip. He had ideas about going out to Indian Wells and 29 Palms and shooting the actual acid trip.

I remember asking Roger, "How did you research this movie?"

He said, "I took a tab of acid and I lay down with my nose an eighth of an inch off the ground for six hours."

I said, "The ants in Jack Nicholson's backyard are no fucking different from the ants in my backyard. How could you stand the smell? It's all horseshit. Bad sewage. It's septic. Don't let him tell you he's on a sewer because he's not. Helena Kallianiotes is next door. Brando was on the bluff. Beatty's around the corner. A bunch of riffraff either way."

Corman said, "It was fascinating."

I said, "I don't know what acid looks like. I still don't know what cocaine looks like. It's mumbo jumbo to me."

I'd been in *Will Penny*, *The War Wagon*, and a couple of other studio films that were now five years ago. I didn't see a lot of progress. Jack had two lines in *Ensign Pulver*, otherwise he's been in nothing. Redford, Beatty, George Segal, Ron Leibman, Bud Cort, and Donald

Sutherland were taking off. Duvall was about to do *The Rain People*. Tony Bill had just done *You're a Big Boy Now* for Coppola, who was preparing *Finian's Rainbow*.

Anyway, we did *The Trip*. I don't think I worked more than four days, because I give Fonda the acid in the house, and then he runs off from me. I chase him into the Troubadour.* I lose him in the Troubadour and you don't see me again until the end of the movie, where I try to find him. The rest of the movie was the cameramen running around town shooting Peter getting into trouble with Susan Strasberg, Max Julian, and Adam Roarke.

1967 becomes an unbelievable year for me. While they're finishing *The Trip*, I do a movie with as funny a script as I've ever read, called *Waterhole Number Three*. The writer and director, Joe Steck, a funny wunderkind, had written a movie called *The President's Analyst*, which Jim Coburn was also in. *Waterhole Number Three*, a western, starts out with Coburn in a card game where he loses everything he's got. He's a gambler who's a slick cardplayer, a card shark, great at cheating, who sucks them all in, but loses the last fucking hand. He's broke. He walks outside, pulls his gun out, and kills his horse. Now he's got nothing. He looks into the lens and says, "So blame me. So what? I want to start from scratch, okay? Is that okay with you? Can we go on now?" He's saying this to the audience. I thought, shit, this works. It's funny. He goes into another saloon, and an old miner's there having a drink. The old miner has an attack. As he dies, he gives Coburn a napkin containing a map to waterhole number three, where there sits a fortune. He spends the rest of the movie trying to find it. Unbeknownst to him, there's a bunch of people also looking for waterhole number three: Timothy Carey; Strother Martin; Maggie Blye, who at that time was in love with Harry Dean Stanton; Jack Elam; and the guy who Jim Arness kills at the beginning of *Gunsmoke* every week, Bob Welke. Tim Carey, the

---

*A famous L.A. nightclub, which introduced Elton John, James Taylor, Joni Mitchell, Carole King, Blood, Sweat & Tears, Albert Brooks, and Steve Martin, among others. Doug Weston, who owned the Troubadour, was famous for making acts perform for a week at a time for a miserly stipend.

guy in Kubrick's movie *The Killing* who kills the horse, is in it. Carroll O'Connor is the sheriff, and I'm the sheriff's deputy. We're looking for the guys who are looking for waterhole number three. L. Q. Jones is another one. Warren Oates. They all find waterhole number three one after the other, except for Coburn, who has the real map. It's a *Mad, Mad, Mad, Mad World* with horses instead of cars. And it works.

Nothing happened after that, so I went back to doing episodic TV, *Gunsmokes* and so forth. I was literally running through the sixties. I would say between 1961 and 1970, I ran forty thousand miles. I was doing four thousand miles a year. In *Run for Your Life*, I replaced John Kerr, who had replaced Ben Gazzara, for the last four episodes as his running character. Fernando Lamas directed three, and Nick Colasanto directed one. Colasanto was an Actors Studio guy who had been part of *A Hatful of Rain*. He ended up being one of the bartenders in *Cheers*.

We were shooting the last weeks of the show, and on a Thursday night, I got thrown against the wall in a fight scene. A doorknob hit right behind my shoulder blade, which later caused my lung to collapse. It's called a spontaneous pneumothorax.

I was in the middle of Malibu Canyon, running Friday morning. I've never been shot, but it felt like I had been shot. Instead of coming home in twenty-nine minutes to do the four miles, it took me about an hour just barely being able to limp along terrified. When I came off the hill, I went right into Dr. Hiken's office, which was near the Malibu Colony where the Bank of America building was. He was a famous marathon runner who was a family M.D. A little older than I was. He lived in the Colony.

It was almost noon, and I didn't have to go to work that day until four. I went in, and he took a picture. He didn't blanch. He said, "Look at the two pictures. This is the left lung, and the screen is completely black, which means your lung is fine. The other side is completely white, which means there's no air in this lung, and the lung is flat and it's just tissue."

I asked, "Well, what does that mean?"

He said, "It's a ninety percent collapse, which means you have basically no air in your right lung. You have little blibs that look like little blisters on the lung. One of them breaks, and all the air goes out of your lung, then the lung seals itself. But all the air, instead of being in the lung, is now in the chest cavity outside of the lung. The lung is trying to work because it's a muscle. But it can't because the air is on top of it. That's why the pain is excruciating. And you only have fifty percent breath. If the other lung were to go down, you'd have about forty-five seconds to live. What's your day like?"

I said, "I've got to be to work at four. I can't miss it. What's the diagnosis?"

Dr. Hiken said, "You have two choices: One is you shouldn't go to work, because if you lose the air from the other lung, you're dead. Choice two is if you have to go to work, I can give you a couple of pain pills, but I can't do anything with the fact that you're going to be breathing like this all day."

I said, "Well, I can get around that somehow."

He said, "What kind of call do you think you'll have Monday?"

"What do I have to have done to me?"

"Tonight we'll put you in St. John's. I'm going to send you to Dr. Ramsey, who's a thoracic surgeon who you know because he removed John Wayne's and Bette Davis's lungs."

I said, "I don't have to have a lung out."

He said, "No, no. Your lung isn't damaged. You just have a hole in it. When you're through with work tonight, he will meet you at St. John's. What time do you finish?"

"I won't finish until midnight."

Dr. Hiken called Dr. Ramsey, who said, "I met Mr. Dern on *The War Wagon*, which was a movie he did in Durango, Mexico, with John Wayne. You tell him to be there at midnight."

I said, "No hospital's going to admit me at that hour."

Dr. Hiken said, "Call this number."

I called, and a lady answered the phone and said, "Yes, Mr. Dern, how are you? I'll be at the hospital at twelve thirty. I'll meet you there. Everything will be just fine."

I finish filming that night, arrive at St. John's, park my car in preferred parking. This seventy-five-year-old nun comes out—they're

Sisters of Mercy there so they have those big Dutch-windmill kind of hats—and takes my hand. She walks me to the door. And this lady comes out in a stunning dress. She takes my other hand, and she says, "Hi, Mr. Dern. I'm Loretta Young. I helped found this hospital." I thought, my God, it's Loretta Young. She had her own TV show then (*The Loretta Young Show*), and she'd just come from filming. It was an hour theater each week. She whisks me upstairs with this nun and puts me down in my bed, making sure I had everything I needed.

Dr. Ramsey's there, and he says, "I have a note from Mr. Wayne to make sure I don't screw up with you. As I see it, on this piece of paper, you've only done three movies. What's the big deal with you?"

"I don't know what it is."

"Well, according to the X-rays, you have a rather full spontaneous pneumothorax, which generally happens to American men more than others before the age of thirty. It's a young man's disease. Young men who are athletic get these little water blisters on their lung, and any kind of blow in the front or the back of the chest wall can break one of these little blibs, and within ten or fifteen seconds all the air escapes from the lung. So we have to get the air out of the chest cavity, and then the lung seals itself. Your alternatives are: I can cut you from here to here and we can go in and cauterize your lung, which means we take a sanding type of machine and we sand your entire lung and get rid of all the water blisters. The water blisters look as if they number a hundred to a hundred and twenty-five on your lung, which means that at any time any one could break. By sanding it, you will have no water blisters left, so they can never break again. And you won't develop new ones at this age." I was thirty.

Dr. Ramsey says, "It's unexplainable to me why you have this many. It doesn't make sense. And you have a lot on the other side, too. Or, you can go home and rest for forty days, and the assimilation of air while you're resting will fill the lung up, and while it's filling up, the air will disabsorb itself from your chest cavity. Or we can do what Miss Young has suggested, since no one must know you're here, nor can they know you were hurt. I will make a little incision right here with a local anesthetic, and I will stick a tube through that hole, and it will go down into your chest cavity, not into the lung, into the chest cavity. I will take the other end of the tube, and I will stick it in this bottle of water on the floor. When the water stops bubbling, that will mean all the air is out of the chest cavity. I will pull the tube out and put you on a rarefied oxygen machine for forty-five seconds, your lung fills up, and you will be at work Monday morning at six thirty, and no one will ever know this went on. We won't even stitch up this little hole. It'll close itself."

I say, "Well, that's the obvious choice."

He says, "So let's do that." He comes at me with a penknife.

"You said I was going to get a local."

"Damn, I always forget that."

A nurse comes in with a needle, and the little nun stands there and says, "Well, boys, do you need me anymore?"

The mother superior's name was Sister Mary Gertrude. "I'll be down the hall or around the hospital somewhere. Mr. Dern, if you need me, just press this buzzer on the wall."

"Thank you."

"The nurses are all nuns," she goes on to say. "So don't worry. You're in St. John's and Miss Young made sure that everybody on your floor is a nun. There are no laypeople here. Some of them are new. They are not saints. Make sure you understand that. Just because they wear habits, they're not saints." She leans way into me and says, "Nor am I a saint, sir."

Now it's just Dr. Ramsey and me. "Now, before I do this, let me sit down here and ask you, what's your lifestyle like?"

"I've never had a cigarette. I've never had a drink. I've never had a cup of coffee, and I don't do any drugs whatsoever and never have." This was before I'd ever had a Vicodin or a Quaalude.

"It puzzles me," he says. "Where did these blibs come from?"

I say, "Well, I'm a runner."

"Yeah, Duke [John Wayne] told me that when you were down in Mexico, you used to run two or three hours every day. Two hours in the morning and an hour at night. I'm not going to ask the obvious question: what are you running from, or where are you running to? Where do you live?"

"I live in the Valley."

"Where do you do most of your running?"

"Well, we train every afternoon at four. We meet at the little cricket ground there at Pickwick Stables in Griffith Park."

He slaps the table and says, "Let's do the operation. I know exactly what's wrong. When this operation is over, it'll take you a few months before you're going to want to run again. But when you start, don't ever, as long as you live, run or move a step in Griffith Park. It is the worst smog-congested area in the continental United States. Anywhere between seven thirty in the morning and seven thirty at night, all those freeways converge together at the corner of Griffith Park, and the smog sits there, and it's the most intense place in the city of Los Angeles." And this was 1967.

"You're breathing nothing but exhaust at a fifty percent level. That's where the blibs are coming from. They're growing bigger and bigger, and any kind of blow at all—a hard slap on the back—and these things are going to break. You just can't train there. A brisk walk of half an hour could have caused these to break. You didn't need a blow on the back. You are a walking time bomb."

He performs the procedure and says goodnight, and I say, "Thank you very much."

"Thank Duke and thank Miss Young."

He left, and I realized after this whirlwind seven hours, where are my people? The one person I had in my life was Miss Diane Ladd, who was in Texas selling *The Wild Angels*, which had opened that day. We just shot it ninety days earlier. It was opening in six hundred drive-ins all over Texas and Louisiana. Who would think you could make a movie in ten days and have it out ninety days later in six hundred theaters? Who would make six hundred prints of *The Wild Angels* and think they would do any business? On the opening weekend, I think it made a million dollars. No movie like that had ever made any kind of money. It was Peter Fonda, Nancy Sinatra, and me. I'm sure Nancy pulled all the money in, because "These Boots Are Made for Walking" was a big hit right then. Peter and I didn't mean anything, although I'm sure Peter meant a hell of a lot more than I did. And any billing that I got above the title, I'm robbing poor Bill Smithers. As far as I'm concerned, it's Bill Smithers whose career I'm having. And I kept thinking to myself, where is Miss Diane?

Monday morning I'm back shooting *Run for Your Life*. The director, Fernando Lamas, was probably as grand a laid-back guy as I'd ever met in Hollywood. I used one-sentence deliveries on everything where I had two or three sentences. I'd break the dialogue up, sneaking little breaths in between. It was all courtroom stuff, so it was plausible. Was it terrible? I think it was. But Fernando really didn't give a shit about anything except nailing the girl who was playing the ingénue.

In the late 1940s and '50s there were the actors and there were the personalities, and then there were guys like Fernando Lamas, who you just know covered the waterfront. He was a guy who was so charming that he talked Esther Williams not only out of a marriage, not only out of the pool, not only into his bed, but into a marriage with him. This is a guy who's in the water with Esther Williams, who had Olympic swimming credentials, on this film they were doing together. They're in this long, hundred-meter pool. He immediately says, "You will go home with me tonight. Mark my words." He's a good-looking guy.

She says, "I'll go home with you only one way. You've got charm, and I've heard how well endowed you are, and that does make a difference, but I'm in a relationship."

He says, "This does not matter to me. I've been in relationships, too. But your relationship is waning. I read the papers and the magazines. I know Miss Hedda Hopper. I know Miss Louella Parsons. We all read the same things. We go to the same parties."

And she says, "This is a hundred-meter pool. I've had the fastest time in the world for several years. You're an athletic guy or you wouldn't have gotten the part in the movie."

He says, "You'll go home with me if I beat you to the other end of the pool, right? That's what you're going to say? When you say go, we go."

She says, "Go."

He beat her by fifteen meters. Fernando Lamas was also an Olympic swimmer, but for Mexico. She had not done her homework. He had.

Roger Corman did a major motion picture called *St. Valentine's*

Day Massacre for Fox. It was a million-dollar movie. He had to use the contract players at the studio. Jason Robards played the lead, and George Segal, David Canary, and Clint Ritchie were under contract. Roger had to use Jack Nicholson and me because we were his guys. Jack and I each got $550 a week instead of scale, which was $375 a week. We knew we could act as good as those other guys.

Roger does a great thing for Jack and me. He says, "Both of you work three days. Jack, you're going to play the cab driver, and, Bruce, you're going to play John May, one of the seven who lined up against the wall and gets shot. So you guys will get paid twenty-five hundred dollars because I'm going to have you both work the first two days of the movie and the last day of the movie."

Roger carried us for five weeks. That was sensational of him to do that for us.

Seventy-five percent of everything I learned about the business, I learned from B movies, because you weren't directed. The guys who were directing them didn't know how to direct. They were just making a scam film to make bucks. They were involved in the deal somehow. In *Psych-Out*, Dick Rush was a serious filmmaker, but he had no conception of how to deal with an actor. He just didn't know what to say to you; he'd just say, "Do it again," or "Try it again," and any kind of enthusiasm or energy he would mistake for talent, and he would love that. He was the most sensitive of the early directors that I worked for, although he wasn't the best. Corman was far superior to him. So what you did was to learn to do it yourself. You learn how to survive and be real and be good and be interesting and exciting and to promote your career and continue on. That's what you learn, and that was 75 percent of the ball game. Now, later, that becomes a problem, because you may get a director you don't trust. So you have a tendency to nod "Yes, yes" to a director, but inside you're fighting him, and you can't give it all to him. That was hard for Jack, and that was hard for me.

In the summer of '68, I go to New Mexico with a new girlfriend* and do *Hang 'Em High*. One of the producers told me, "You tickle the shit out of Clint Eastwood. He and his costar Pat Hingle love you.

---

*Though still married, Dern and Diane Ladd were in the final throes of their marriage.

They need a guy who will give leverage to the bad guy in this movie, and they'd like you to play it." Ted Post, who had directed me in a *Rawhide* and was a friend of Clint's, directs the movie.

There's a little girl named Inger Stevens who's the female star of the movie, and she took her life right after the end of filming. I don't know why. She was pretty. She had a nice ingénue career. She was still on her way up. It was tragic.

Hang 'Em High has the greatest single stunt ever performed in the history of movies. Not by Clint, but by Ben Johnson. We hang Clint at the beginning of the movie, and we ride off and leave him. Ben Johnson comes over the hill and sees him hanging alone. He rides toward him full-out. Pulls a knife, rides, stops his horse dead as he slashes the rope, dismounts, and before Clint hits the ground, catches him. No cut. Only Johnson could do that. He was the greatest cowboy who ever lived, and I mean bona fide five-time world champion. Greatest roping cowboy who ever rode, and he got a part in a movie simply because he was a wrangler on *Rio Grande* and John Ford saw him do a stunt on the second day of the movie and said to John Wayne, "Who the fuck was that?"

Wayne said, "Oh, that's Ben Johnson. He's the best horseman who ever lived."

Hang 'Em High ended up being the most recognized movie with Bruce Dern in the first twelve years of my career. Most people bring up that movie to me because Clint basically emerged from the spaghetti westerns as a result of it.

Miss Diane and I were now having big problems about my remaining in the household. She had been offered a play on Broadway costarring Cicely Tyson and David Steinberg, who was about to become a big comedian, and directed by Sidney Poitier. It was called *Carry Me Back to Morningside Heights*. Diane went back to New York, and Laura stayed with the granny in Santa Monica. Sydney Pollack sent me a script, *Castle Keep*, and offered me one of two parts. I went to Novisad, Yugoslavia (now Serbia), where *Castle Keep* was being shot. The family, once again, was split, as it had been since it first began.

Tom Gries calls me and asks, "Do you want to do another movie with me?" Tommy had directed four *Stoney Burkes*, and that's where

I got to know him. "This fall, the New Orleans Saints are having their first season. We have a script called *Number One* that's going to star Heston as an aging quarterback for the Saints. Everybody knows they're no good. We're going to travel with the team the first eight weeks of the season, and you're going to play his wide receiver who's in his last year and really wants to get out. They've all been picked up from other teams because they were in the expansion draft."

So we traveled with the Saints the first eight weeks. One thrilling thing was they opened the season against the Rams—and I was a Rams fan—in New Orleans. The Rams kicked off to the Saints. First game, first play they ever had in their existence.

John Gilliam, who later had a great career with the Vikings, caught the ball and ran 104 yards back for a touchdown. First play of the Saints' history. In the movie, we go through the season, and they lose, and they lose, and they lose. By the end of the movie, the number-one draft choice, a black kid, has taken over as quarterback, and the team has a future. But they don't win any games. The beauty of the movie is when the black kid gets hurt in the thirteenth game and Heston has to play in the last game. It's his last hurrah. So they go out and play hard. They win the game 17 to 14. Heston's not a hero. They play decently enough because they play as a team.

From *Number One*, I went on to do *The Cycle Savages*, where I made $1,750 a week for three weeks. That means $5,250 to star in this movie. I played a real bad biker, and Chris Robinson played an artist and the love/romantic star of the movie. Melody Patterson was the good-looking girl star, and you just knew the filmmakers were going to have a scene where I was going to have my way with her after I took care of the artist.

I had to blind him and cut his hands all up so he could never paint again. Typical Bruce Dern storyline in the sixties. I start out really horribly nasty, then turn into not really that bad a guy. There was a scene where a detective grilled me and showed me I really wasn't as tough as I thought I was. One scene. So they went out and got a guy who had been a legitimate movie star—Scott Brady. *Shotgun Slade*, that's what I remembered him as. He was a good actor. I thought, God, today I get to work with Scott Brady. That was big stuff to me. He was in a TV series, and he was in a lot of good movies. I mean, he was up there with Jimmy Stewart and always stood in there with Robert Ryan and guys like that. He was good. He played a lot of sidekicks but starred in a lot of what they called B movies. I saw all those movies. He was with Jeff Chandler, and he was with Neville Brand. He was a good-looking guy and menacing.

So he came in, and they paid him thirty thousand dollars. I didn't care. He was only there for one day, but his name meant something. It was like when director Patty Jenkins said to me my name meant something in *Monster*. That's why they wanted me in the movie. I don't know who it meant something to. You could put my name above the rubber machine in the Texaco station. No one's going to buy one because it said Bruce Dern. But Scott Brady, he brought people. I was excited because I was going to work with him. The one thing I got from Gadg at the very beginning of our relationship was that every day I went to work, I thought, we're going to do something nobody ever did before. And that's what I've hoped for on every movie I've ever been on.

· 7 ·

"You Are Not a Leading Man"

I t's the week before Christmas, 1968, and my agent calls: "Bruce, you won't believe this. I got a call from Sydney Pollack."

I said, "What are you talking about? Sydney Pollack? I just finished with him in January."

He said, "He's doing another movie, and he wants you in it. He says he apologizes because it's not much of a part. It's certainly not an improvement over the last part, but he offered you the Scott Wilson role and you didn't want to take it because you didn't want to be in Yugoslavia five months."

"Do you blame me?"

"No, it ended up being seven. You were smart. He's doing a movie called *They Shoot Horses, Don't They?*, and he said you and a girl named Bonnie Bedelia, who hasn't acted before, are going to be partners. It's about dance marathons, and he wants you for two reasons: one, you play a country bumpkin and you win the contest; two, he needs somebody who can show the actors what it's like to go

77

take after take after take because Bonnie is pregnant in the movie and you've got to haul her every day, derby after derby. Twice each day, they're raced twelve laps around the floor to music. The last three couples are eliminated. Sydney wants to shoot it like that. He's going to eliminate the couples except for the two starring couples, Jane Fonda and Michael Sarrazin, and Red Buttons and Allyn Ann McLerie. Everybody else gets eliminated, including Susannah York."

"Susannah York should've won an Oscar for *The Killing of Sister George*. He's going to eliminate her?"*

"He's going to eliminate whoever finishes last. He can't eliminate you because you and Bonnie win the contest in the book. And you're not going to be last."

The first day on the set I see this big dance hall that they set up with grandstands all around. Johnny Green, the musician, is sitting at the piano playing Johnny Green songs. Gig Young is at the mike as the emcee. Susannah York, I had no idea what a tremendous actor she was. She was flat-out great. There's Jane walking around with Al Lewis from *The Munsters*. Severn Darden. There's Felice Orlandi. Art Metrano. Michael Sarrazin.

I meet Bonnie, who is eighteen. Sydney doesn't rehearse. He wants to shoot. The first morning, we're all on the dance floor. Everybody's dancing too hard except me.

Sydney stops and says, "No, no, Bruce, you and Bonnie keep dancing. That's Bruce Dern and Bonnie Bedelia. I want everybody to look at the way they're dancing. What do you notice?"

Some wag says, "They're dancing too slow."

"And why are they dancing too slow?"

"I don't know, but it doesn't look good in the movie. It looks like they don't give a shit."

Sydney asks, "Bruce, why are you dancing so slow?"

I say, "Because we're going to be doing this until April first, and it's

---

*York went on to be nominated for an Academy Award for this movie, as did Gig Young, Jane Fonda, Sydney Pollack, and the art director, the costumer, the editor, the writers, and the composer. Only Young actually won an award, however.

January fifteenth. Franklin Lenkowski set the world record for dancing seventy-three days without sitting down."

The wag says, "Oh. You mean it's called moving as slow as you can for as long as you can."

"Right. You get a six-minute break every fourth hour six times a day. In that six minutes, you've got to shower, go to the bathroom, eat whatever you want to eat, although you can eat out on the floor. All day long, you've got eight to nine thousand people in the stands, cheering for you, not cheering for you, just watching you. You're bugs in a zoo and they're watching you and they're betting on who's going to drop and who's not. There's five hundred of you at the start, and at the end, whatever two are still standing win it."

Twice a day, at lunchtime and at midnight, they stop dancing, and we line up at a start line, and we race. Twelve laps. The last three couples around the floor after the twelve laps are eliminated. We do that twice a day every day until there's no one left except one couple. That couple wins five thousand dollars for seventy days' work. In the meantime, there are prizes each night for the couple that wins and for best costume or talent—people would break out and do a jazz number. So if you were really good, you could win yourself thirty-five, forty thousand bucks in three months. It was outlawed on the Santa Monica Pier and Pacific Ocean Pier in L.A. in 1936 after the incident in the movie when the kid killed the girl. It's a true story.

On the East Coast, Francesco LoVecchio ended up being world famous for doing something else. He holds the world record for marathon dancing of one hundred forty-five days and a few hours and turned out to sing a song called "Mule Train," changing his name to Frankie Laine.

While I'm doing this movie, Sydney is cutting *Castle Keep*, next door to Tommy Gries, who is looking at dailies for *Number One*; assembling their movies right next to each other. I'm feeling proud. Then comes the most heartbreaking day of my career, the only time I've ever felt sad enough to cry in front of somebody else about the movie business.

The fifth day of shooting I'm sitting in a rest period between scenes. Sydney comes over and says, "How do you feel? How many miles would you say you've run today already? I've got at least seventy-five percent of the actors saying they can't do any more today."

I say, "Sydney, it's three thirty. Normally I run fifteen to twenty a day. I feel like I've done four or five."

"So you think these people got more in them?"

"Sydney, this is their fifth day. If they quit now you'll never get them through three weeks. You'll have to shut down. There's no scenes where they're not on their feet except where Gig Young is screwing Jane in the back or some other little girl, and that's two days' work."

Sydney asks, "What'll I do?"

I say, "You can risk making about seventy percent of them run one or two days but then they're gone for the movie because they will mentally break down when their bodies are exhausted. They're not running for a gold medal."

"But they're running for cash, their salaries."

"Sydney, they're actors, not athletes."

He says, "Let me talk to you about another problem. I'm not nuts about Michael Sarrazin's work. I've called Redford. I talked to Beatty. I've talked to a couple other people. You see actors all the time. Who do you know that could play this role? I'm thinking of switching this weekend and recasting Michael's role."

I look up at him, and the tears are running down my face. "Sydney, you're looking at him."

He says, "You are not a leading man."

I take a deep breath and hang with it. He walks away from me. Monday, Michael Sarrazin is back, and Sydney yells at him every day for three weeks. Tries to replace him five or six times. He has nine guys turn the role down. Never once does he come to me. I've never gotten over it to this day. Sydney actually said to my face, "You are not a leading man."

I can't think of a movie Sydney's done where there wasn't a Redford or a guy like that. I was never in that category. Although he thought of me, he never thought of me on a grand scale. There are people in your life who will never give you a shot at grabbing the gold ring. Sydney was one. He's one of the directors who I would have loved to have had that chance from, because he demands you push the envelope every single shot. Had I been able to have that opportunity with him, I might have gotten some really great work. I'm saying I'm an actor who was blessed with certain kinds of unique abilities who had a chance to be a truly great actor and hasn't been yet. That's my thing with Sydney Pollack. I've done better than some of the actors I've worked with, and I haven't had a chance to work with some actors who could have made me better.

It's still coming. I hope.

A few years ago, when I was doing some television work for the opening of the documentary A Decade under the Influence, Sydney and I were on a panel together onstage. I told him the story from They Shoot Horses. He remembered it, but never thought that I'd been bothered by it. I was shocked. As we were walking out the door, he put an arm around me and turned my head so I'd look him right in the eye. He said, "Jesus, man. I'm so sorry. I had no idea." That's a guy who was a mentor of mine, and he was also the director of that James Whitmore TV episode I did when our child died. So he has tremendous game.

One day on They Shoot Horses, Jane Fonda came up to me and said, "Have you seen Peter's new movie?"

And I said, "No."

She said, "Well there's a guy in it, Jack Nicholson. You know who he is?"

I said, "Yeah, I kind of know who he is." This is after having done seven movies with Roger and Jack.

"He's in this movie with Peter, and, of course, Peter's the best thing in it. It's Peter's movie. But this guy Jack Nicholson, he's really something. He's fabulous in it. Somebody said you should tell Bruce Dern that because he'll be happy for his friend who nobody knows. His work is really extraordinary."

Surprisingly, she never mentioned Dennis Hopper.

I said, "That's good. What's the movie called?"

She said, "Easy Rider. It's a drive-in movie, but it'll do real well. And Jack Nicholson, he could be a star. He's real funny and he's real good. He's a special talent."

"That's good."

"I thought you should know that. Do you really know him?"

"Yeah, I know who he is. I suspect I'll get a note in my box if he gets any kind of reviews."

"Oh, he'll get reviews. He'll win the Academy Award."

"That's doubtful. No one in the Academy will see a movie like *Easy Rider*, another fuckin' motorcycle movie. Tell me about it, I've only done two billion of them."

I thought Jane was an enormous talent, and yet she was still married to Roger Vadim and had just finished *Barbarella*. I wondered why she was not doing *They Shoot Horses, Don't They?* every movie instead of *Barbarella*.

I didn't dare eat lunch on *They Shoot Horses*. I felt subservient to Jane Fonda, because she made me feel that way. She didn't treat me as an equal yet. I wasn't Michael Sarrazin. What can I tell you? A lot of times I'd run on my lunch hour. All the other movies, like *Support Your Local Sheriff*, I'd eat with the wranglers or the cowboys. I never felt I was really on a movie set. It was like the day I did *Gunsmoke*. Here's Bette Davis in the commissary. I'm going to sit down and have lunch with her? Or when I did a pilot for Dick Powell called *Adamsberg, U.S.A.*, and there's Charles Bickford, Lorraine Day, Dennis Morgan, Michael O'Shea, Charlie Ruggles, and Gene Raymond. They were all big stars in their own right. I was going to sit down at the commissary and eat lunch with them? I didn't belong there.

I will say that on *Support Your Local Sheriff*, a couple of times Jim Garner said, "You gonna eat lunch?" I would say, "I think I'll go run." I didn't realize that what he was saying was, "Let's go eat lunch." But he said, "Are you gonna eat lunch?" I was feeling that I didn't belong.

· 8 ·

Star of the Second-Best Two-Headed-Transplant Movie of 1971

In the summer of 1969, I meet Andrea Beckett in a class I'm teaching. Lee asks me that summer if I would teach at the Strasberg Institute he's opening in L.A.

Andrea went from a town in North Dakota to New York to become an actress and a model. She did it the hard way. She didn't know anybody. She had a little acting class in high school. She modeled for Bonwit's and magazines. She took acting classes and then came to California. She was a widow at twenty-four years old. She had married her high school sweetheart, who later died in a car accident, and she said, "I'm not a widow. I can't hack this." She came to California with her friend in a '66 Corvette convertible. She was a hottie and still is a hottie. Went to work for Petersen Publishing and enrolled in an acting class that I taught. I was doing *They Shoot Horses, Don't They?* I was living with Susan Stevenson, who was an extra in movies, and Andrea took her spot, and we've been together since. She's a rock. She gets it.

She gets it as fast as anyone I've ever known. She's the best friend I've ever had.

Andrea's an artist. She's a painter, a very successful one. She's always been an artist. Every house we ever had, she's just gone to the nines on it. *Architectural Digest* did it right to the top. Been in every magazine there is with what she's done with the home we've lived in and other people's homes.

She bought into the whole idea of what I did from the beginning. Nothing interferes with my work, and a good sex life stimulates art. A good sex life stimulates anything. A bad sex life will affect human performance. It's the only thing in the world like that where something is leaving you; both men and women are actually losing—what is it? Red cells? White cells? I don't know. I always had biology classes during the World Series.

You've got to get the sex part of the relationship right the first night. The first night. You've got to say, "I'm into this, this, this, and this. It's all not gonna happen tonight, but these things could come out at any time. Accept it or we can't make it." I really believe that. If both people can accept and understand that, then the morals, the intelligence, the downtime, the athletic endeavors, the drive, the emotional capacities, all the other things will fit in. If there comes a time when the playroom part of the bedroom is not there enough for both people, there is going to be serious trouble in that relationship down the road.

They'll grind it out, but they'll *grind* it out. My first two marriages were ground out. It was more my fault. I was the pig in the relationships. I was the bad guy, no question about it.

I respect Andrea enormously. She's as close to the perfect lady as anyone I've ever known, in terms of having her priorities in the right place, her attractiveness, her durability, and accessibility to me. Her ability to bend, not break, is her greatest attribute, and that was essential with me. It's taught me to be the same way—and I'm still too selfish. My marriage to Andrea is successful. I'm deeply in love with my wife, who I hope is deeply in love with me.

During this time, Lee Strasberg, Anna, his wife, Andrea, and I are going to Rams exhibition football games, and we develop a relationship where he and I are very one-on-one. I was closer to him then than

I ever was to Kazan. Lee and I would have long talks. He explains the difference in their two theories about me. And he knows about my being upset with the fact that I wasn't included in *Splendor in the Grass*. He explains to me that it wasn't an oversight that my name wasn't on the screen in *Wild River*. He explains to me Gadg's lack of understanding about how I sat with my family and how he didn't get that and how he would never get that. Lee was a New York Giants fan. When the Giants played the Dodgers in L.A., I'd pick him up and we'd go — just like fans.

He went to a couple of my movies with me. I would say, "Just talk to me. Let's sit way back here." We'd go at two in the afternoon when no one was in the theater. "Talk me through the scene. Tell me what you see. Tell me what you don't see." One was *Support Your Local Sheriff*. The other was *Silent Running*, which was the last movie we ever saw together. *Silent Running* blew him away.

Lee said, "I can't imagine teaching a student to do what you did. How did you do it? You're talking to a box."

I said, "No, I'm talking to a guy in the box. I'm like Señor Wences on *The Ed Sullivan Show*."

He said, "I've watched you teach. The ideas you gave were absolutely brilliant. I just don't think they'll work in my school."

I said, "They won't work in any school, because the students are not ready to receive them at the age you teach."

He said, "If I had a perfect world, I'd try to teach students never younger than thirty-five years old. I'd be broke."

Andrea and I had been living together about four months, and we decided we wanted to get married. Andrea won't have a shot of any kind, so she wanted to get married in Nevada because they don't require blood tests there. We were going to Tahoe in October after I'd run in the American Fifty Mile Championship at Rocklin outside of Sacramento.

The end of September, Maurice Smith, a producer, called me and said, "Look, you want to make $1,750 for ten days work?"

I said, "What do I have to do?"

"I want to make a movie called *The Incredible Two-Headed Transplant*."

"I don't want to do it. Call my agent."

And he said, "You've got to do it. There's no one else to do it. We've got Berry Kroeger."

I said, "Who the fuck is Berry Kroeger?"

"He's done every weird fucking science movie ever made. You'll know him when you see him. If there's a movie with a crazy doctor with a limp, he's done it because he's got a limp."

"You ask my agent, Ronnie Leif, what he wants to do."

Leif called me and said, "Okay, here's the deal. I've got $1,750 a week for two weeks, and you only work ten days."

"Ronnie, ten days is two weeks. What are you talking about? They don't shoot Saturdays and Sundays. I've got $1,750 for two weeks, we've got $3,500."

I figured that's the money Andrea and I can get married on. So I do the movie. At the same time, Roosevelt Grier and Ray Milland are doing a movie in which Grier is a two-headed man.* And Rosie Grier is a big person. It's easy to mount two heads on him because he's six feet nine and weighs 340 pounds. I had known him since college, when I was at Penn and he was at Penn State. He was national champion in the shot put and also was a great football player and was one of the fearsome foursome of the Rams. The year before, he had been in the room when Robert Kennedy was shot, and he was the guy who physically picked up Sirhan Sirhan and slammed him against the bar. And Ray Milland is an Oscar winner. The audience is going to see their movie, not my little movie where I'm the doctor who creates this guy, a seven-foot kid who went to Southern Cal as a basketball player, who has a little actor strapped on his back. The big guy is the nice guy, and the little guy who's the other head is the bad, sick guy. They run around creating all kinds of mayhem.†

---

*Called *The Thing with Two Heads*, it used the tag line "They transplanted a white bigot's head onto a soul brother's body!"

†Called *The Incredible Two-Headed Transplant*, it used the tag line "This brain wants to LOVE . . . this brain wants to KILL!" Neither of these movies ought to be confused with the later Steve Martin comedy, *The Man with Two Brains*, which also starred Pig's Dad (James Cromwell).

My costar, who played my wife, was Pat Priest, who was on *The Munsters*. She was pretty and a great dame. Her mother, Ivy Baker Priest, was the secretary of the treasury, whose signature was on all the currency. Now Pat Priest is a player, and I'm about to marry Andrea.

Pat said, "Why don't you stop by on the way to work some morning? My girlfriend and I have coffee before she drives me to work. Have you seen her?"

I said, "Hey, babe, I'm getting married this fall. I'm out of that. I don't do that anymore."

She said, "Bring Andrea by. We work out, have a little brunch, and we all get together."

I said, "Hey, babe, I'm not up for that. How do you work all day? I can't do it."

Andrea and I never got together with Pat there or anywhere else.

Andrea and I got married off the money from *The Incredible Two-Headed Transplant*. That was the end of my bona fide B days. That wasn't a B. If you're going to call *The Wild Angels* a B movie, this was a Z movie.

· 9 ·

Jack Job

I t's early 1970, and Andrea and I have been married three months. I'm doing a TV show on a rainy, pissing-down, horrible, thunder, lightning, rainy cold January day at Fox called *The Land of the Giants* for Irwin Allen, who would later go on to do *The Poseidon Adventure* and *The Towering Inferno*. But now he's doing *Land of the Giants*.* He's a nice man.

I get a phone call. In those days, a phone call meant you had to go to the wall of Stage 9 and pick up a phone. Jack Nicholson says, "Dernser."

"Yes sir."

"What are you doing March fifteenth?"

---

*The show was exactly what it sounds like. A ship full of earthlings crashes on a parallel earth where the humans are all giants. In this especially weird episode, Dern guest-starred as Thorg, a time-traveling changeling.

"I don't have a fucking idea. I know I'm in the line collecting sixty-five with all the other tuna fishermen in Santa Monica. What are you doing?"

"I'm doing a movie, Dernser, and I owe you one."

"What do you owe me one for?"

"Because you put me in *Rebel Rousers*."

"You wrote me a part in *The Trip*."

Jack says, "No, I didn't. I wrote myself a part in the fucking *Trip*, and Roger wouldn't let me play it. I never told you it was for me. I'd have been a lot better than you were because I wrote it myself and I understood it."

"I wasn't bad in the part."

"I'd have been better."

"Yeah, okay. So what do you want?"

"I'm going to send you a script this afternoon. You go home tonight. You're not watching the Lakers game, you're reading my fucking script. There's two parts in the script. One is a basketball coach, and the other an English teacher who's married to Blackie (Karen Black). You can play whichever one you want to play. I've got a hunch which one you're going to play. But you're going to call me in the morning, and you're going to tell me which one you're going to play, okay? You're going to work for a thousand dollars a week, and you're not supposed to tell a fucking soul what I'm paying you. I'll give you two per diems for shooting in Eugene, Oregon, and it starts March fifteenth. What are you doing at Fox?"

"I'm doing *Land of the Giants*."

"Jesus Christ. What the fuck is that?"

"It's a TV show."

"Oh, my God. Stop working on the small fucking screen. *Land of the* fucking *Giants*!"

"Well, we can't all be in *Five Easy* fucking *Pieces*. What is that about?"

"It's about five of the easiest pieces of ass that I ever got."

"I figured it would be something like that. But you're on your way now, Bud. What do you got to worry about?"

"Right now I'm directing this fucking movie *Drive, He Said*. You read the script. You tell me what you think. But you've got to be in it, Derns."

The script comes. I read it, and I'm puzzled by it. I love the script. It works. It's a good movie. And there's a note in it about who the cast people are. Karen Black's in it. Bill Tepper's in it as the basketball player. Never heard of him. Just says Fairfax High School, third team all-city. Michael Margotta. I don't know who he is. He's in it as the roommate. No Coach Bullion cast yet. No history professor. I don't see Harry Dean Stanton's name. I don't see any of the guys that were in *The Trip*, *Wild Angels*, *Psych-Out*, or *Easy Rider*—Luke Askew or any of those other guys that I thought were around Jack. I said, "Shit, this is a movie he's casting himself that Jeremy Larner wrote. Jeremy Larner will win an Oscar the next year for *The Candidate*. Who are these guys?"

I chose to do the part of the basketball coach. And I went up to Oregon, and the first day I was there, I went and saw Jack.

Jack said, "I'm glad you made it. You gonna work tomorrow, Dernser? You're fucking brilliant."

I said, "Right now I'm on my way home."

"What do you mean?"

"You told me on the phone the terms of the deal."

"Yeah, what about it? You want more money now?"

"No. You said I could have two per diems."

"Yeah. You got two per diems."

"No, Fred Roos said that he could only afford to give me one, and if he had to give me another, they were going to take it out of his salary."

Jack turned and looked at Fred Roos. "Give him another per diem."

Roos said, "It's for his wife."

"I don't give a fuck who it's for. I told the man he could have two per diems. He's only getting a thousand dollars a fucking week. This man's in big movies."

Roos asked, "What big movies has he been in?"

"He's in movies that are coming out. Some horse movie he did. A western about shooting horses. *Will Penmanship*, or whatever it's called. Who gives a shit? He's in big fucking movies. Bigger movies than you or I have been on. With big stars."

"Well, who are the stars?"

"Carlton Cheston."

Roos said, "But Jack, I don't have a budget for that."

"Give him his two fucking per diems and quit fucking with my actors, will you?"

Jack was always a guy of his word. He wanted me to be in the movie. Whether it was because he felt he owed me or because he felt I was best for the role didn't really matter. I was in the movie. And he gave me an opportunity to be really good. He encouraged me to push the envelope all the time. Each scene. I was rough on him a couple days when I saw him playing basketball instead of directing. Not pushing himself as hard as he would push other people. But his directing was just magical. Nicholson, even though it was one time out, gave me the single best piece of direction I've ever had for a moment in a movie, and I gave him the single best moment I've ever given in a movie, even though both scenes were only three seconds long. I had to go around the corner and walk down the hall, but within that three seconds, I gave him something he'll never get from another human being.

My character, Coach Bullion, sees some puss walking down the hall, and he snaps his fingers in her direction. We shoot it, somebody says we didn't get the sound, and Jack says, "Come on. You'll see a moment of pure genius once every two decades. That's it. If you don't get the snap, who gives a fuck. I don't care. We saw what he did." It says everything about why I came to Hollywood to make movies. That's a Dernser. And maybe Dean did it once and maybe Brando's done it twice. That's it. If that doesn't say what we're in movies for, if that doesn't say what this character's about or what this scene's about or what this movie's about, that's him. Jack said, "The man didn't utter a fucking word."

In another scene, Jack said to look exhausted at something. It's just a pantomime, but basically, I'm absolutely frustrated. I'm in my player's face. It's halftime in a semi-final game. I'm trying to explain something to my star player, who just isn't getting it. He's worried about his roommate, who's trying to beat the draft. He's worried about the fact that he's not scoring and he's got a six foot nine guy he can't get around. He's worried that he went to Fairfax High School and he can't play big-time college basketball. He's worried about puss, he's worried about Karen Black. He's worried about all these things. And I get frustrated.

Jack says, "At the end, instead of acting like that, just put your hands on your knees and turn your head to the side, looking into the camera. Look right into the lens, utterly frustrated." And it was great. It's perfect. He was absolutely right.

Of all the directors I've worked for, I miss the experience of Jack directing me more than I do anybody else. I was quite touched when I read in some magazine recently an interview with him where he said, "I would very much like to work with Bruce Dern again." I really liked that, because I was the only one he singled out. It was very touching to me. I have a couple of books in which the authors said one of the things that seems to be disappointing in Mr. Nicholson's work is that in the later years he doesn't seem to challenge himself with the actors he works with as much as he did earlier. Where are the Bruce Derns? Where are the Nurse Ratcheds? It's not his fault. He doesn't pick the people he works with. Jack's a guy who always defers to his director. If you work for Mike Nichols, you don't tell Mike Nichols, "Get me Bruce Dern." Mike Nichols knows where I live. He knows how to get hold of me. I would love to work with Jack. I miss that relationship. There are things that I've really missed since the sixties and early seventies. I miss working with Jack as an actor. I miss terribly working with Jack directing me. And I miss Roger Corman directing me in a big movie, or directing a big movie. Period. In other words, I'd want to work for Jack twice: once with him as a director only and once as an actor. But *Drive, He Said* was a great experience for me, and I thought it had tremendous potential as a movie. The movie was not particularly well received. It wasn't well distributed. Why, I don't know.

By the middle of July, there were three projects that were on the front burner in town that all the guys in my age group—directors, writers, and actors—were keenly aware of. One was a script to be directed by Monte Hellman called *Two-Lane Blacktop*. One was a Vernon Zimmerman–directed project called *Deadhead Miles*. One was a movie Robert Aldrich was directing called *The Grissom Gang*. Within the same day, offers came to actors on all three projects. The first one was *Deadhead Miles*, where I met with Alan Arkin, Vernon Zimmerman, and Tony Bill. It was strange, because I'd never met with an actor before to play a part in a movie. I came out of the office and rode down in the elevator with Arkin, assuming I had the role. That was the last time I ever assumed I had a role in my career. I did not get the offer. Paul Benedict got the offer and played the role. Vernon Zimmerman directed it. I don't know what happened to the movie.*

I was called in to meet with Martin Baum by my agent, Ronnie Leif, who was told by Baum, who was running Fox or Seven Arts, that I was going to play the starring role in *The Grissom Gang*. We went over to have a meeting with Baum to solidify the deal. We sat in his office, and he got Robert Aldrich on the speakerphone. I don't know where Aldrich was, but he wasn't in Hollywood. Baum said, "Bob, I've got Bruce Dern in my office, and we just want to firm up the deal and have you say hello to him." Robert Aldrich had directed me in *Hush, Hush, Sweet Charlotte*. So I thought it was kind of like pleasant feelings. Well, I didn't get a pleasant voice on the phone.

I said, "Hello, Bob, how are you? How are your kids?" All his kids — Elita, Alana, and Bill Aldrich — they all worked on his movies. They were in their teens or twenties, and they'd all worked on *Hush, Hush, Sweet Charlotte*.

Aldrich just said, "They're fine."

Baum said, "So, we're going to make Bruce's deal."

Aldrich said, "No. I want Scott Wilson. I don't want Bruce." Right in front of me.

And Marty Baum turned to Paul Lazarus, who was his assistant then, and said, "Get Scott Wilson's agent on the phone. I'm sorry, Bruce, it's just not going to work. That's the way it goes sometimes." Marty Baum's one of my agents now. He's ninety-two years old, and he walks to the office every day. He's a fabulous guy.†

---

*Not much. It remains to be seen whether this was truly a missed opportunity.

†Dern dodged a bullet here, as the movie did so badly that Aldrich could no longer produce films, just direct them.

In the meantime, just before lunch that day, I got an offer from pro- ducer Michael Laughlin to star as the lead in *Two-Lane Blacktop* for a thousand dollars a week for twelve weeks, playing G.T.O., the main character. Twelve thousand dollars for the movie. The other stars were going to be James Taylor and Dennis Wilson. Obviously they were looking for music star power and not actors. I was going to be the actor. Monte Hellman was the director, and I knew Monte because he had been Roger Corman's script supervisor when Roger couldn't get Bonnie Pendergrast. And Monte was good. He was a writer and direc- tor, an avant-garde, underground, bona fide guy. He had wanted to direct this movie for years and years and years, and it finally was going to get done.

So Ronnie said to Laughlin, "I'll get back to you after lunch."

Laughlin said, "You can't give me an answer now? Because that's the offer. It's not going to get better than that."

Ronnie figured he's got two hours. He can go to lunch. Think about it.

Laughlin said, "Are you going to accept that offer? Because that's the offer."

Ronnie said, "I'm not going to accept an initial offer, for Christ's sake. Let me think about it a couple hours. You can't do better than a thousand dollars a week? That's what he got on *Drive, He Said*."

Laughlin said, "Yeah, that's right. Last month he worked for a thousand dollars a week. That's what he's worth. That's what he's going to get."

"Yeah, but that was one of four stars in a movie. This is a movie that's being done for the same kind of budget, a million dollars, but he's in every shot and he's the star of it. Can't you come up a little bit?"

"That's the offer. Take it or leave it."

"I'll get back to you after lunch."

Ronnie knew we had to go to the Bob Aldrich meeting, and Ron- nie would play both ends against them. We came back from Aldrich, and Ronnie said, "Well, I'm going to have to call him back and tell him I want a little more money."

I said, "Call him back and accept the fucking part. Who are we kidding?"

"I'm nothing as an agent if I can't get at least a hundred dollars a day more than this. This is ridiculous. What do you need an agent for then?"

"Exactly. That's the point."

So he called, and Michael Laughlin said, "We cast Warren Oates. I told you before lunch. We made an offer. You didn't take the offer. We moved on."

And Ronnie said, "You didn't give me a chance to negotiate."

"Yes, I did. I told you you had an offer of a thousand dollars a week for twelve weeks. That's twelve thousand dollars. And you said you wanted to think about it. I said that's what it is. It's not going to change."

"You can't do business like that, Michael."

"That's the way it's going to be from now on. That's the way I do business, and I'm going to turn this business around and change it. This is the new breed here. It's the seventies. That's the way we're going to do business from now on."

"Well, you're not going to do business like that with me or anybody else."

So I lost three jobs in one day and was dead on the vine.

· 10 ·

Saying No to Coppola

A month after that *Two-Lane Blacktop* incident, I got a letter from Fred Specktor, who was at William Morris.

He said, "Dear Bruce. I've watched your career for about eight years. And it's my opinion that you have been both marketed and sold wrong since *Marnie*. I'd like you to come in and talk to me. Would you do that?"

I called him up, and he said, "Why don't you come in tomorrow?"

And I said, "Why don't I come in now?"

Before I saw him, I wrote down names on two index cards. He still has them in his desk. On one index card were all the directors who would hire me, and on the other index card were all the directors who wouldn't hire me. I went in to see him, and I said, "Don't squeeze me in with someone behind me, because I'm here with my life. I'm not leaving this office to go back to Ronnie Leif. I may not sign with you, but I have no career after the story I'm about to tell you."

Fred said, "You don't need to tell me. Agents know what the projects are. But you have to look at it as a positive."

"How is that?"

"You were offered starring roles and lost every one of them. What does that tell you?"

"That I'm no good or, at least, not as good as I think I am."

"Neither one. It tells you that you have a lame agent."

I told Fred my history and explained what had happened on each one of these projects.

He asked, "Why did this happen? Why did that happen? All these movies you've got coming out, everybody knows about you and *Drive, He Said*. Everybody knows how good you are. I want you to go home and think about my representing you. I want very much to represent you."

"Really?"

"Yeah. You go home and you think about it."

"Well, I've got two cards here I want you to look at. These are the people that won't hire me."

He looked at the card and flipped it over and looked at the other side. He said, "There are seventy names here." It included Stuart Rosenberg, who wouldn't hire me or even read me. Bob Aldrich, who fucked me. Monte Hellman, Michael Laughlin. Various people who'd turned me down or wouldn't work with me. Alan Pakula, Robert Mulligan. Various directors who had never hired me. Television directors who I couldn't get in to read for. Producers. Franklin Schaffner, John Frankenheimer. Some guys who I would eventually work for. I gave him the other card.

He said, "What's that?"

I said, "These are the guys who will hire me."

"Billy Graham's on here. He'll hire you?"

"Yeah, well, he did four episodes of *Stoney Burke*, so he'll hire me. And he did a pilot for a series. He hired me for that. Leslie Stevens, he should hire me. Burt Kennedy. John Wayne seemed to have liked me the one time I worked for him. Sydney Pollack hired me twice. Some TV directors. I don't think Mark Rydell will hire me, because I went against his word when I was doing a *Gunsmoke*."

Fred said, "You look for the laugh too often. There's only twenty-four names here, and there are seventy that won't hire you. What's going to happen to your career?"

I said, "Well, if you'll work those twenty-four, those twenty-four might pick up another twenty-four. And if you eliminate twenty-four of the seventy, we'll be just about even."

"It's an interesting theory. Because if you operate on a fifty-fifty theory, in fifty years we could be in pretty good shape."

The other day I talked to him and said, "Freddy, we're in the thirty-fifth year of the fifty-year plan."

And he said, "We're not yet even. I'm about four directors off in catching the bad ones that won't hire you. But we've said a lot of kaddish over the list of seventy. Just in terms of people going down in flames. We're getting closer and closer and closer."

So that day in his office, I said, "What am I going home for? Sign me. I'm signed."

He said, "I'll tell you what, Brucie. I don't sign contracts with any actor. When an actor wants to leave, he leaves. What's a signed contract going to do? You're at William Morris. They like that. But with me, it's just a handshake."

And he took me down the hall and introduced me to Lenny Hershon, who handled Walter Matthau and Jack Lemmon. He introduced me to as many people as were there, and he said, "This is my new client." Every single guy he introduced me to knew at least one thing that I had done already. I realized that morning, God, what if I'd been in that building? I might have gotten three out of five jobs. And it was just such a wonderful feeling.

I went home to Andrea, picked her up, and swung her around in the house. I said, "You know, I'm part of another family. So are you now." These people knew who I was. And they talked about a little piece that I did in *They Shoot Horses* that had just come out three months earlier, and they knew a moment that I had in *Castle Keep*. They hadn't seen *Drive*, but they knew about it. Somebody in the hallway mentioned they'd just seen a rough cut. And I felt I finally had an agent.

A week later, Fred, me, his wife at the time, Kathy, and Andrea were out for dinner. We're having our first dinner together. And he said, "So Brucie. I get two phone calls today. One is from Fred Roos."

He's a little younger than me. Two years. Fred Specktor's three years older than I am.

He says, "Yeah. Francis wants you to come in and see him next week."

I said, "Okay. What for?"

He said, "Well, he's preparing this movie, *The Godfather*, and they're going to test a bunch of people up in San Francisco."

And I said, "So?"

"Well, he wants to test you."

"What does he need to test me for? He's seen all the films I'm in. He knows who I am."

"Well, they want to test you. They're testing everybody."

I said, "Horseshit. He's not going to test Marlon Brando."

"Oh yes he is."

"Oh no he's not."

"Oh yes he is."

I said, "Well, I'll test the test before or the test after. He tests Jack and then Brando will test the test after me. Okay?"

He said, "Well, I think they're planning to do that."

"I'll go in the car just before Brando's limousine. And Jack can follow in his little Messerschmitt car."

He says, "I think it'll be like that."

I said, "Horseshit, Fred. Jack Nicholson will test for nobody. Particularly that fat fucking guido."

And Fred said, "You know you've got to be more respectful to these people, Brucie, because Francis Coppola's going to be big stuff."

"Well, I hope he's a little bigger than *Finian's Rainbow* or *You're a Big Boy Now*. Two movies I couldn't get a reading for either."

"Well this *Godfather*'s going to be a big movie. There's a lot of important people involved with it."

"I'm sure there are. On the island next to Sardinia where they come from, I'm sure they're very important."

He says, "Oh, don't think that the mafia's in everything."

I said, "Particularly they're not in our business, are they, Fred? And why do you think he puts the word Ford in the middle of his name? Does that legitimize anything? Does that make him legitimate?"

He said, "Brucie, you've got to stop that stuff."

So, I went to Francis's office. He said, "I saw some stuff from *Drive, He Said*. Just fabulous."

I said, "What'd you see?"

"I saw some of the basketball stuff."

"Uh-huh. What else did you see?"

"Well, that was it."

"How'd you see that?"

"Fred Roos showed me some."

"Really? How'd Fred get it?"

"Well, I don't know. Fred's the producer of the movie."

"Where's Fred right now?"

"He's back at his office."

I said, "Fred is the casting director, Francis. How'd Fred get any film from the movie?"

He said, "Well Fred . . ., you know, Fred's . . ."

"Fred's what? Jack Nicholson didn't give you any film from that movie to look at."

"Well, I didn't say he did."

"What did you see of me?"

"You're the coach or something, right?"

"Right. What'd you see me do?"

"Oh, I saw you coaching on the sidelines. You looked good."

I said, "So what do you want me to do?"

He said, "I want you to be there this weekend. . . . I've got Al Pacino, Bob Duvall."

"Yeah. What are they doing?"

"We're going to do some screen tests of scenes. Guys working together. Method actors and all that."

"Yeah. And what are you going to learn from that?"

"I'm going to learn who I'm going to use in my movie."

"Francis, let me say something to you. Who are you using Bob Duvall with?"

"Well, I have a couple of scenes I'm going to do with him and Al Pacino. I'd like to do some scenes with you and Al Pacino."

"Francis, I'm not going to be involved. You've seen film on me. You know what I can do. I think I'll take a pass."

"Why is that?"

I said, "Loyalty. You did a movie called *The Rain People*. In it, Bob Duvall was as good as an actor can be. You have a history with Bob Duvall. Why on earth would you test me for any role that you're testing Bob Duvall for? He's a terrific actor. He's never gotten any kind of a break. He needs one. My time will come. I've done a movie. I'm consistent. I don't test. I don't read. I don't read well. I'm not dyslexic, but I'm not good at reading and looking down and then looking up and looking down and looking up."

Coppola said, "Well, you could memorize and then read."

"No. It's called a read. I don't read. I don't test well. I don't know what a test is supposed to do. All I know is when you test or you read, it gives you an excuse not to hire me. You have the advantage."

"Why shouldn't I? I'm the employer."

"That's exactly why. It's a collaborative art. It's not an employee and employer. It's an art form. It's a collaboration."

"Well, that's highly unusual. With that attitude, you obviously are not going to have much of a career."

"That's okay. Maybe I'll just go back and work for Mr. Strasberg and Mr. Kazan and hang in there."

"Well, that's a choice. I can understand that."

I said, "Fine. I can understand this about Bob Duvall: If you don't hire him to play the role of Tom Hagen in *The Godfather*, you might end up with a note in your box someday that smells like fish. And there's two things that smell like fish, Francis. And one of 'em's fish."

He just looked at me like he didn't know what the fuck I was talking about. And I never tested. I saw Francis three years later. We had a discussion. I've never seen him since that day, and it's my loss because he is a fabulous director. *Godfather II* is an opera.

Anyway, back at dinner, Fred said, "Then I got a second call today. Much more disturbing."

I said, "What was that?"

He said, "It was from your mother."

I said, "My mother?"

He said, "Yes. And this is the way the phone call went: I get on the phone. My secretary says, 'Fred, you want to talk to somebody named Jean Dern?'

"I said, 'Put her on. Hello, Mrs. Dern, how are you?'"

Now, my mother had half a tongue because she'd lost the front half of her tongue to cancer.

"Mithter Thpecktor?"

"Yes, Mrs. Dern?"

"That would be Fred Thpecktor. Would that be Thpecktor of the Jewith variety?"

And Fred says, "Yes, Mrs. Dern. It would be of the Jewish variety."

"I thought tho. You know, twelve yearth ago, my thun Bruthie wath in a Broadway play. Wath with that immigrant director Mithter Kathan. And he changed hith name to Thtern, which wath very upsetting to me. And to my father Mithter McLeith. He tried to make uth believe it was a typographical error. But we never believed him thinth he was five yearth old. Now I just wanted to make sure that his new reprethentative Mr. Thpecktor ith who he thays he was, that you were the point man for the Ithraeli contingenthy in Hollywood. Ith that true?"

Fred says, "Well, your son overestimates my value. But I do feel that I'm quite competent at what I do."

"Are you ath powerful ath Mithter Mayer?"

He says, "Mr. Mayer's not here anymore."

She says, "How about the man who is across the thtreet from me, Mithter Balaban?"

"I'm nowhere near as powerful as Mr. Balaban. He owns sixty percent of the movie theaters in the United States."

"But he's not a legitimate bithnith man."

"How do you feel that, ma'am?"

She says, "Mithter Balaban never leavth hith houth."

"Why do you hold that against him?"

"Well, becuth he duth bithnith on the telephone. And wuth a terrible influenth on Bruthie when he wath growing up becuth he taught him to gamble and do bithnith on the telephone. That'th not legitimate here in Glencoe. Do you do bithnith on the telephone, Mithter Thpecktor?"

He says, "Yes, unfortunately it's the heart of my business. If it was in person, and occasionally it has to be in person, it's done by handshake."

"Oh. And do you ever do bithnith with Chrithtian people?"

"As little as possible, Mrs. Dern."

She said, "I wouldn't trutht a goddamn Chrithtian if it wath the last perthon in the world. I can conthider Bruthie in good handth."

"Yes, you can."

And she said, "Well, it wath nithe talking to you, Mithter Thpecktor of the Jewith variety."

"Thank you, Mrs. Dern." He was laughing.

She said, "You're laughing, Mithter Thpecktor. I thound funny. I only have half a tongue cuth I thmoke five packth of Chethterfieldth every day and I'm not going to thtop. I gueth that'th it for today." And they never talked again.

She died during the making of *Marvin Gardens*.

Fred said to me, "I'm going to ask you to do something for me. It's going to be hard to swallow. You're not going to want to do it, but it's the only way we're going to change the image of you, because you can't keep playing these guys that you're playing or your career's not going to go where we want it to go."

I said, "What's that?"

And he said, "No more television."

Well, what Fred was saying to me was that you cannot continually be cast in people's homes in episodic television as a bad guy. They're never, ever going to forget you as that or forgive you for that. And you're going to constantly be cast, if you ever get on the big screen, as a villain. So if we're going to do it, let's get paid for it and do it in a big form instead of a little form. Or you may never be able to outlive it.

My most memorable TV roles were sadistic. The *Hitchcock* I did with a squirrel and Pat Buttram was a bad guy. The *Virginians* I did were all memorable bad guys. The *Gunsmoke* I did, the most memorable was when Warren Oates and I kidnapped Miss Kitty. Mark Rydell directed it, and it was probably the meanest episode that was ever done. I did one where I was Bette Davis's son where I was fairly sympathetic. It was so traumatic to me that Bette Davis was playing my

mom on a TV show. It was a crusher. So the more memorable performances I gave on television were performances where I played
mean-spirited people. However, at the end of the decade, I was working my way toward being positive. Fred just meant that we had to
change the collective thinking.

I said, "I have to make a living."

Fred said, "I don't care. No more television. Call up your mother."

"I can't call her up. What's she going to say? 'Ith thith my thun
Bruthie? I don't have a thun named Bruthie.' He's studying to be an
actor in New York."

She never forgave me for the Stern thing. She thought it was horseshit. She thought I changed it for one play to get recognized.

She died believing my name was changed for me. Strasberg,
Kazan, Actors Studio leftist theater group, commies. Andrea and I
wrote her a letter. I asked her for five hundred dollars. She wrote me
back a letter in which she said, "The answer to the five hundred dollars is no. I will not give you five hundred dollars. I have a tight budget
on the money that your father bequeathed to me." She didn't ever use
the word "left." "Bequeathed." And, "I don't ask my father for money,
although he lives next door to me." She couldn't stand living in the big
house by herself where all the kids and her memories were, so she
built another big house next door to him, but it wasn't nearly as big as
the big house. There were five houses all together on the sixteen acres.
In a row. All on the lake.

She said, "But I'll tell you what I will do. If you and Andrea will
move back and live next to me I will put you through law school. Take
care of you and Andrea very, very well for the rest of your lives. And
Andrea can run the Winnetka Garden Club and be involved in
Chicago doing whatever she wants to do. And you can get this acting
bug out of your system, doing plays and being involved in the Goodman Theater in Chicago."

And this is after having done major motion pictures, sixty-five television shows, theater, and twelve years in the business. I can get this
acting bug out of my system by doing little plays at the Goodman Theater and being put through law school. This from the woman who
owned one-third of Carson, Pirie, Scott & Co.

Right after I did *Drive, He Said* in 1970 and before I went to Fred Specktor, I did a movie called *Thumb Tripping*. If you go to the Chartoff/Winkler credits, I don't think it appears. Bob Chartoff was there every day as the producer.

We shot in Big Sur, and it was about this hippie couple (Michael Burns and Joy Bang) who were traveling around in a bus and they picked up hitchhikers. I was one of the hitchhikers they picked up, and oh boy, did they make a mistake picking me up. That was the last straw for Fred. When he saw that movie he said, "Brucie, we cannot do this kind of stuff." I had a knife, and I wanted to do everything bad to the couple, particularly to her.

It's pretty easy to play those roles because of the fact that you're angry you're cast in these roles in the first place. You get so annoyed that everybody else in your generation is emerging as a movie star. It's not the stardom. It's not the money. It's the fact that they're getting opportunities to do the best parts.

Fred called me up and said, "Bob Chartoff wants you to come back to Big Sur for two days next week to do it again."

I said, "What?"

He said, "They never finished the movie because they fired Joy Bang."

"You're kidding!"

"No, they finished the movie with another actress named Meg Foster." Meg Foster was a pretty good actress. She had catlike eyes.

Fred said to me, "Bob and Irwin"—meaning Chartoff and Winkler—"are good guys. Someday they may turn out to do really well. So do this, Brucie. You don't want to piss them off."*

"Yeah. Why would I want to piss them off?"

"Well, they want you to go back and do this for nothing."

I said, "Fred, come on. We've been together one week. Now the first thing you're sending me on you want me to do for nothing?"

He said, "Be smart."

I said, "Come on, Fred. Who are you working for?"

---

*They did go on to bigger things, including producing many Martin Scorsese films, and all the *Rocky* pictures.

"Be smart and listen to me."

"Do I have to do this?"

"No, you could demand what they gave you before, a thousand dollars a week."

"Well, can't I just get paid prorated? It's two days. Can't they give me four hundred dollars?"

"Well I suppose I could ask for that."

I said, "Two hundred dollars a day. I'll drive up in my car. It's not going to cost them any airfare. They're going to pay for our hotel room for two nights. We'll stay where we stayed before. That's a hundred and thirty-nine dollars or whatever it is. Give me five hundred dollars for a night at the Lodge and two days' work. That's it. Five hundred dollars."

I did it, but we flew up. Andrea and I were in the airport. We'd been married not quite a year. And Bob Chartoff was in the airport. He's going to go back on another plane, and he wants to borrow money from me because he doesn't have his credit cards with him and he has no cash. He needed sixty dollars or something like that. I just remember the incongruity of it all. Here's a guy who wanted me to go up and work for nothing. Gave me two days of pay for what really amounted to a repeat performance. And he's hitting his actor up for money in the airport. It was just funny. Chartoff and Winkler are good guys. I never worked for them again, but they were always very kind to me.

· 11 ·

I Killed John Wayne

I passed on *The Godfather*, not because I didn't want to be in it. Of course I wanted to be in it. But I was so angry that Francis Coppola wanted to use me as a wedge to get Robert Duvall to work for no money in a part that I knew he was going to play, but Francis was fucking with him. I hate that. They used me the same way in *Cuckoo's Nest* and *Jaws*.

On *Cuckoo's Nest*, Jack Nicholson told me, "Derns, I'm going to do the role. But they're going to try and get me down off a million dollars. I've not gotten a million. I'm getting a million dollars. And they're using you."

I told Fred Specktor, my agent, that. Fred said, "Are you sure?"

I called Jack back and said, "Are you monkeying with me?"

He said, "Nosiree. They're not going to give you the role because I'm going to do the part."

"You mean you're eventually going to back down?"

"No, I'm not going to back down. They're going to give me a million dollars. Michael Douglas won't do the movie without me because
there's nobody else that can play it except you, and they're not going
to give you the part."

"What if I do it for fifty grand?"

"They're not going to pay you fifty grand to do it, because in a
pinch he'll let his dad do it because he did it off-Broadway."

"That was twelve years ago."

Jack said, "I don't give a shit. The only guys that can play McMur-
phy are the dad, me, or you, but the dad can't act anymore. The dad
knows it. The kid knows it. But the kid don't know how to negotiate.
And I'm getting a mil. So sit back and relax and tell Fred to calm down
and not let you get in a bidding war with me. Because Jackie's getting
a mil."

Fred says, "What do you know about Mike Gruskoff?"

I say, "Well, he used to be my agent. He brought me out here. He's
a good guy."

"I notice here on your list he's a guy who would hire you."

"Yeah, he might hire me. He doesn't hire people, though. He's an
agent."

"Not anymore he isn't. He's a producer. He's producing this
little . . . he calls it a science fiction movie. Do you know who Douglas
Trumbull is?"

"I don't have a clue."

"Well, they want you to meet him."

So I went out to the San Fernando Valley to a garage behind a guy's
house. It was a little duplex kind of house. I went into this garage, and
it was like Santa's workshop. Guys with big binocular-type glasses on
with one lens sticking out. I had been places where guys wore things
like that, but they were mostly looking at money. ("Is this bill for
real?") These guys were looking at pieces of film. And it was like a
magikan's workshop. Or magician. I call them magikans. We got in a
Volkswagen and drove down to San Pedro across the Vincent Thomas
Bridge.

We went to Norm's Landing, where there was an aircraft carrier docked. We went down in the bowels and raced little cars around. Douglas Trumbull took my hand and explained all this stuff to me and what was going on. I still hadn't read the material. We got back in the Volkswagen, and on the way home, with Douglas driving, Gruskoff read the script to me.

He said, "You're the eighteenth guy we've been to. We started with Paul Newman. Nobody wants to do this fucking thing." I mean, he called it a fucking thing. How do you think that makes me feel? And I haven't read it yet.

So Gruskoff's reading it to me, the descriptions, the liner notes, and everything. Tennessee Williams wrote the best liner notes ever. I mean, the things between dialogue. Patty Jenkins wrote fabulous liner notes. And then Gruskoff says, "We've got to stop here." We stop at a phone booth. There were no cell phones then. He gets back in the car and says, "You're going to get a thousand dollars a week for twelve weeks doing this movie."

And I said, "Okay."

He says, "And you start Monday, and we'll work until April."

"That's great."

"And you're the star of the movie. What do you think of that? Your old agent came through for you, right? Saw you in *Shadow of a Gunman*, saw you in *Sweet Bird of Youth*, started representing you, got you your first TV show, *Naked City*, got you a *Route 66*, brought you to California, got your first TV show in California. Got you two movies: *Hush, Hush, Sweet Charlotte* and *Marnie*. Then went off to another agency. Now I'm getting you your first starring role in a movie. How about that? Your old agent, Gruskoff. Not bad, huh?"

I say, "Yeah, but I got a thousand dollars a week last year."

He says, "From who?"

"From Jack Nicholson."

"For what?"

"For a movie called *Drive, He Said*."

"*Drive, He Said*? *Drive, He Said*? It ran one week. That's the one they took to Cannes where Mick Jagger's baby cried all the way through it. I was there. It was the premiere. They had a red carpet thing, and it was a big deal and all the BBS* people were there and Karen Black and the two young boys [Tepper and Margotta] and Jack and Fred Roos and all the people were there."

I thought, those cocksuckers. They went all the way to Cannes, the whole troupe of them, but nobody asked Brucie to go and have a shot at international press. No one asked Coach Bullion to go. Not a soul. And Mick Jagger's kid cried all the way through the movie so Jack always claimed that's why the movie never made a dime, because it got a horrible reception and nobody heard the words. I don't know how long the movie ran, but it didn't do well financially at all.

So we drive along. Now we get off the freeway, and we're in the Valley and heading out toward Canoga Park to Douglas's garage there. Gruskoff says, "Stop here." And we pull into a doughnut place. It has a phone.

I say, "Jesus, you make a lot of phone calls."

So he goes in, makes another call, comes out, gets in the car, and says, "I'm giving you $1,250. Fred says you should be proud of him."

And I told him he should be proud of *me* because I'm the one that got the $1,250. I'm hearing guys are getting half a million, and I'm working for $1,250 a week. It's not a problem for me, because I'd just gotten $1,000 a week.

I went into the workshop, and I asked Douglas, "Can I take the script home please so I can read it and know what I'm doing?"

"Yeah. We'll start Monday."

We start shooting *Silent Running*,† and one day, about three in the afternoon, Fred calls me. He said, "Brucie, how well do you know Douglas?"

And I said, "Douglas the director? I've known him five days."

He said, "We need a favor from Douglas."

---

*A maverick production company founded by producer Bert Schneider, director Bob Rafelson, and attorney Steve Blauner.

†A low-budget, independent film, *Silent Running* was directed by Douglas Trumbull, the special-effects supervisor from Kubrick's *2001*. It came out six years before *Star Wars* and is considered one of the truly great films of the science-fiction genre. Dern plays Freeman

I said, "What's that?"

"I need you to get out of the movie for two days."

"When?"

"March seventh and eighth."

"What for?"

"I've got a request. I've got to go back on my word with you."

"What are you talking about?"

Fred said, "You've got to leave your set on a Tuesday night after work and fly to Santa Fe, New Mexico, on a Wednesday morning. You've got to work Wednesday afternoon, and there's no way for you to fly back from Albuquerque until Thursday morning, and you won't be able to work until the end of the day Thursday. So you'll have to miss work all day Wednesday and unless they can find something for you to do in the afternoon on Thursday, you're basically going to miss at least a day and a half, maybe two full days of work. But BS them into thinking you could work on Thursday afternoon."

And I said, "Jesus, Fred I'm in every shot every day. There's nothing for them to do without me. Nothing. There is one scene where the guys talk about me and how crazy I am. But by March seventh those guys are all dead."

"Do your best. And don't tell them what it is. Just tell them you've got to go to the dentist or something."

"I can't do that, they're going to catch me."

"And don't talk to Gruskoff about it. Get Douglas's permission first."

"Well, what is it?"

"I can't tell you now. It just happened. But you've got to do it. I'm breaking my word to you. You're not going to like it, but it's more money than you've ever made."

Lowell, a futuristic park ranger minding earth's last forests, sealed in gigantic domes aboard a freighter in space. When ordered to destroy the domes and return home, Lowell is forced to choose between his crewmates and his beloved forests. He chooses the forests. Trumbull went on to be the special-effects supervisor for many of the biggest sci-fi films of all time, including *Close Encounters of the Third Kind*, *Star Trek: The Motion Picture*, and *Blade Runner*.

"How much money is it?"

"I don't know, but it's going to be more than what it is right now."

"How long do I work?"

"Six weeks. But they need you for an afternoon in March. Three hours' work. It's a master shot and a close-up and then an offstage. And it's a magic-hour shot. So if they don't get it the one day, they'll get it the next day, but I told them they only have one shot at you as you're doing another movie. The problem is, what do you look like in the movie you're in March seventh?"

"Fuck, Fred, that's seven weeks from now. I have no idea what I'll look like in the movie. But it'll be seven weeks beyond where I am now so I'll probably have a full beard."

"Well, you can't have a full beard in this movie because it's the first time we meet you in this other movie."

It was then that I realized Fred didn't really give a fuck about what my acting problems were or anything about continuity. So I go to Douglas with a very vague plan right after I get off the phone.

I said, "I've got a dilemma."

He said, "Whatever you need."

I asked, "Can you shoot anything without me?"

He said, "Yeah, I can shoot a lot of things. I can shoot pneumatic arms. I can shoot drones doing different stuff. I can do three days of drone work without you being there. I could just have your pants leg. I can do an operation on your leg. That can be half the day with the intricacies of this, that, and the other thing."

So I said, "Okay. You really can do that?"

He said, "Yeah. Do you really think this is an advancement in your career?"

I have no idea what Fred's talking about. I don't know what I'm being considered for. I just know it's Fred Specktor, and Douglas had met Fred by this time. And he liked him. Everybody likes Fred because he's a player. He just gets it.

So I go home and a script is there. There's no title on the script. I see the names of the writers, Harriet Frank, Irving Ravetch. These people are well-known writers who have written big movies for thirty-five, forty years.* The first page says, "Opens on a one-room schoolhouse." And there are twelve kids in the schoolhouse. Ten boys and two girls. None of them over twelve years old. And it's 1886. A guy walks into the schoolhouse, he's six feet five, and weighs about 280, and is seventy years old. His name is Mr. Anderson. He says to the teacher, "I've got a problem. All of my men have just run off to the gold rush. And I got nobody to drive my cattle herd to Montana. I need every kid who can chew a plug of tobacco and rope and ride. And we've got to leave a week from today."

The schoolteacher says, "Well, you ain't going to find them in here, Mr. Anderson. Not as long as I'm a teacher."

He says, "Well, ma'am, that leaves me one choice. I'm going to have to go to the parents of these kids and ask their permission, and I'm going to have to take you with me."

He takes them all out in front of the schoolhouse. He says, "Fellas, you got a choice. You can stay here and listen to this all summer long or you can learn to be cowboys by the time the leaves turn." Of course, they all want to be cowboys. "Every now and then you'll be scared and you'll have things scare the hell out of you. Something may come upon you the likes of which you'll have never seen before nor will you ever see again. And that'll come in the form of the most wretched human beings you'll see as long as you live. When they'll come, we don't know. But believe me when I say they're out there. They want one thing and it won't be you. It'll be that."

He points to five hundred horses and eight hundred head of cattle. I skipped about fifty pages and got to this one little scene by the river crossing where I have to work. I didn't need to read any further. I put it down. I called up Fred.

I said, "I don't have time to read the rest of it tonight because I've got to memorize all the shit I have to do tomorrow. But there's no discussion."

He said, "Do you understand why I have to go back on my word?"

---

*Norma Rae; The Long, Hot Summer; Hud; and The Dark at the Top of the Stairs to name a few.

"Fred, this is the baddest ass that ever lived."

"Go to the last nine pages with me on the phone."

So, I go through pages 111 to 120. And I see what happens to my character.

Then he says, "Now go to page seventy-three."

The first line on seventy-three is said by Longhair, my character: "Turn around, you son of a bitch. I want you to see this coming." And Mr. Anderson's line is, "No." The liner note says, "With his hands trembling, both of them broken, and his nose shattered in five places, Longhair, with sweat pouring onto the ground off of his face and blood coming out of his nose, his ears, and his eyes, raises the gun and simply shoots Will Anderson three times in the back until he drops dead."

I said on the phone to Fred, "Fuck! I kill John Wayne?"

He said, "That's right, Brucie. We're on our way."

"I can't do this."

"If you don't do it, the guy who does do it is in for life. And that guy is Vince Edwards.* You are here because of two people: Mark Rydell,[†] who has begged me to insist that you do this role, and Duke himself, who insists that you be here because he thinks you're funny and he wants you to entertain the people until you get to this point. He wants Longhair to be entertaining and unpredictable. I've already accepted, and I've already made the deal, so you have no choice. What did Douglas say?"

"Douglas said he'll shoot drones doing mechanical things from now until the next thousand years."

So on my second day of shooting *Silent Running*, I got *The Cowboys*.

The next day, Douglas asked, "Did you get any more information?"

I said, "Douglas, I'm going to whisper this to you and I don't want you to tell a soul, except Marty Hornstein, the first assistant, to make sure I'm clear the seventh and eighth of March. And I'll try and be back on time."

---

*Vince Edwards was, at the time, the star of the long-running television show, *Ben Casey*. After the show ended, so did his career.

†Rydell, the director, knew him from *Gunsmoke*, but he'd also directed episodes of *Ben Casey*. He went on to direct *The Reivers*, *The Rose*, and *On Golden Pond*, among others.

He said, "Don't press it. The seventh and eighth you just won't work. But I do need you on the ninth. So if they don't get the magic out of the seventh, you make sure they get it on the eighth. Who's the cinematographer?"

I said, "Bob Surtees."

He says, "Robert Surtees is your cameraman? You know he's the greatest western cameraman that ever lived."

"Yeah, he's awful good. He also shot *The Last Picture Show*. Pretty good black and white. Mark Rydell is the director." He wasn't so sure who Mark Rydell was.

I said, "He's good." I told him the short story of the movie.

He said, "God, that's touching. I mean these little kids have to become men."

I said, "What they really become is *Lord of the Flies*."

We're filming *The Cowboys*, and in the first scene, I'm trying to get Wayne's character to hire me. Duke says, "Who recommended you?"

I say, "Mr. Leeds recommended me to you, Mr. Anderson."

He says, "Really? And how long ago did you meet him?"

I say, "Oh, about six weeks ago. I was down yonder at his ranch."

"And you rode all the way up here just to see me? If that's the case, you rode a long way for nothing, because I ain't interested in hiring you."

"Really? Why is that, sir?"

"Because Leeds died four years ago. So you're a liar. And I don't cotton to liars."

"Well, I swear on my mama's sainted grave that I ain't a liar."

Duke says, "I'd question that somebody like you ever had a mama."

I look around and I say, "Well sir, if you're going to coin a phrase 'had a mama,' I guess I'd say I had yours about five years ago."

Wayne just breaks up laughing. He's up on a horse and he turns around in the saddle, and the sun is sinking, and you can't really see the expression on his face because he's got that goddamn lid hat that comes out to here. He looks pretty fucking great on a horse when he's up there all six foot six and 285. He looks around and says, "And that, ladies and gentlemen, is exactly why this prick is in this movie. It ain't gonna be in the movie. But that's why he's the guy that's gonna kill John Wayne. Because that's clever goddamn thinking, ain't it?" Everybody breaks out and applauds. And then we go to take two.

We've got one shot left. It's now ten after five, and the bottom of the sun has just hit the horizon. Duke's close-up is the magic-hour shot. It's him silhouetted in the sun as it's setting. The ultimate Marlboro Man shot. Rydell and Surtees are running around looking where to put the camera. Wayne doesn't say a thing. He just sits there. He's all by himself. Not a PA in sight, because he's across the river. You've got the mountains, you've got the sun, and you've got Duke, and 114 people over here waiting to wrap it at the same time. It's early in the movie. It's their first or second week of shooting. Duke's sitting there. Now the sun is halfway down below the horizon, so Wayne's hat is just below the rim of the sun. Now it's an absolutely perfect shot, and they're still futzing with the sticks. All of a sudden, you hear, "Mr. Rydell!"

"Yeah, Duke?"

"Mis-ter Ry-dell."

"Yeah, Duke?"

"Whe-ere you from?"

Mark is very quick, every bit as quick as yours truly in his own way. He says, "I'm from 167th and the Grand Concourse in the Bronx."

"Really. How far did you have to walk to see a real cowboy?"

"Well, I guess a pretty long way."

"You tell that old geezer who's wandering around with you with the goddamn box on the sticks to set it in the ground. Face me. It's a goddamn lock-off shot. It's Marlboro time. It's cocktail time. Stick it in the sand. Point the sumbitch and shoot it. It's a standard John Wayne shot. Shoot it, and let's get out of here. I'm never gonna say another word to you the entire movie, but if you can't shoot this fucking close-up you don't deserve to be making cowboy movies."

Mark says, "Stick it in the ground."

Surtees goes plunk, plunk, plunk, roll, snap, done.

We were out of there.

John Wayne knew exactly the pressure that I must have felt, knowing I was going to kill him. He knew he was an icon. He believed the audience would hate me forever and ever. He was correct. I never lived it down. I will never live it down. He died in other movies. A Japanese sniper shot him in one movie, and he died, but I don't think an identified person ever took him out. If he died because of wounds that's one thing, but certainly no one ever shot him dead one on one.

For our scene, he was a little polluted at eight thirty in the morning. He had bullet packs put on him, which he'd never had put on him before. He was a huge man. John Wayne was a big, big man in more ways than just that he was a huge star and a magnificent guy. He sat on a horse big and walked big and lived big. Loud. Big booming voice. He was a little nervous that morning. He'd never been shot in the back. And he wasn't easy about that.

The day before for the whole day he just beat the living hell out of me—pounding me against the tree, breaking my nose, and almost killing me. And having a ball doing it. Duke's longtime normal double, stand-in, was a guy named Chuck Roberson. Chuck had been with Duke for forty years. But he couldn't double him anymore because now they were both in their seventies. So he had a double named Walter Wyatt, who was the national bulldogging champion, and the strongest man I've ever dealt with.

So instead of John Wayne having to do it, they had John Wayne's double for my close-ups so he could move me around. Wayne would sit there and watch it. Well, Walter Wyatt comes in, and Mark Rydell and Wayne are sitting there, and Rydell says, "Okay, action." Wyatt has to grab me by the shoulders, and I've got to start swinging at him and fighting with him. Now this is a guy who's the best steer wrestler that ever lived, but wrestling Brahma bulls. He's got to get off his horse, grab a Brahma bull by the horns—they've got these big horns, we're talking about 1,500-pound beasts—and turn their necks so this entire beast gets slammed to the ground. And these are just as angry as any bull in a bullring. These are nasty, angry beasts. Most of them have never been thrown in their life or rolled over, which is why they're prime stock in rodeos. Walter Wyatt never failed to turn one over. Well, he goes whomp and grabs me and I'm just frozen in my tracks. I cannot move.

Rydell says, "Come on, Bruce, make a fight of it."

And Wayne says, "Uh, excuse me, little guy from Illinois, how 'bout a fight?"

I say, "I can't move."

Wayne says, "Walter, give the guy some slack. This is awful. What can we do? We're going to have to get another actor. This guy is pathetic."

I just couldn't move.

So, Wayne says, "Well, I'm going to have to get in there."

I say, "Oh, god, no. Walter, just let me get a punch off."

Walter's the sweetest, nicest guy in the world. He turns to Wayne and they're rolling all this time, and Walter says, "Should I just throw him once?"

Wayne says, "Throw him once? If you throw him once, you'll kill him and we'll have no movie. Shit, we've done most of the movie. Just drop him into the tree, break his back, and walk away."

And I'm thinking, I'm not a Brahma bull. So Walter let up, and then we made a fight out of it. Duke came in, and he did his stuff and we worked it. But for about a minute and a half I literally was in a vise. I'd never had anybody just totally control me so that I couldn't do anything. I'm not a tough guy. I'm not a big fighter or anything like that. I just said, "You know, as soon as I can get this goddamn hand on my gun it's coming out, because I'm going to kill this son of a bitch as fast as I can."

So when we finally got to it and I could pull that gun out, I didn't hesitate. I jumped the gun as fast as I could, and Wayne turns and walks away from me. After the beating that I got, he just took three steps and, as soon as that gun cleared my holster, I said, "Turn around you son of a bitch. I want you to see this coming." He wouldn't turn around, so I just shot him in the back. He never knew it was going to come then. Mark Rydell didn't know it was going to come then. Nor did anybody else. I was lucky he printed it, because he never thought John Wayne would be shot in the back. But he loved it, because that's the first shot. Then he turns around, and I give him two right in front of him. And that's the only time I've ever been in a theater in my career where I heard an audience gasp. They actually gasped.

Wayne told me it would happen. He said, "They'll all gasp."

And I said, "Why? Because it's you?"

He said, "No, because it's halfway through the picture and they'll never expect it. That's why the Ravetches put it halfway through the picture. Scribes are always right when they're good."

And I loved that. He called them scribes. I've called them scribes.

When I got back to *Silent Running,* Douglas Trumbull asked me, "Who was the lead in the movie?"

"John Wayne."

"Oh, you get to do a John Wayne movie. Didn't you do a movie with John Wayne?"

"Yeah, *The War Wagon.*"

"Well, that's quite a privilege. And at the end of the movie does he kill you?"

"No. The little kids kill me. Douglas, you know what happens on page seventy-three of the movie?"

"No, what?"

"I kill John Wayne."

Douglas just sat in his chair. He called his father, who was way the hell in the cargo deck on the aircraft carrier, probably a hundred yards away. He grabbed the megaphone from Marty Hornstein, the first assistant. He goes, "Dad." The father comes all the way up in one of the little golf carts. "Dad, you know what Bruce is doing in this next movie? He's killing John Wayne."

The father said, "If he kills John Wayne in a movie, he's going to kill our movie. We've got to come out before he kills John Wayne."

Gruskoff comes down about an hour later. The father goes up to Gruskoff, and Gruskoff turns white. Gruskoff immediately goes off the aircraft carrier onto Terminal Island, where he gets to a pay phone. He calls Fred Specktor. "You took a job for Bruce where he kills John Wayne?"

Fred says, "Yeah."

Gruskoff says, "Oh, we've got to replace Bruce. He can't be in a movie where he kills John Wayne. The only way he can do that is you guarantee that movie comes out after us."

Fred says, "Here's John Wayne's home phone number. You call him up and you tell him that."

Of course, Fred gave him some bogus phone number. Gruskoff never called him. But Gruskoff fought, Universal fought. Everybody fought.*

---

*Ultimately, Universal lost. *Silent Running* came out the next year, two months after *The Cowboys*, and, despite good reviews, didn't do that well at the box office because of Universal's mishandling of the movie. It has since become a cult classic.

· 12 ·

I'm Still Sorry,
Burt Reynolds

B ob Rafelson had always kept an eye on my career since seeing me in 1959 and '60 on Broadway. He liked my work in *Drive, He Said*, and he had just seen both *Silent Running* and *The Cowboys*. He said, "I have a script that I'm going to give you called *The Philosopher King*,* written by a guy named Jacob Brackman. There are two roles in it. I'm thinking of three guys to play two roles: Jack Nicholson, you, and Michael Parks."

This was very odd to me, because I knew Michael Parks pretty well. I wasn't a good, sit-down, let's-go-have-dinner friend of his, but we'd grown up together in the business. He was always an actor you had to contend with, because he was brilliant. He was a terrific guy and had suffered tragedy like I had. He had a wife who took her life, and he had a little girl who was run over on a tricycle and died. What I didn't

---

*The title was later changed to *The King of Marvin Gardens*.

121

understand is why I was being brought in and told I was going to compete with him. Obviously Jack was in the movie.*

So Curly Bob says to me, "Well, the obvious casting in *Philosopher King* is for Jack to play the flamboyant role and for you to play the nerdy kind of role. But I don't want to do the movie that way. And I've convinced Jack not to do the movie that way. I want you to go down the hall to Harold's† office—I've got some people I've got to talk to at lunch over at Columbia—when I come back, I want you to have finished the script and tell me what you think."

There was no going home to read it or anything like that. I don't think he wanted it out of the building.

"And don't call your agent. Just read it."

Rafelson came back from lunch, and I went in and we talked about it an hour or more. He said, "Did you see what I mean about the two roles?"

And I said, "Yeah."

He said, "Now, what if it were you and Michael Parks?"

Then I understood what he meant. If Jack decided not to do the movie, he was going to do it with me and Michael Parks. It wasn't that I wasn't going to be in the movie, it was whether he could sell Jack on playing this other part. He was not going to do a movie with Jack playing my part because he'd done that in *Five Easy Pieces*. And Jack had done that in *Easy Rider*. Jack was on his way to a career where that personality was going to be exposed several times, and Bob knew that. That's Jack's game face, and Jack does that very easily. That hadn't been my game face. And I hadn't done that real easily. That part of my personality was exposed in real life, but not on the screen. And Curly Bob wanted a surprise.

I said, "Well, I could do David, the Jack role, easier than I could do Jason. But Jason would be a challenge and more fun for me and I'm much closer to Jason than I am to David in terms of who I am."

He said, "Well, you go home and we'll see what happens."

---

*Bob Rafelson cowrote and directed *Five Easy Pieces* with Nicholson but made his fortune creating the *Monkees*.

†Harold Schneider, Bert's brother, was associate producer of *The King of Marvin Gardens*.

I had no idea whether I'd do it or not. On the way home, I stopped and called Fred and told him what had happened. By the time I got home, I had an offer of twenty-five thousand dollars, which I thought was fair. Twenty-five thousand dollars to star in a million-dollar movie. That's what they pay you now to star in a million-dollar movie. And that's what they paid you thirty years ago.

Rafelson did convince Jack to play the role. I don't know if Jack was particularly happy playing the role or whether he liked playing the role. I do know that he was a wonderful partner in the course of making the movie. Ellen Burstyn was a fabulous partner. I never really got to know Julia Anne Robinson very well. That was a tough time in her life. She was only twenty, twenty-one years old. She was involved in a horrible kind of love triangle in which she was the girlfriend of a guy named Lenny Holzer, who was the heir to a great fortune and the husband of Baby Jane Holzer, who was a Warholesque girl. Lenny used to helicopter down in the evenings from New York City to be with Julia. Curly didn't like that because he wanted us to be a family and didn't want Julia to have any outside distractions because she wasn't really a very well-trained actress. It was kind of an incestuous family situation on *Marvin Gardens*, but I loved it. Outside of *Black Sunday*, *Smile*, and *Gatsby*, it's probably as fun a film as I've ever worked on. But the competitiveness of Jack and myself and Curly Bob was kind of the allure on the movie. We had a terrific amount of fun. The crew was great—just a group of people who wanted to make a great movie. We were stuck in Atlantic City. And this was two years before gambling came to the resort town.

I don't have a can't-miss actor who I always have to see. I will see the worst wretch imaginable, man or woman, for a moment, if that moment is pure. We're all only as good as our next moment. Geoffrey Rush's performance in *Shine* is the best continuous moment-to-moment behavior I've ever seen. The only danger in working with somebody as gifted as a Hal Ashby or a Bob Rafelson or a Frankenheimer is they print so many takes that they will borrow from take one, take two, and take three, and put those three takes together to satisfy their need, but rob you of the purity of the consecutive behavior. While the audience may get the benefit of what looks to them like the best overall take and the movie may be helped by that, you end up looking at something that is not your best overall work. And that's hard to live with.

For example, in *Marvin Gardens*, Jack and I have a scene in which I have to tell him that I love him and to go along with me on this dream. It's a long scene, and Curly Bob would take a long take and shoot it in a master with coverage off the master. So you're doing a master and coverage all in one take. But they'd run four or five minutes. The last scene, in the bedroom before Ellen shoots me, is a nine-minute master. What you're really seeing in the master is the gun traveling around the room. That's what the focus is on. Where does the gun go? Well, it starts with Ellen and it ends with Ellen. But it includes Jack and a close-up of Jack. Julia and a close-up of Julia. Me and a close-up of me. And Ellen with the gun lapsing in her hand after having shot me and then going into the bathroom and not being able—which wasn't planned—to turn the shower off. Curly, because of that accident, just stays on her not being able to turn the water off and having Jack futzing away his chance at redeeming himself and saving the movie and everybody's life, costing me my life with that crucial line I say. "Oh, I can see it now, major headlines. Matron slays three in seashore love nest." Pissing Ellen's character off because she looks seventy at thirty-eight or forty, whatever the fuck she was. And it's masterful filmmaking. But instead of saying, "Well, let's pick up and go on," Bob just says, "No, we're going to do it again."

So we start at nine thirty in the morning, and at five in the afternoon we finally get it. The same thing with the scene downstairs where I have to go up to Jack, take him by the shoulders, tell him how much I really love him as a brother, put my arms around him, and hug him full on, and he hugs me back by putting his arms lamely on my shoulders. But you know, that's Jack. That's what he'll do today. I'll see him and he'll hold me at arm's length, and that's the biggest hug he's ever given anybody. Even puss. When he hugs a girl, it's like that, too, and God forbid he kisses anyone until he gives them five breath mints. He's just not going to let you physically get close to him. I can't imagine what sex with the guy would be like.

So we're doing the scene, and after six or seven takes, we both stop, and Curly, Jack, and I are standing there. And László Kovács is over there with the camera. It's night. And we've been there an hour and a half now. Rehearsal for a half an hour.

So Curly says, "So. We'll do it again."

And I say, "Well, that'll be number eight."

Bob says, "Yeah, something like that. What's the difference? We've got all day. You've got nothing else to do. Your mom's dead."

My mom had died two days before. I say, "Yeah, that's clever. What do you got for Jack?"

"Well, he don't have a mom."

Jack says, "Oh, yeah, that's cute."

Now these are guys who'll eat you up: Rafelson, Dern, and Nicholson. We've got Ping-Pong every night after work. And I'm the second-best. Curly don't play well. He's into weights and stuff like that. He's a giant of a person anyway. He's very deceiving-looking, Bob Rafelson. He's six feet three and he's all muscle. He wears those big welder's glasses. Jack is a good Ping-Pong player, and I can barely return the ball.

So we're standing there, and Curly says, "We'll do it again."

Finally, about the fourteenth take, I'm pissed and Jack is pissed. Now, Curly's his friend. I like Curly. He's a nice guy. But I don't go back with him like Jack does.

Jack says to him, "What is it with you?"

I say, "Yeah, Curly, what are you looking for?"

Curly pinched the skin on his arm. "What do you see?"

I say, "I don't see a fucking thing."

And Jack says, "What's there to see? Some big Jew arm."

Curly says, "That's right. A big Jew arm. And what do you see on it? Nothing. When you see goose bumps, that's when we got the scene, and we'll move on to the next one. Take fifteen is up. Let's go."

He stands back. And you've got to understand, this is in the days when nobody's heard of a video monitor. Nobody says 185, or whatever numbers they're hollering out. I don't know what the hell they mean. Anamorphic or whatever they're saying.

So we go again and again. We get into the twenties. Finally take twenty-two. God. Jesus Christ almighty, it's about time. Curly says, "Okay. Out of this room into the living room." And I turn. Jack turns. We look at Curly. He says, "Open the drapes. Let the light in."

Take twenty-two is not a whole lot different from take one or twelve or fourteen. And we both say, "Curl?"

He shows us his arm. "What d'ya see?"

I say, "Nothing. What do you see?"

Jack says, "I see the same Jew arm. With maybe a couple of little pimples or something."

So we say, "What do you see?"

All BBS movies had to be made for not a dime more than a million dollars. Abe Schneider, who was Bert's dad, was still president and chairman of the board of Columbia Pictures, and BBS's deal was they were allowed to make any movie they wanted to for seven films for a million dollars each. Columbia would never look at a foot of film. Bob and Steve Blauner would get the answer print, do the final cut, get everything. Columbia would give them five to one—five million dollars of prints and advertising if they stayed under a million dollars and released the movie in at least a thousand theaters. After *Easy Rider,* that was the deal they made because *Easy Rider* showed that they could make money. The first one they did that with was *Five Easy Pieces. Last Picture Show* was the second movie. *Drive, He Said* was the third movie. *Marvin Gardens* was the fourth movie. *A Safe Place* came after *Marvin Gardens.* That's Henry Jaglom's film. Then *Gone Beaver* was to be the sixth, and Peter Davis's *Hearts and Minds* was the seventh.

We say, "What do you see, Curl?"

Curly says, "Well, I'll tell you what I see. Fifteen mil. Fifteen million fucking dollars. That's what I see. You'll make that. Derns told you he loved you, and you fucking believed it. That's fifteen mil. Derns and Nicholson hugging with real love on the screen, celluloid, history, Oscars, fifteen fucking mil for goose bumps. Next fucking setup please. Bring in the Burstyn woman." That's the way he talked every day.

One of the defining moments in a friendship that I've had in my career happened on *Marvin Gardens* between Jack and me, which solidified to me that he was indelibly my partner for the rest of my life, regardless of where his life went or my life went. Forever, this would be a mark of his humanity to me, and the fact that he was a special, special person.

We were doing a scene in the Atlantic City convention hall, the Miss America Pageant scene, and at the end of it, Ellen finishes playing the organ and Julie Anne comes down off the runway, and I come up and get them in a little furniture cart thing. I'm driving, Jack's next to me, and Julie Anne is in the back with her gown and her sash and her flowers with Burstyn. As soon as they're on, I have to drive off. Ellen was trying to hang on for dear life, and the car jerked, and Julie just went over on her head. I went about twenty feet and stopped, and everybody ran to the girl, and Jack didn't move. He just put his arm around me and said, "Are you all right, Derns? Are you sure?" He was more concerned about me, because he knew what I was going through, than he was about the girl on her ass. And that was the most heavyweight thing in a crisis that anyone had ever done for me in my life. It was the most positively wonderful moment, because his first concern was for the perpetrator rather than the injured person. He went to the person that he knew would feel guilt for the fact that he drove and caused the person to fall off, rather than the person who was injured. She was fine; nothing happened to her, but no one knew that at the time. Jack's first instinct was for the guy who had driven off. And the fact that he would have that as his first instinct made me fall in love with him for the rest of my life. No matter what he does. He can drown my puppy, and I'll still understand him a little bit.

It's the noblest thing I've ever had anybody do for me in my life. It just shocked me that somebody in a crisis situation would make that choice. I hope someday that I'm a big enough person to make that choice in a similar situation. I hope that I behaved that way somehow when our little girl died, but I don't know because I was alone when I got there, after it happened. And I tried to behave that way once Miss Diane got home. I don't know that I did, but I hope so, but that was after the fact. This was at the fact.

Curly Bob and his then wife, Toby Rafelson, lost a daughter when a wall heater in their Aspen home exploded. She was fourteen. Steve

Blauner had a baby who was two and somehow got a bib string tangled in a feeding chair and got hung. Dead. And I had a child drown in a swimming pool. It was an odd kind of a bond between the three of us.

I had a good time with Jack on *Marvin Gardens*. Jack is tireless. He'll go as many takes as you'll go. He won't drop until you drop. He'll get frustrated quicker than some actors will, but so do I. But he won't sacrifice performance for frustration. He's a perfectionist. I'm a perfectionist. We're certainly equals on a set. He's a little bit more competitive than me in front of the camera, but not to the point of disturbing his work or my work. And he's the best teammate who's ever worked with me. Any actor who says he's hard to work with because he's too competitive isn't that good an actor.

The weekend before we finish shooting *Marvin Gardens*, Jack, Jake Brackman, and Curly Bob go to New York. I get a phone call about one in the morning. Andrea and I are in the hotel, and we still have Monday, Tuesday, Wednesday, and Thursday of that next week to shoot. And they call me up at one thirty laughing their asses off, and this is the quote I get . . . "Dernser. What are you doing?"

I say, "Well, I'm sleeping. Trying to get some sleep because it's Super Bowl Sunday."

"Forget the fucking Super Bowl. We just got you in there."

"Got me in there where?"

"You just won the National Society of Film Critics Award for best supporting actor for your piece of shit performance in *Drive, He Said*."

I say, "Oh yeah, sure. Are you going to tell me forty critics are going to sit around the Algonquin Hotel and say Bruce Dern is best supporting actor for *Drive, He Said*? A film that was never seen anyplace but Croatia."

Jack says, "No, it's true."

I say, "How many votes you need, one?"

Jack says, "You gotta be here Saturday night because they give out the awards."

"How do you know I won?"

"They name the winners before the show, and you won."

I was delighted. I said, "Well, thanks very much."

He says, "So can we tell them you're going to be here, or are you going to be running back to Winnetka or some other goddamn place none of them have ever heard of?"

"No, I'll be there. What else am I going to do? Go back to Malibu and eke out a living? What do you get for it?"

"A piece of paper in an envelope."

"Oh, that'd be nice."

So the following Saturday I went to the Algonquin, but I did a horrible thing. As I walked into the room, I was struck by two things. A guy I had known for some time, who had done a couple of wonderful things for me, who had been a known fugitive and was thought of as a very, very bad man, got up and hugged me, shook my hand, escorted Andrea to where he was going to sit next to her, and was there to protect Bert Schneider. It was Huey Newton. The room was shocked. He'd just come out of seven years of solitary confinement at Folsom. He was free. He had also stopped being a revolutionary and wasn't underground anymore. And he was at the National Film Critics awards dinner, which sucked the life out of that room. And he wasn't asked to be there by anybody except BBS's Bert Schneider.

The second thing was that sitting next to the wall, looking me straight in the eye, were Dinah Shore and Burt Reynolds. For some terrible fucking reason, I just nodded and shined Burt on instead of going over and putting my arms around him. I gave him a "What are you doing here?" look. He got over it. I never got over it. It was the shittiest thing I ever did to another person. We'd known each other eighteen years. I had worked with him in television. We never spent anything but lunches on sets together, but we knew a lot of the same people. Dinah Shore was quite the hierarchy to me. Miss Shore was a class act. Burt belonged with her. Burt's a class act. I'm in a different kind of category than Burt and Dinah Shore and that Hollywood kind of royalty. I never got to that level.

My mother died while we were making *Marvin Gardens*. She died two days after calling me and telling me that she was pleased because she had read that I had won the National Film Critics Award for *Drive, He Said*. She thought somehow it was more prestigious than it was, because "national" meant somehow the president and people like that had to do with the voting. God forbid, it had been the New York Film Critics Award.

· 13 ·

Saying No to Woody Allen

In December of 1972 Stuart Rosenberg is directing *The Laughing Policeman*, starring Walter Matthau, and they want me to star in it. They offer me $35,000. Matthau got $350,000. I got thirty-five grand. That means I was about one-tenth as good as Matthau.

Walter Matthau was a bit of a bully, not to me and not to the actors, but to the people behind the camera. Or as he referred to them, "the little people." He wasn't rude to them or mean to them, he just would pick on people like a wardrobe person for no reason at all. He'd go into a shot. And his tie wasn't straight because he'd pull on it because it was hot. The script supervisor would say, "Fix your tie." And he'd say, "Well, where is wardrobe? Wardrobe's always fucking around and screwing it up," when just two minutes before, I saw him pulling on it. So it wasn't wardrobe at all. But he would never take the blame. Despite that behavior, he was pleasant company. He was a good guy to bet with because he knew sports real well. He was very educated and had run the half mile when he was in high school. We had that to talk about. Generally he was a pleasant guy to do a movie with.

He did a wonderful thing for me, for which I will forever be grateful. He allowed me to go above the title with him in the movie. It said, "Walter Matthau and Bruce Dern in *The Laughing Policeman*."* I'd never had that. This was a big studio and a big star. It wasn't an independent little $300,000 movie like *The Wild Angels* with Peter Fonda. So Walter allowed that, and I was very, very grateful.

We were partners in the movie. The first day at work I got in the car. And he said, "I saw you at the Lakers game last night. You're a fan, huh?"

I said, "Yeah, big-time. Last year was it for me when they won it all."

He said, "Yeah, you were a pretty well-known runner in college, weren't you?"

I said, "Yeah. Now I run with my mouth."

"I heard you gamble."

"I heard about your gambling, too. I heard you bet both ends of the Yankee/Oriole doubleheader the last day of the season."

"Yeah, at the first game I lost fifty grand, second game I had no money. It's the last game. Baltimore's in last place. Yankees have got to win it. And Bert Schneider, who I was doing a project for, was there, but he wouldn't loan me any money. I said to Bert, 'I'll tell you what, I'll put up my salary for the whole series. I'll work for free if I lose the game.' So that's what I do. Bert says, 'If you lose, you will work for free every day until next June.' The guy, Hoyt Wilhelm, normally a relief pitcher, throws a goddamn no-hitter. I worked for free every day. Wouldn't give me lunch money, wouldn't give me a goddamn thing. So be careful, kid. Let me ask you another question. This movie you just did, were you the king or were you Marvin?"

That was the way we got on the whole movie. What was most interesting was Stuart Rosenberg doesn't ask me to come in, doesn't ask to shake my hand, doesn't ask to meet me or anything. But, on the basis

---

*Despite the title, *The Laughing Policeman* is not a comedy. Rosenberg, the director, also directed *Cool Hand Luke*, and later, *The Amityville Horror*, *Brubaker*, and *The Pope of Greenwich Village*.

of *Silent Running*, *The Cowboys*, and *The King of Marvin Gardens*, which had been out in theaters two months, I'm starring in a movie for a guy who seven years earlier wouldn't even interview me for *Cool Hand Luke*.

At the same time, there is talk in Hollywood about *The Great Gatsby*, which is casting. Director Jack Clayton is in town staying over at the Beverly Hills Hotel.

So Fred Specktor said, "Have you got a formal picture of yourself in family scrapbooks or something like that?"

I said, "Yeah, my sister's got some pictures of me in high school, college, stuff like that."

"Have you read *Gatsby*?"

"Yeah, I read it."

"Remember the part of Tom Buchanan?"

"I am Tom Buchanan."

"Yeah, but we don't have any film showing you as Tom Buchanan. Get a picture of yourself as Tom Buchanan by tomorrow. Get it in my office, and we'll blow it up and slip it under Jack Clayton's door, because Bob Shapiro, who is with William Morris in London, is a good friend of Jack Clayton's, and he has an idea that you could play that role because Clayton saw *Marvin Gardens* and thought you were wonderful and has this wild-ass thing that maybe he could make you into Tom Buchanan. If he likes your picture, then we could get you in to meet with him."

So my sister sends me a picture that *is* Tom Buchanan. We slipped it under Clayton's door and got a meeting with him. He walked in the door, shook my hand. He was talking to somebody else, who was leaving. He had a couple of assistants around, and his wife, who's kind of heavyset, with an exotically beautiful face.

Jack Clayton had done a movie early on in the '60s called *The Pumpkin Eater* with Anne Bancroft, and it was a fabulous movie. Later, after *Gatsby*, he did a movie called *Something Wicked This Way Comes*, with Jason Robards. I think Miss Diane is in it also.* It's a good movie. He was quite a gifted filmmaker.

---

*It was based on a Ray Bradbury novel, and Diane Ladd was indeed in it.

He said, "Come in here."

So I go in the bathroom.

"Put your head in the shower."

So I put it in the shower.

"Put this sweater on. Look in the mirror. You got a comb?"

"No."

"Haya, take a comb out of your purse. Come in here. Comb Bruce's hair forward. Part it here. Put it over this way. Oh my God, look at that. Is that fantastic? Look at this picture."

Haya said, "Well that's the same guy in the picture."

He said, "That's you in the picture. How long ago is that?"

I said, "Twenty years ago tomorrow."

"Really. What are you doing on May twenty-sixth?"

"I have no idea. I'm finishing a movie with Walter Matthau called *The Laughing Policeman*."

"They're making a movie of that? Those are the Martin Beck books."

Martin Beck was a fictional detective in Stockholm that solved a bunch of crimes, but the writers transposed the story to San Francisco.

He said, "I used to love those. They're great. That'll make a wonderful movie. When would you be done?"

I said, "We'll be done about the twelfth of April."

Clayton asked, "Are you getting a lot of offers because of your magnificent performance in *Marvin Gardens*?"

Like a schmuck I said, "The movie was good, but I wasn't quite as good as I should have been."

He said, "It's the best performance I've seen an American actor give in a long time. You shouldn't second-guess yourself like that. Have you read the *Gatsby* script?"

"No. Is it close to the book?"

"That's the trouble with it. It's right out of the book. This kid, Coppola, he's so busy doing *Godfather II*, he just copied it down literally right off the page into a screenplay. He could have done it in four hours. I don't think he spent much time doing it. He's a good writer, and he took the right things, but it's basically just what the book is."

I said, "A lot of people tell me I am Tom Buchanan."

He said, "Well that's exactly right. You are Tom Buchanan."

"Is that a compliment from you?"

"Where I come from, Tom Buchanans rule my country."

"Well, where I come from, they rule my country too. Especially the town I live in."

Clayton said, "Someday you'll tell me about that. It was nice meeting you, Tom. I look forward to seeing you in May."

It was all convoluted to me. I don't trust anybody when they say anything like that. Clank clank, you're in my movie. It's all horseshit.

As I was leaving, Mr. Clayton said, "You know, when you first came in here, you were asking trivia questions with one of my assistants. Do you play movie games?"

I said, "Yeah, but I'm not nearly as good as Joey Walsh."

"Who's Joey Walsh?"

"He's a friend of mine, and he's the best at movie trivia."

"Well, do you like movie trivia?"

"Yeah."

"Well, look at Mrs. Clayton."

"Yeah, she's beautiful."

"What movie did she star in?"

"God, I have no idea."

"Look at her."

And I looked at her. "I have no idea. I couldn't tell you."

He said, "She starred in the biggest movie ever made."

I looked at her, and I was embarrassed. She hadn't been in any movie I'd ever seen. I said, "I'm embarrassed. I'm sorry. I don't know. Should I know?"

"Yeah, I guess if you went to movies."

"How long ago was that?"

"Fifteen years."

Now I'm pissed off at myself.

He said, "I'll give you another hint. She's the biggest star her country ever had."

"And she's your wife?"

"Yeah. She only made eight movies and never acted again."

I asked her, "How old were you when you did the movie?"

"Nineteen."

I said, "Wait a second."

He said, "We've got to go out to dinner, so you've got to go. You tell me May twenty-sixth when I see you."

During the Second World War, Jack Clayton had been a 007. He was a commando. He was one of Montgomery's guys who worked in Tangiers and Tunisia and a lot of places like that as a spy. And he was one of the guys that was used as a fake Montgomery. If they killed anybody, it would not be the real Montgomery. This is where he met the man who was the Israeli father of this girl who would later be his wife, and he'd known her since she was two or three years old.

He said, "I'll see you in May."

I said, "You're not kidding about that?"

He said, "Jack Clayton doesn't kid. And this is my wife, Haya Harareet."

I said, "My god. You're Charlton Heston's girlfriend in *Ben-Hur*."

And she said, "That's right."

I looked at her, and I flashed back. In *Ben-Hur* she's absolutely beautiful, but she had to be much heavier when I saw her. She had a big caftan on. She was on the set every day, and she was the sweetest, nicest lady I've ever been around. So supportive of the movie. Such a grand dame. Such a fabulous ambassador for Israel and everything about it. I never saw her after filming the movie except when it opened.

Gatsby is fun. It's camp. Everybody had their families there. Mia's married to André Previn. She's got a slew of kids. Little Soon Yi came along on that movie as a basket baby. We were in Newport, Rhode Island, for six weeks, New York for ten days, and then we went to London for two and a half months, where we shot at Pinewood. What was done at Newport was the green light at the end of the dock, the cottage, and the big parties in the mansions at the Vanderbilt estate and the Gatsby house. What we did in New York was the trip across the Triborough Bridge into the city, and shooting in the Plaza Hotel. And then in London we did the big party scenes. At Pinewood, they built the drive to New York from West Egg to East Egg and the slag heaps and the Dr. T. J. Eckleburg sign and the garage set where Myrtle gets killed. It was eventful. I felt that I was in the hands of craftsmen. Jack

Clayton was tough to work for, but he was interesting. It was an incredible, unique experience. I'd never worked with British people before. What was interesting was the camera crew, the sound crew, people like that, all came to America to shoot in Newport. Yet when we turned around to go to England, we were not allowed to take one crew member, not one.

Gary Liddiard, the makeup man for Redford and me, and Bernie Pollack, Sydney's brother, the wardrobe guy for Redford, had to do us in a hotel. They were not permitted on the set in England. It's just the rule. The law. We allowed their workers here, but ours were not allowed to go there. Annabel Davis-Goff, the script supervisor, was about to become Mrs. Mike Nichols before Diane Sawyer, and she had dual citizenship because she was Irish and American, so she was allowed to work both places. She was the only continuity that we had. We had great cameramen, but they had to be paid as standby cameramen and were not allowed to work. They weren't even allowed to do second-unit work in England.

When I went to England, it was an all-English crew. But it was fun, and I met a guy who would become just about the best friend I have in my life. His name is David Tringham, and he was our first assistant director. And he's the best first assistant I ever worked for. He went on to do movies like *The Bounty*, but his first job, he was twenty years old, his first day of working in the movie business, was as the third assistant director or what you would call in the states the set PA. You're on the set. You're not back at the trailers. The difference is, his first day was on *Lawrence of Arabia*. He was in charge of the Bedouins, the day the bodyguards rode in with Lawrence. The first thing they shot was the first shot of the second half of *Lawrence*, where he had all those nasty guys in pitch-black robes riding with him. And they broke for lunch.

David Lean would wait for cloud formations and the perfect kind of sky. John Box was the set designer who won a bunch of Oscars and was fabulous. He also did many of David Lean's movies, and later did *Gatsby*. A formal British lunch, an hour and a half, is served on linen and silver, even in the middle of the desert, but Tringham had his in like twelve minutes. He came back, went over to John Box, and said, "I have a problem."

Box asked, "Tell me, what's the problem?"

"The Bedouins. They've vanished. They're gone. Camels and all. And there's no footprints."

They had to get in a plane and travel twenty-two minutes to find the Bedouins. They'd gone twelve miles out in the desert. When they got down on the ground, the interpreter talked to them. They said, "You took picture of Bedoo with camera. No, no. No one said you were going to take our picture. You take picture of Arab Bedoo, the soul is gone forever. We don't come back."

So they convinced them to come back, but they had to pay them after every take through the entire movie or they were gone. That was the only way they'd stay. Cash. And that was Tringham's first movie.

David was so good that he became the first assistant director on *Ryan's Daughter*. Anyway, he became my best friend. I don't see him nearly enough, but we talk maybe twice a month.

Gatsby cost seven million dollars. The movie was produced by a Broadway impresario who'd never produced a movie before or after, David Merrick, who I thought was perfect to produce a movie. It was also produced by Robert Evans. So it was a perfect combination. How well they got along, I don't know. There was probably a great deal of friction, but Robert Evans was also the head of the studio (Paramount) at the time. He was the physical producer of the movie. There were some brilliant things done in the marketing, like getting Ralph Lauren to make all the men's clothes for nothing so he could introduce his Polo line of clothing. Theoni Aldredge did all the women's clothes.

There was a gaffe in the movie in the casting, which was unavoidable. Ali MacGraw was Evans's choice for the movie, obviously because he was married to her. Or had been married to her. I forget where Steve McQueen came in and where Evans left off. Ali tested. Katherine Ross tested. Mia tested. Redford wanted Katherine Ross because he had done *Butch Cassidy* with her. Jack wanted Mia, who won out. She's among the classiest ladies I've worked with in my life. There are five or six in that group. I include her with Miss de Havilland, Miss Bette Davis, and Lee Remick. I include Miss Lynn Fontanne, though I never worked with her. I would certainly put Mia in that class. Ann-Margret would be another one. Mia Farrow is just a cut above the rest of the ladies I've worked with in the industry. She walks alone.

I can't even get into what she must have gone through with the little clarinet player. He's clever. He makes interesting movies. He's bright. I turned down a part with Woody Allen. Jerry Orbach ended up playing the role.* The producers asked, "Can Woody please call you on the phone?"

And I said, "It's not personal. I've never met Woody Allen." But there's no script or anything. He doesn't send you a script. It was to do with the issue of money and living in New York on your own dime for ten weeks and getting there on your own dime when you knew you were only going to be in a couple of scenes, and having to be there every day in case they needed you. And getting no money for it. It wasn't resenting that he got money and I didn't. He'd earned that. I just couldn't hang in there.

I'm a Woody Allen fan, but I'm more of a *Sleeper* Woody Allen fan than I am an *Annie Hall* Woody Allen fan. I mean, those are wonderful movies, but I like the wildness of the *Sleeper* movies. His imagination is so wild. Then, later on, it's all gotten a little confusing for me. I don't know which Woody Allen we're dealing with anymore, but that's okay. He's quite gifted, especially for a Knicks fan.

Mia has nothing but class as far as I'm concerned, and she can be quite a gifted actress when she wants to be. She started *Gatsby* in her fourth month of pregnancy. Did not tell anyone. So by the time we got to England, they were cutting the silk dresses every day. She was showing obviously, and if you look at the last half of *Gatsby*, there's not a shot of her below the chest because she was out to here. That was tough on Redford and tough on her. But it was her choice. She was in control of it. Had she told them, someone else would have been cast. That to me is a tremendous act of courage and bravery, but to the detriment of the movie. Other than that, I don't think the movie was miscast.

---

*The film, *Crimes and Misdemeanors*, garnered three Oscar nominations as well as six BAFTAs (from the British Academy of Film and Television Arts), and won numerous critical awards.

I question making the movie. It's been made four times, the last time with Miss Sorvino for TV. F. Scott Fitzgerald did not write *The Great Gatsby* to be a visual experience for an audience in a movie theater. He wrote it much like J. D. Salinger writes his things—for the mind's eye of a reader. You don't write the last sentence of *The Great Gatsby* to be put on the screen. That's impossible. "Beating against the shores," or however that line goes. I mean, how magnificent is that? How do you put that on the screen? It's a cerebral line, but we all understand exactly what it means, which is that we don't understand at all what it means. It's just something out there beyond our grasp. The question is: why do we continually have to make it? I guess *Gatsby* is the great American novel. And we have to see it on the screen.

When we went to Chicago for the opening of *Gatsby*, Fred Specktor went with me. We stayed at the Drake Hotel. I took Fred out to see my grandfather's house. Fred was just wandering around the house.

I said, "Come on, we've got to go back in town now for the opening."

And he said, "No. I want to sleep in any bed just one night. Any bed in the house. I want to say I did it."

"No, Freddy. I couldn't do that to them. They're all gone now. I can't let you do that. They're up there looking down. We may get hit by lightning."

"Come on, Brucie. What do you want me to do?"

"Only if I get to sleep in one of the beds in your house."

"Oh, no way. Absolutely no way. I mean, I've got a brother who's a rabbi. You just can't do it."

Gatsby was a joke because it didn't make the kind of money they thought it would make, and it was sold so fabulously well. Everybody put Evans down because of the way it was sold, but he did a fantastic job of selling it. Bob Redford didn't go out and help sell it enough, and that was a big, big problem. It fell to me to sell. They didn't want to see me, they wanted to see Bob and Mia.

· 14 ·

And I Said No
to Bertolucci

Everybody knows I like buttercream frosting on birthday cake. In May of '74, I get a birthday cake and a manila envelope with a script delivered to my house. The frosting on the cake says, "Smile." I don't know what it means. So I smile. I open the envelope and the script says, *Smile.** I sit down. I start to read it. I go through it in ninety minutes. Done. I read every word. All the liner notes. Everything. I get to the next to the last page. "And now, 1974's California Young American Miss is . . ." You turn the page. And the page says, "Lest you forget, dear reader, there were two Lombards. One was *Gable and Lombard* and the other was just *Lombard*." That's all it said on the script. Meaning that no way are you going to know who the winner is

---

*A wry satire on beauty pageants, this forgotten gem rests easily alongside director Michael Ritchie's other insightful takes on America, competition, and the wayward male made during the same period, including *Downhill Racer*, *The Candidate*, *Bad News Bears*, and *Fletch*. Scripted by notable TV writer Jerry Belson, the cast also included a very young Melanie Griffith and Barbara "Agent 99" Feldon.

or are we going to decide until the night of the show. The emcee was told just before he went onstage and Michael Ritchie rolled the camera. He and Jerry Belson went backstage. Belson was the dirtiest, sneakiest, most fabulous fun guy to be with in your life, and really ingenious as a writer. He just plain got it.

We couldn't have done *Smile* without Tim Zinnemann and his acute genius for doing things. He was the first assistant director on it. He'd run it. And he was like a walking producer in the field. In *Smile*, they actually put on a beauty pageant for three days, which we filmed as part of the movie. The actresses developed their own talents to be filmed for the movie. We needed 2,500 extras every day for the three days. Santa Rosa is a town of 75,000, or 80,000. Three high schools. An hour and twenty minutes north of San Francisco. Right in the middle of Sonoma County. Thousands of people were standing in line to be extras, and once you locked them in, you had to keep them all day. So at the end of the day, you give away TV sets or a car, and you get the local merchants in on it, and everybody ends up making a little money.

Well, Tim Zinnemann comes up with a plan. We'll get Phil's TV Store to give away a big color TV. In the gym, we'll turn over a big spread to all the extras who will have a sit-down lunch and be treated like kings. But I tell you what else we're going to do. We're going to charge the extras to be extras. There's going to be an admission fee to get in to see the show. So instead of paying them to be extras, Zinnemann charged them. And then had more money through the fee for the extras to pay for everything. It was ingenious. And they never balked once. They gave away thirty TVs at the end of each day, and with your ticket, you had a raffle ticket. So you were paying to get a raffle ticket, but in essence, you were paying to be an extra in the movie for which there was no remuneration. That's just ingenious thinking. And it wasn't cheap. The public paid fifty dollars to be an extra for three days in a movie. They're featured constantly. You see the same faces. Andrea's in there, and Jerry Belson's wife Joanne, Michael Ritchie's wife are in there. His twins are in there. They didn't have to pay, of course, but all the other people paid and they loved it.

Michael Ritchie is six feet nine, and he's got the most baby face you ever saw in your life. I love him. I worked for him first on *Big Valley*.

The star on the series, Barbara Stanwyck, called him "Pablum" because he was a twenty-three-year-old kid. He and John Landis were roommates at Harvard. Ritchie was brought to Hollywood in 1962 to direct *Profiles in Courage*, which was a Kennedy family series based on a book that John Kennedy wrote. Michael was head of that series and directed it. After that was over, he stayed and began directing episodes of *Big Valley*. Within five years, he was directing *Downhill Racer* with Bob Redford. And he directed a good movie no one ever talks about called *Prime Cut*, with Gene Hackman and Lee Marvin.

In the spring of 1975, I had both *Smile* and *Posse* coming out. One was a UA picture, and the other was a Paramount Picture. Jeffrey Katzenberg and Mike Eisner had just come on board at Paramount to work for Barry Diller, who had just taken over. *Smile* came out and died. Just died. Terrible opening. UA did a very poor job of marketing the movie. The studio was in a big state of flux then.

I was now doing *Family Plot* with Alfred Hitchcock. I went out and stumped for *Smile* as much as I could, but my mind was really into *Family Plot*.

David Picker, of all the producers that I worked for, was the best in terms of taking care of the people that he worked with, from the grips to the craft service to the stars to the extras. Did it better than anyone. David mentioned a couple of rules of thumb that were interesting. One was, "I'll never make a trek movie, where you go from A to B." And two was, and when I was thinking about doing *Big Love* for HBO, it took a lot of thought because of the sentence he laid out to me, and he laid this out to me thirty years ago. He said, "As an executive, when I was running United Artists, and if I ever get back to being an executive again, or just as a producer of films, I'll never buy a television star for a movie. Because you never buy anybody for a film that you can get for free in your living room." And I never forgot that.

Around this time, Bertolucci asked me to be in *1900*, and I turned it down. I was probably a sap. Donald Sutherland played the role, and he's a wonderful actor. I was terrified of playing a revolutionary terrorist in a movie where I had to do the things that that character had to do during the rise of fascism in that time in Italy. I had to rape a deaf girl and smash the kid's head. I just didn't see myself doing that, and yet it was such an honor to be offered the role by Bertolucci himself.

At Universal, Steven Spielberg used to hover in the back on *Family Plot*, and Hitch would always turn to me and say, "Bruce. Who is that boy?"

And every time I tell Steven this story, he always says the same thing, "God, I get goose bumps."

I said, "That's Steven Spielberg. Look, Hitch, he just wants to talk to you for ten minutes. Five minutes."

He said, "Well, what does he want?"

I said, "You're his idol. He just wants to sit at your feet for five minutes and chat with you. He doesn't want to ask you anything technical, he just wants to tell you what a fan he is and he appreciates your style and your filmmaking ability. If there's any pointers you could give him, he'd really appreciate it."

He said, "Isn't he the boy that made the fish movie?"

I said, "Yeah, he is."

And Hitch looked at me. "I'm panicked."

I said, "Why? He's not going to do anything to you. He's going to be quite a good filmmaker."

He said, "I could never sit down and talk with him."

I said, "Why not?"

He said, "Because I look at him and feel like such a whore."

I said, "What do you mean, such a whore? Get over it, Bud."

I sat next to Hitch every day for ten weeks on *Family Plot*. On the first day, I pulled my chair right up next to him, and I said, "I don't give a shit if you like this or not, but I'm sitting next to you for ten weeks, because I'm not going to miss the opportunity to sit down with a guy who's been so helpful in my career, giving me the starring part in his movie. Why, I don't know."

He said, "You know why, Bruce."

In all our conversations, he's never looking at me and I'm never looking at him, because he's looking at the set.

"You know why you're in the picture?"

"Tell me again. I like to hear it."

"Because you're unpredictable. I know the frame's perfect because

I have it in my office. And my setup is perfect, but, within the setup, I have to be entertained. And you're entertaining, Bruce, and you're unpredictable. That's why you're in this film. Get on with your question."

I said, "Why do you feel Spielberg makes you feel like that?"

Hitch said, "Because I'm the voice of the *Jaws* ride. Universal paid me a million dollars. I took it and I did it. I'm such a whore. I can't sit down and talk to the boy who did the fish movie."

I said, "Well, maybe you'll give the money back."

He said, "Was the fish movie any good? I've never sat through a whole movie, including one of my own."

It drives Steven Spielberg nuts when I say that Douglas Trumbull is a genius along with Alfred Hitchcock. Douglas looks through the eyepiece and sees magic.

Spielberg asks, "But why does that give him status along with Mr. Hitchcock?"

Because with both men, every day I was excited to go to work for one reason. And I'll throw Frankenheimer in there too. Every day I went to work, I thought just maybe we might do something nobody had ever done before.

I talked that over with an actor one time where he said he had the same feeling. I did two movies (*Will Penny, Number One*) with him in two years, and that was Charlton Heston. We were talking one night in 1986, eighteen years after I worked with him. I told him my experiences with Douglas and Hitch, and he just snapped his fingers and said, "I know exactly what you mean. I had it once in my life. As much as I adored Willy Wyler on *Ben-Hur*, I only had it once. And that was on *Touch of Evil*. Every day I went to work with Orson, I thought, just maybe . . . Did we do it every day? No. But there was always that chance."

In the summer of '75, I did *Won Ton Ton, the Dog Who Saved Hollywood*. It was written by Cy Howard and Arnold Schulman. Five years earlier, they had written a script that was really funny called *Lovers and Other Strangers*, with Anne Meara and Jerry Stiller and Harry Guardino, Diane Keaton, Bonnie Bedelia, and Bill Macy. It was just funny shit. It was about a wedding gone bad. These guys were wonderful writers. It was fabulous, and it did very well. Then they wrote this movie, and it was the funniest thing I had ever read. They wanted me to star in it, and David Picker produced it. I thought it was just going to be terrific. Art Carney was the lead in it.

The movie was about the making of Rin Tin Tin into a movie star. I was playing Darryl Zanuck as a young kid, trying to make a German shepherd into a movie star. My character, Gordon Potchuck, is running this studio. There were vignettes where all these old-time movie stars from the 1920s and '30s were playing themselves for a day. So, for sixty days, every day, you have excitement because one of these people is on the set. One day it was the Ritz Brothers, another day it was Groucho, another day it was Rory Calhoun. Ron Leibman was in it, and he was fabulously funny.

Leibman, Jane Fonda, and I all got in the Actors Studio the same night. Leibman was in *Where's Poppa?* He was also terrific in a movie where he wasn't funny but he was great because of his sense of humor. It's one of my favorite sports films of all time, *Phar Lap*. He was also in *Norma Rae* with Sally Field. He's big stuff.

Madeline Kahn was just wonderful. I felt so out of my league in that movie. W. C. Fields said it: "Don't work with kids and animals." Man, was he right. I remember in one scene, sitting at a table at dinner one night, where they have five nominees for a Best Actor Academy Award. Four of the guys are sitting at one table. The fifth one is Won Ton Ton, the German shepherd, who's with me at my table. They introduce all their names, and of course, Won Ton Ton wins.

At my table, my date was Gloria DeHaven, and I can't believe that this woman, who was then fifty years old—this is 1975—was as sexy as she was. The other people at my table were Phil Silvers and his date, Ann Miller; Cyd Charisse and her date, Red Buttons; and Mickey Rooney and some fabulous-looking blond Marilyn Maxwell type. Just great-looking dames with guys.

Anyway, Won Ton Ton wins the Oscar, has to get off his chair, run down through the aisle, and go up on stage, where Art Carney gives him the award. Won Ton Ton pisses on Art Carney's leg while he's getting the Oscar, and he has to do it three or four times.

Michael Winner directed the movie. He is a very, very, very funny man, but not the right guy to direct *Won Ton Ton*. He directed *Death Wish*, but that's not *Won Ton Ton*. And Cy Howard is married to Jack Warner's daughter Barbara. So old man Warner is represented there by his daughter's husband. I was thrilled to be a part of it. It was the first time that anybody ever paid me six figures on anything and David Picker was my friend. I just had fun on it every day.

Anyway, at our table, Phil Silvers is out cold. He's facedown in his dish. It's take three, and Won Ton Ton is going up and does it the same every single time. We had two German shepherds. One was the beautiful close-up German shepherd, and the other one, Gus, could jump through things, over tables, and do all the stunts. These were German shepherds that were making big, big bucks.

About halfway through the third take, Won comes back and sits down at the table, and Ann Miller says, "God, German shepherds are so smart. I mean how can they do it, take after take?" Phil Silvers is facedown in his soup. He's been out for all three takes. He wasn't supposed to be like that. But he was, and nobody wanted to wake him up. They just shot him like that. Nobody gave a shit. It was perfect. He's Phil Silvers.

Ann Miller says, "Dogs are so smart."

Phil Silvers lifts his face out of the soup and says, "Oh yeah? If they're so smart, then why are they dogs?" And drops his face right back into the soup. It was the funniest thing I'd ever seen in my life. It was so Phil Silvers. And it went on like that every day.

One day, Groucho Marx was in a scene. He came in with Zeppo's ex-wife, who was married to Frank Sinatra. This woman looked beautiful to me. The only woman I've seen that looked like her was Mia Farrow. They looked very similar. Just a great-looking blond. Beautiful soft skin. Groucho was in a scene of an open casting call with the Ritz Brothers, and they were going to do their little number. One of them had these big overlapping shoes on. So one of the brothers was standing there telling Michael Winner what they were going to do in the scene, Groucho gets a hammer and a couple of long nails from a grip, and nails this guy's big shoes to the floor. Unbeknownst to him.

So Mike Winner says, "Okay, everybody let's go. Is everybody ready?"

And this Ritz Brother turns to go, and he flies right out of his shoes.

Groucho looks down with his big fucking cigar and says, "Aha! I think I have the answer. You're not as bright as you thought you were! Maybe you're not really a Ritz Brother. Here. I'll get one of my brothers to bring you some crackers."

All this shit was never in the movie because we weren't rolling. It wasn't a part of it, but it was really fun.

On *Won Ton Ton*, I was out of my element in terms of expertise at high-level inventive comedy. I never thought of myself as being funny. I still don't. I think of myself as witty and clever, but Art Carney and Madeline Kahn are both funny folks. I don't think Madeline thought of herself as being funny. She was just funny. And sexy and nasty but without ever advertising it or broadcasting it. She had a fabulous figure. She was as pretty as she wanted to be. She could be a mess if she wanted to be. She was a wonderful, wonderful actress.

It's funny because I worked with her and Barbara Harris back-to-back. Both were actresses that had no confidence in their own ability at all. And both were amazing comediennes. Look at Madeline in *Paper Moon*, *Blazing Saddles*, and *Young Frankenstein*. Look at Barbara Harris in *Nashville*. They were both rather unheralded comediennes who were cute, adorable, pixie-ish, and worked all the time in their genre in our age group. And were terribly insecure at what they did. It was unusual that I had them back-to-back like that. They were girls that were highly unusual at what they did.

· 15 ·

Le Dern Hot

I went to France to do *The Twist* in 1975. We arrived in Paris on Armistice Day, the eleventh of November. Everybody said, "Oh, great, you're going to the City of Light." Well, they must have meant electric light, because we got there on Armistice Day and I left the twenty-fifth of January and I never saw the fucking sun. I never saw it. I just saw grim, wall-to-wall gray. But it was fun, because it was director Claude Chabrol. Stéphane Audran, Claude's wife, and I were the two stars, along with Ann-Margret. Chabrol was wonderful and a big devotee of Hitchcock. I guess that's why he hired me. I never quite knew. He couldn't have seen *Family Plot*, because it wasn't out yet. I'd just finished it that summer.

I was quite enamored of the French workday, which started at eleven and went until seven with no lunch. You just shot eight straight hours, and the caterers served lunch all day long and you took whatever you wanted and kept working. I liked that. There was no break. I don't like the break in the middle of the day. And the crew seemed to like it. The crews were very tight-knit. Everybody knew everybody. In the studio, it was the walking lunches, but when we shot outdoors, there was a lunch. Chabrol was a big gourmet and a great cook. The days we would shoot on location, lunch was a big deal. You started at seven in the morning, and you worked until dark. The whole day was planned around what restaurant we would eat lunch in. It was like an hour and a half to two hours. Chabrol was a nifty little guy. He had a wild imagination. I had only seen one of his films called *Landru*, which was fabulous.

I ran in a bunch of French races because we were there in the wintertime. They ran a lot of cross-country then, because France had the two best milers in the world. The French were knocked out that here was an actor starring in a movie for Claude Chabrol, running in the midst of two thousand cross-country runners, and I'm right up there in the front with a Santa Monica Track Club shirt on. And they thought, Santa Monica. Is that someplace in Spain? I said, no, it's Santa Monica, California. Claude came out to the race, and they all got excited. They had a big picnic lunch. It was fun that way. But the city was grim.

I didn't really enjoy my time in Paris. I enjoyed making the movie, but I speak no French at all. And as soon as they yelled *Coupez*, or cut, I didn't know a thing that was going on. No one spoke English except in the dialogue.

Stéphane was a wonderful partner. But it was a strange, odd movie. It was released as *The Twist* in the United States, but in Europe it was released as *Folies Bourgeoises*. I don't know that it even played in the States much at all. Three things happened during it: first, it made me familiar with Isabelle Adjani, so, later, when I did *The Driver*, at least I knew who she was; second, it made me familiar with Johnny Hallyday and Sylvie Vartan, who were the two singing rages; third was getting to work with Chabrol every day, who had great ideas and wanted to do things with the camera. I didn't really get what the movie was getting at until about two-thirds of the way through. I've said earlier, one of the wonderful things about going to work with Douglas Trumbull and Mr. Hitchcock was, on any given day, you went to work excited because you thought you might do something no one had ever done before. Well, that was also the wonderful thing about Claude Chabrol.

The camera was always up to stuff. There were days where he had a camera hanging on two cable wires.

He'd say to me, "If I can give you shoes that look like street shoes, but are really sneakers underneath so you can run, can you keep up with a camera if I drop it on a cable and have you run, for example, through the bois and carry on a conversation with yourself?"

I said, "Yeah."

He said, "So my wife, meaning your wife . . ." that's the way he talked to me, "pisses you off."

"She pisses me off every day."

"She pisses you off every day. She's playing your wife, but she is my wife, but she's playing your wife. She pissed me off this morning. She pissed you off. You talk out loud like I talk out loud all the time. So you run away to get away from her to get on the other side of the parkway. You go with your mistress. You go to her place and you fuck all morning. But then you have to come back to her. You talk about it out loud to yourself all the time. You run across the park talking. I can't run. But I see that you run, and by the time you get across the park you see the mistress. Then you're fine. Could you do that? Could you stay with the camera if I have it on a downhill slope all the way so the camera goes very fast. It goes about eleven, twelve miles an hour. Can you do that?"

I said, "Yeah, I can do that. But can you do that?"

"Yeah, I can do that. You can run twelve miles an hour for five hundred meters?"

"You can't run a camera five hundred meters downhill."

"Watch this."

So we'd do stuff like that. That was exciting because there's nobody on the camera. Chabrol takes a helicopter with a big telephone pole on it, hovers the helicopter, puts the telephone pole at an angle and has a guy wire all the way to another telephone pole at the other end of the park. On the wire is this tiny little Arriflex with a short lens on it. I start running. My job is to stay about ten feet in front of the camera for five hundred meters across the park and talk out loud to myself with dialogue based on what's written, but I don't have to say what's written, just talk about how much she pisses me off. And it works and it's fabulous. We do it in two takes. Sometimes, the camera would get ahead of me, but the camera can swivel because Mr. Rabier can make the camera turn back at me if I stumble. And this was thirty years ago.

By the end of the movie, I determined everybody had somebody else that they were monkeying around with. Not me. I had Andrea. Stéphane had a ski instructor. The script supervisor had someone. This one had that one. So at the end of the movie, I made up a program. I had little matching T-shirts made with numbers on them like soccer players. Number one went with number six. Number four went with number two. So you'd get a scorecard of the players that matched with the other players. Stéphane had a number one, the ski instructor had a number seven with a one in italics. Seven goes with one. They got the biggest kick out of it. Everybody knew. Nobody cared.

Andrea and I and Roger Smith and Ann-Margret went to the Crazy Horse Saloon. I didn't know Ann-Margret when I was growing up, even though we grew up in the same town. She went to New Trier, and I went to New Trier. But when I was a senior, she was just coming in as a freshman. So we weren't in the same building at the same time. They invited us to go with them to the Crazy Horse. The four of us. We were just getting to know them.

So we're sitting in the Crazy Horse and out come these girls who are outstanding-looking girls. A chorus line like the Rockettes. They're naked except their beavers are merkins, which are fake beavers. They're introduced by a guy who's dressed like a fairy in a tutu. But he's big. He's about six feet four and weighs about 350. He's got little cupid lips on. He does his little number and the girls dance and they go offstage and between numbers he entertains you. He's dexterous. He can move. He's not just a big fatty. He dances around. We're at the first table. He comes down to our table and he picks me up in his arms and carries me up on stage like a little baby in his arms. He keeps saying in English to me, in his arms, "Be a good sport. Don't be an asshole. Be a good sport." I couldn't move. I mean, I'm six feet one, and I weigh 180. There's 150 people dining in one of the more famous clubs in the world. And I'm embarrassed. I'm pinned to this guy who, now I'm finding out, is also one of the strongest men alive. I can't move, and he's kissing me on the face with these big ruby lips. He's twirling me around in his tutu, cradling me in his arms like a little fucking fetus. He's dancing around for maybe three minutes, and he finally brings me back to the table and sets me in my seat. There are three people at my table who have made a lake out of their tears from laughing so hard. My wife is almost choked out. Roger Smith and Ann-Margret are just beside themselves. They have never laughed so hard in their lives. I am speechless. I'm shocked. I don't know what to do. I don't know what to say. I can't move. The place is standing up. Everybody's applauding. And I feel I've been set up worse than anything ever in my life. To this day, they deny they had anything to do with it. I can't believe they didn't. It had to have been set up. And, for that, I will be indebted to them forever simply because it's too good a story not to have happened.

We were there at Christmas. Roger Smith goes into the big department store in downtown Paris, Le Printemps, to buy Christmas gifts for all the people that work for Ann-Margret and him. About eight employees. He's a piece of work, Roger Smith. When I came to Hollywood, he was the biggest international star in the world, television-wise. He was the star of 77 *Sunset Strip*. It wasn't Efrem Zimbalist Jr., it was Roger Smith. He was the guy. When he met Ann-Margret and fell in love with her, he said, "I'll give up what I do. I'll step back. I love you. I'll marry you. I'll manage your career and I'll take care of you the rest of your life." He did it. He put his money where his mouth was, and he's taken care of her since. And she's had a fabulous life and a fabulous career, at least from where I sit. He's devoted to her, and likewise, and she's had some rough times. That was 1964, so they've done over forty years. Pretty good.

But in Paris, he wears a full length . . . not a mink, but some kind of animal, to the floor. He walks into this department store to get gifts for his people. He's not good with public contact. In Paris, particularly in the winter, Christmastime, there's all these gypsies running around the city. This gypsy woman comes up to Roger in the store. She says, "Money for the baby. Money for the baby. Please, money for the baby."

And he goes, "No, no, no, no! I only speak English."

She says, "Schmuck, I *am* speaking English."

· 16 ·

Dr. Death El Demento

One day after New Year's, 1976, I come home from work, and in Paris at the hotel, I get a package with a manila envelope and a bunch of pages in it but no cover page, no first page, no letter. It was just script pages without numbers on it. No phone call, no nothing. So, I didn't look at it. Andrea and I went and ate dinner at Maxim's, where the violinist serenaded us with Andrea's favorite song, "Fascination," on her birthday.

I went to work the next morning. We were working out in the Bois de Vincennes. It was drizzly gray. Typical. Andrea came out to see me. We had a guy who drove us around. His name was Michel. What was interesting about Michel, or any driver I've had in a foreign country, was he would eat in the back with the other people. You ask them to eat with you, they will not do it. That's not their place. I'm shocked by that.

Andrea comes to the set and says, "You got a phone call from Fred, who asked if you got an envelope last night. You're supposed to call him right away."

"I'm in a field."

"He said it's urgent."

So I go to Chabrol and explain what's going on.

He says, "Ah, Monsieur Specktor, he treated me with honor."

I say, "He wants me to give him a phone call."

He says, "Phone booth about two kilometers. Lunch about half an hour. Go make the phone call."

I take Michel, my driver. We go to the phone and I call. In L.A. it's three in the morning. I wake Fred up.

He says, "What are you calling me at three in the morning for?"

I say, "Because Andrea said you called."

"I didn't call you, Brucie. Don't call me at this time in the morning. Oh, no, that's right. They sent you a thing. You're supposed to call Bob Evans."

"Bob Evans?"

"Yeah, they offered you a movie last night. You call Bob Evans. He's producing the movie for Paramount. You have to be there on the eighteenth of January."

"Fred, I'm working here until the twenty-first of January. I can't get out of this."

"No, the Super Bowl's the eighteenth. You have to be at the Super Bowl because they have to shoot you in the blimp tied into the press box on the day of the Super Bowl. There's no second day, Brucie. You have to be there because they pan up off the press box to you in the gondola."

"Come on, it's a matte shot."*

"Brucie, the gondola of the blimp is crushing the press box at the Super Bowl. They have to see some of it. They have to see the announcers like Tom Brookshire. They have to see Bob Short, the president of Goodyear. Robert Shaw will be running down the stands. It's one shot. They have to do it that day. You have to be there. You've got to tell the little frog you've got to be out of there."

---

*The easiest and most common way to do a shot like this would be a matte shot, meaning you'd shoot the actor against a bluescreen and combine it with Super Bowl footage later.

We are family—left to right—
brother Jack, Bruce (age 2), mother
Jean MacLeish Dern, sister Jean,
and father John Dern (1938).

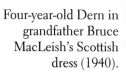

Four-year-old Dern in
grandfather Bruce
MacLeish's Scottish
dress (1940).

Dern (age sixteen) with father John Dern at the Glencoe, Illinois, family compound (1952).

A sixteen-year-old Dern in front of the family home on the shores of Lake Michigan in Glencoe, Illinois (1952).

Premier half-miler Dern running for the University of Pennsylvania in 1956 at age nineteen.

Dern as the not-long-for-this-world Loser with Peter Fonda in *The Wild Angels* (1966).

Dern as Asa Watts, aka Longhair, the man who killed John Wayne in *The Cowboys* (1971).

Spaced-out Freeman Lowell (Dern) on his mission to save Earth's vegetation in Douglas Trumbull's *Silent Running* (1971).

Icons of seventies' cinema, Jack Nicholson and Dern play brothers David and Jason Staebler in Bob Rafelson's *The King of Marvin Gardens* (1971).

Two future Oscar nominees, Dern with daughter Laura celebrating her seventh birthday in 1974.

Dern with an uncharacteristically animated Alfred Hitchcock on the set of *Family Plot* (1975).

Returning Vietnam vet Capt. Bob Hyde (Dern) finds his wife, Sally (played by Jane Fonda), changed by the antiwar movement in Hal Ashby's *Coming Home* (1977).

Birthday boy Bobby Lee (Dern) with Ann-Margret and Helen Hughes from *Middle Age Crazy* (1979).

In the Michael Ritchie film *Diggstown*, Dern plays the nefarious fight promoter John Gillon, seen here with costar James Woods (1991).

Old guard meets new guard—Dern and Matt Damon on the *All the Pretty Horses* set (1999).

Dern plays Thomas, the only sympathetic male in *Monster* (2003), which featured Charlize Theron's Oscar-winning performance.

"But what if the little frog doesn't give a fuck about the Super Bowl? What if he doesn't even know what it is?"

"Read the script and then call me up with complaints. Let me go back to sleep. Call Bob Evans."

I got off the phone, and I said, "Shit, I can't call Bob Evans without reading this fucking script."

I didn't know what *Black Sunday* was. I didn't know it was a big hit book. It had just come out at Christmas. And Thomas Harris was still working at the *Waco Journal*. *Black Sunday* was his first published book.* So I went home. I read it. I couldn't put it down. I read every fucking page. Michael Lander, my character, was everywhere. But he was nuts and there was no getting around it—from the first page, when he apologizes in the documentary, to when he goes into the office of the guy at the VA and sits there waiting, and the woman makes him wait the whole day.

She says, "Take a number."

And Lander says, "Take a number? I've been coming in here once a month for two years and I'm always taken right away because my name is an L. That's the twelfth letter of the alphabet. Not the twenty-sixth letter. Why do I have to take a number? I'm twelfth. I'm here on time. Every week I go twelfth."

"Take a number."

Thomas Harris is so great with the way he writes, the inner things. I immediately bought an American copy of the book and read it. It's all in the script. Ernie Lehman, who wrote the script, also wrote *Family Plot*.

I got him on the phone before I talked to Bob Evans. I asked, "What do I need from the book?"

He said, "Read it. What Hitch allowed you to do in *Family Plot*, Frankenheimer will allow you to do on *Black Sunday*, plus you've got Ivan Moffatt, who's rewriting my script. You know him from the Colony, and he'll do whatever you need."

---

*Thomas Harris, the novelist, is perhaps best known for *The Silence of the Lambs*. His first book, *Black Sunday*, was written while he was a reporter, and it attempted to get inside of the mind of an American terrorist working with Palestinian terrorists.

Ivan Moffatt was big, big stuff to me. He'd written some of *Castle Keep*. And he wrote a little bit on *They Shoot Horses, Don't They?* So I knew that flexibility was going to be there. I couldn't put the book down. I was excited. And I said, you know what? Frankenheimer lives in the Colony. I'm going to call him. I'm not going to call Bob Evans. So I called.

I got Frankenheimer's number. It's now about 11 P.M. my time, which is 3 P.M. L.A. time. I call Frankenheimer's house, and I don't get him, I get Evvy, his wife, who was a Kazan actress. Gadg loved her. She had a nice part in *Splendor in the Grass*. She was in *Dark at the Top of the Stairs*. She was in anything Gadg would do. He really liked her. She was pretty, and she had that great name, Evans Evans. I just called her Evans squared. She was very, very pretty and a great dame. She was a little loose, and she loved hamsters. When I called, one of the hamsters had just gotten in the fireplace and the fire was on, so it was kind of dicey whether I was going to get John on the phone or whether Freddie, who was hamster number three, was going to be toast.

She says, "He's at the office."

I ask, "But where's the office?"

"Freddie number three is close to the flames."

"Why don't you turn the fire off?"

"It's real logs."

"You're not supposed to burn real logs in the fireplace, Evvy."

"Yeah, I know, but John's not here. He's at Paramount."

So I call Paramount, and Frankenheimer says, "Why'd you call me?"

Now I don't know him very well at all. All I know is, when I'm in the Actors Studio in 1960, he's there observing, and he is one tough motherfucker, John Frankenheimer. At that time he is the king of *Playhouse 90*. He is the most astute, well-rounded, live-television director going. Franklin Schaffner, George Roy Hill, and John Frankenheimer are the three wunderkinds of *Playhouse 90*. Each one has an assistant. Frankenheimer's assistant is Syd Pollack. They alternate the *Playhouse 90s*, which are done once a week. This is ninety minutes of live TV. Nothing to cut to. It's live. You can't go to a commercial. Frankenheimer did *Of Mice and Men* with Lon Chaney Jr., who was a known alcoholic. Chaney behaved himself all week long, and then panicked after the rehearsal, the night of the live show, and showed up drunk ten minutes before airtime. Frankenheimer warned him.

He said, "You have no idea what'll happen to you if you don't sober up in ten minutes."

Lon Chaney thought he sobered up, and they went on the air. He walked on the stage, and the first thing he had to do was walk out to the barn where the chickens were. He's live in front of fifty million people in America. Frankenheimer goes, "One!" Meaning camera one on Lon Chaney. There's nothing to cut to. Lon Chaney walks through the backdrop of the set and Frankenheimer says, "Stay on him." He walks into the audience, and America didn't turn him off. Frankenheimer says, "Stay on him. Watch him die." They didn't cut. He started groping crew people, technicians. He's walking among cameras backstage. The set is gone. The chickens are running all over. Frankenheimer goes, "Stay on him. He's almost dead." He says, "Call Forest Lawn." This was Frankenheimer, man. He was the absolute best. And finally they got Chaney back after he'd lost a catastrophic seven minutes. He was wonderful for the rest of the performance. And won an Emmy.

So anyway, I said to Frankenheimer, "I don't even want to know why you picked me. "

He said, "Are you telling me you're going to do it?" Just like that.

"Yeah, I'll do it. Absolutely I'll do it."

"So what do you want to know from me?"

"Why me?"

"Because there's only one guy who can do it, and that's you. Because you are Dr. Death. And this is a movie about Dr. Death El Demento. But we don't want to see any of that. We don't want to see a sign of Dr. Death El Demento. We want to see passion, love, compassion, spirit, enthusiasm, and above all, cleverness and creativeness. You bring us that, we'll have a hit movie. You bring us anything less than that, and you'll sink this fucker to the bottom of the ocean. You'll have the most fun you'll ever have. Shaw is the most competitive person you'll ever meet in your life. But luckily for you, you don't have one scene with him. It's the Deutsch you're going to have problems with, because she's the real deal."

"What do you mean?"

He said, "She hates us."

I said, "What do you mean?"

"Juden."

"I'm out of that."

"I'm not. Bob Rosen's not. Evans is not. Bluhdorn's not. Paramount is not. Gulf and Western's not."

"How bad is she?"

"Waffen."

"What do you mean Waffen?"

"Whole family Waffen. Super Waffen. Every male in the family dead Waffen."

I said, "What do you mean?"

"North Africa Rommel Waffen. Proud of it. Scrapbooks to the ceiling. Prussian tank commanders. North Africa. Montgomery. Rommel. The whole thing. They were Tank Corps. But she'll describe it to you. She'll give you battle plans. She'll tell you everything. Their job was to paralyze the Allies on the North African continent. You know something? They did a goddamn good job of it. They'd have pulled it off, too, if they'd have gotten the gasoline."

"John, we're making *Black Sunday*. This is 1976. That was 1943."

He said, "Oh yeah, right."

I asked, "But is she good-looking?"

Long pause.

"John, are you there?"

"Be here on the eighteenth."

"Do I have to call Bob Evans?"

"No. Let Fred Specktor call Bob Evans. You'll drive to work with me every day."

"Do I have to?"

"You live four doors from me. Why wouldn't you want to?"

"Because they just put in the diamond lane and there's only two of us. Takes three."

Long pause.

"We'll get around it."

"How many days do we work?"

"At the blimp place, sixty."

"Do I have to fly it?"

"Only at the Super Bowl. You have to look like you're taking pictures of the Super Bowl."

"What do you mean?"

He said, "I need a shot with you at the controls crashing into the press box. One shot. It'll last eight seconds."

I said, "I can't do that."

He said, "You're gonna do it whether you can or you can't. You're going to do it or you're going to die looking like you're going to do it." Click.

That's my real introduction to Frankenheimer. Sixteen years earlier I walk out of the Actors Studio. I have a Zundapp motorcycle sitting outside in the rain. I come out, and this blond, good-looking, nasty-looking girl like I like, comes out, lifts her skirt up to her waist and cranks her leg over my motorcycle. Sits on it, grabs the handlebars, kicks the starter with her high-heel shoes on, but can't kick it over because there's no key in it. Now Frankenheimer's a great-looking guy. And he's like six feet four. He comes out, grabs her by the back of her shirt, jerks her off there, and says, "Get the fuck off that motorcycle. Where do you think you're going?"

I say, "What's going on?"

He says, "It's my wife. And who the fuck are you?"

I said, "It's my motorcycle."

"That's my wife. What's she doing on your motorcycle?"

"I have no idea." I saw right away where his radar was. "I don't even know her. I've never seen her."

"Bullshit. If she's on your motorcycle, she's been on other stuff of yours."

"No, no. You've got it all wrong, Mr. Frankenheimer."

"And furthermore, why'd you call me Mr. Frankenheimer?"

"Because you're a great director."

"You don't know if I'm a great director. How would you know? I don't know myself. I'm learning."

And that was it. He went off in the rain, literally dragging her up the street. This wasn't Evans Evans, this was his first wife. I never saw him again until Super Bowl Sunday. After that, I became a really good friend of his. But he was a very aloof, arrogant, standoffish guy who was never given his due as a director because in 1966, about a year after he did *Seconds*, they ran him off. And I don't know why.*

In *Black Sunday*, you have Robert Shaw, who comes to the movie having done *Jaws*, for which he was greatly underappreciated. One of the most underappreciated actors in my generation is Roy Scheider. A guy who was consistently good, brilliant once. The three greatest performances I ever saw that I could not have done were the David Helfgott performance in *Shine*, given by Geoffrey Rush; the Murray Abraham performance in *Amadeus*; and the Roy Scheider performance in *All That Jazz*. Those three performances are genius performances. I had a shot at *Marathon Man*, but I didn't take the role. I think there was some conflict with *Marathon Man*. I felt *Marathon Man* somehow overlapped *Black Sunday*, and yet Marthe Keller was in both movies. I don't know how that could have been unless she was finishing one and doing the other at a similar time because Bob Evans produced both movies.

Anyway, *Black Sunday* was, for two and a half months, the most fun movie I ever worked on, because of my proximity to Frankenheimer, the fact that we lived four doors from each other, the creation of the diamond lane, and that we had to drive fifty minutes from our houses to the blimp base every day. You couldn't use the diamond lane then with just two people. Now you can do two or more. The diamond lane was created because of the gas crunch.

Frankenheimer devised this plan that we could use the diamond lane and therefore wouldn't have to fight the traffic to get to work every day. So props made us a dummy and we got a chauffeur's cap and a livery jacket from wardrobe, and I'd drive and John would sit in the passenger seat, and the dummy would sit in the back dressed in a little jacket. We'd put a paper in his hand so he could be reading. We'd drive

---

*It could have been any number of things. He always said he liked directing live television better than making movies. He went through a messy divorce in 1962. He was also a strongly political filmmaker, and he drove his good friend Robert Kennedy to the Ambassador Hotel on the day he was assassinated. He was also rumored to have developed a drinking problem due to any or all of these other stresses.

er, I jump up and drive the boat, and they see it's me and
shot, it was far enough away that you couldn't see that it
Frankenheimer left her there. He couldn't switch people
ng back and forth because there wasn't enough time for
e a half mile away each time. So he let her stay, and the
he boat ran into the bridge. He didn't get under it in time,
t down and cut her face, and Frankenheimer was beside
rest of the night. He couldn't shoot; he just wrapped,
allowed himself to let her be there, and she was hurt and
a little bit. When she came to, she wanted to work the rest
t, and he couldn't do it. She could do it, but he couldn't do
shattered by the fact that he let that happen on his watch.
ith Jack on *Marvin Gardens*, it was a moment of truth, and I
nkenheimer for that. But I saw a sign of weakness in him that
ething go beyond his control when it was within his control.
s no reason to have her there. It could have been any other
He shouldn't have had an alcoholic skiff captain named Buzz
he boat at four thirty in the morning who'd been drinking all
g. Buzz had a buzz at four o'clock when he came to work that
n. It was stuff that should have been shot by people who knew
ey were doing; it should have been a stunt man. Frankenheimer
ed money because instead of paying a stuntman two hundred
for the night and then for the boat, he got the guy and the boat
hundred bucks. It was just Hollywood cheapness.
ring *Black Sunday*, Frankenheimer was all excited about Hitch-
ecause he knew I had just done *Family Plot* and that I still had
relationship with him.
e asked, "Could you ever get Mr. Hitchcock to come down and
a sandwich with us or come visit the set, because I never met
"
said, "Doubtful. Why would he come down here?"
Frankenheimer's feelings got really hurt, and he said, "Because I
always told he loved *Manchurian Candidate*."
I said, "Doubtful he sat through it. That's not to hurt your feelings,
he just doesn't see movies, including his own."

in the diamond lane and just whip down to work every day; we'd make
it in about forty-two minutes, instead of an hour and fifteen because of
all the TRW traffic and the airport.

The Goodyear blimp is in Carson, and that's where we had to
shoot many, many days to simulate the airfield down in Miami,
because it'd be crazy to shoot it all in Miami right around the blimp
operations. At that time, there were only three Goodyear blimps in the
United States: one in Carson, one in Houston, and one in Lakeville,
New Jersey. The one in Florida came from New Jersey.

My first day with actors in the movie, the first time I'm on screen
in the movie, I got the whole key to the character of Michael Lander
and the whole idea that Frankenheimer had described to me on the
telephone about Dr. Death. The scene was with a terrific guy and a
very good actor named Jimmy Jeter, who I hadn't seen since '59.
Jimmy was a pal, and in the scene, I'm going to take some pictures of
Jimmy, yet little does he know he's going to be a Baco-Bit in about five
minutes.

I realized the whole key to playing Michael Lander is not to go
after the maudlin part of it, but to go after the happy-go-lucky side of
terrorism, to the terrorist, which makes him all the more frightening to
an audience and to everybody around them. That's the only way you
can go when you're making a movie that could, to some people, look
like a training film. That was my concern. And John and I a couple of
times in the car would talk about that. I was more concerned about it
than John was. He was caught up in the fact, hey, it's the biggest novel
in the world at the time, and First Amendment this and First Amendment that, and I was concerned with hey, wait a second, John, this
happened in 1972, you know?*

Frankenheimer's the best timeline director I ever worked with, and
maybe that ever made movies. Just go back and look at the original
Manchurian Candidate. In *Black Sunday*, it's great because there's no
suggestion of a timeline until they're in the Algerian's room after

---

*The book was widely seen as a fictionalization of the attack on the Munich Olympics in
1972, even though the two had little in common beyond sports and a handful of Palestinian operatives.

they've shot him dead on the beach, and they can't find a clue, and they're all frustrated, and Fritz Weaver says to Robert Shaw, "Let's go, we're out of here, there's nothing going on here." And at the last minute, Shaw picks up a *Sports Illustrated*, looks up at Weaver as they're all leaving the room, and says, "What is this thing called the Super Bowl?"

We cut to the field. The head of the NFL, Pete Rozelle, and the two executives from each team are standing there. One is Joe Robbie, and his first line is "Cancel the Super Bowl? That'd be like canceling Christmas. You can't do that."

The head of Goodyear is there. "Well, if it can't be done, then he certainly can't come."

"Well, he asked to come. It's an election year. He has to come. He's going to come. He's the president of the United States."

"The president of the United States is going to come to this football game? Well, then there's no air travel whatsoever. Nothing can fly."

"What do you mean nothing can fly? He comes in a helicopter."

"Oh no, absolutely not. They tried that. They had the photoelectric cells, you know, they had that at Munich. You have no idea what these people are capable of. They can do anything."

Suddenly, in about thirty seconds, you realize, Jesus Christ, these people are better than we are. And we don't know who they are. You want to talk about pure excitement? In *Black Sunday*, when they grabbed that woman hostage in the street, that's an actress, but they didn't tell her they were going to grab her.

The police knew, but the Jewish people on the porch, where they were playing "Hava nagila," didn't know. The mayor knew. The police had staked out the alley; nobody on the beach knew. The camera crews, Nestor Almendros's crew, Haskell Wexler's crew, knew; Johnny Alonzo, who was our guy, knew. The day of the Super Bowl, the producers flew down the eight best cameramen alive, and each one had an assignment that day. You only have one day, one shot, three hours of the game. There's no take two. And one of the shots they had to have was that live shot of Shaw running down the stands during the game and crossing the field during a play. Nobody knew he was going

to do that. Not the police, n[ot] the stadium police, not Tom[ ]Shaw, Frankenheimer, Hask[ell]would have let the filmmakers [ ]took off when the Steelers got [ ]the beginning of the second ha[lf]jump over the wall and onto the[ ]the half. The police knew it was [ ]ing a movie there, and they kne[w]They knew he wasn't a terrorist.

My copilot on the blimp was N[ ]tain. He's the first guy I have to kill. [ ]telling me exactly what to do with t[ ]left, pull the ballast right." You're w[ ]thing above you because the gondola [ ]all above you. So you can't see shit. A[ ]neath you.

The blimp can only do sixty knots, [ ]above four thousand feet, because that'[s]can take. It's a big bag, there's 267,000 [ ]one chamber. Every year it goes into the [ ]late April to be repaired because it's got hu[ ]When it goes to San Francisco to cover a ga[ ]golf tournament and you see it go up and d[ ]on freeway overpasses and just pepper it with[ ]thinking one or two bullets are going to take [ ]it with a howitzer to take it down.*

We had a little boat accident during a cha[ ]harbor. When we were doing the longer shots, [ ]had my skullcap on, and Marthe sat in the bo[ ]down there. We came to this drawbridge that wa[s]

---

*The Goodyear blimps currently in use have only two ballon[ ]lope. All three compartments carry helium under low pressure. [ ]is held in under pressure and tears the balloon as the air rushe[ ]hole. The low, closely regulated pressure in a blimp doesn't bl[ ]hole a bullet would make.

as we get clos[ ]her. On one [ ]was me, but [ ]and keep go[ ]it. They wer[ ]guy driving [ ]and she we[ ]himself the[ ]because he[ ]out cold fo[ ]of the nig[ ]it. He was[ ]

Like w[ ]loved Fra[ ]he let som[ ]There w[ ]person. [ ]driving [ ]night lo[ ]afternoo[ ]what th[ ]just sa[ ]bucks [ ]for tw[ ]

D[ ]cock [ ]a clos[ ]

H[ ]have [ ]him[ ]

I[ ]

was[ ]

bu[ ]

So I called Hitch that night, and I asked, "What would be the chances of meeting?"

He said, "Better chances of you bringing him to the Bel-Air Hotel. I would go over and have a drink with him."

So we did that. I couldn't believe it. I said to Frankenheimer, "Tonight, on the way home, I want to stop so we can have a drink with a friend of mine at the Bel-Air Hotel."

He had no idea, no idea. We went there, nobody was there, and he says, "C'mon, let's go home," but he was my prisoner, I had to take him home, I had the car. Three minutes later, in walks the Penguin with his wife, Alma, on one arm and his driver, Ernie, on the other arm. Hitch was so gracious, and all he talked about was how Frankenheimer did *The Manchurian Candidate* and the camera mounts and the racing part of *Grand Prix*. They never talked about a thing Hitchcock did. He was there maybe twenty minutes, and I never said a word except when I thanked Hitch for coming.

In the car, on the way home, Frankenheimer had nothing but tears in his eyes the whole way, and he said, "That he would come and do that, and I know you didn't prod him."

I said, "I didn't prod him at all. I never knew he saw *Grand Prix*. He hates cars."

Frankenheimer said, "But how about when he asked why I chose to leave the light on in the booth in Madison Square Garden instead of turning the light off when Raymond assembled the rifle?" That's what Hitch was interested in.

Hitch had asked, "Why would you leave the light on so that the adversary could know where the protagonist was?"

And John said, "Because that's what you would have done."

That's the biggest smile I ever saw Hitchcock give. Hitch said, "Absolutely. If the light was off, the audience loses its point of view as to where the protagonist might have gone, but if the light is on, you know that the protagonist is still at work. If the light is off, the audience might lose its concentration that the bullet could still be fired. If we fail to realize that the bullet might still be fired, then the vice president is no longer in danger because film is about danger, and if you remove danger, there's no reason to make a film, is there? Even in comedy, danger has to lurk underneath, or it can't be funny."

Frankenheimer said, "Bruce, what a lesson I got, even for the rest of this movie. He said I constantly have to keep the audience thinking of the danger that you pose everywhere you are. Incendiary, it always has to be incendiary. What we have to do is keep amping up the pressure that you have on her and that she has on you. At any minute, she could snap her fingers and you could crumble."

The point is, as despicable as Michael J. Lander might be in *Black Sunday*, he still has breaking points. Thanks to Thomas Harris, the greatest speech I have in all my movie career is when I break down at the door in *Black Sunday* when Marthe Keller insults me and tells me that I'm just a total loser and can't get it together enough to fly a fuckin' blimp on Super Bowl Sunday. It's acting that was very hard to do. I had to do that breakdown scene three times because there were two camera malfunctions. It's a seven-minute scene so it's twenty-one minutes I had to go through that kind of trauma digging up, you know, a child dying in a swimming pool with all that grief I had to go through combined with all that tough dialogue.

In *Black Sunday*, I have a third of a long scene with dialogue in which I am one hundred percent, moment-to-moment behavior. I have a whole scene that lasts twenty seconds that is one hundred percent, moment-to-moment behavior. I have another scene in which there's no dialogue, which is about half a minute, which is one hundred percent, moment-to-moment behavior. It is a scene where it came and totally overwhelmed me. I never saw it coming, never planned it. I'm up in the blimp over the stadium, and Up With People, which is this musical group, starts singing "God Bless America," and I just got tears in my eyes. It overwhelmed me, and it was wonderful for the character because you suddenly realized he's still in America. It touches him that these people are still what he really cares about. But he's too far gone. It's just a reaction, but it's pure that whole shot. Frankenheimer didn't plan to stay on it. It was supposed to be a cut. That's the beauty of being allowed to have a director, an actor, and a cameraman all in sync on the same film at the same time. They trusted me, I trusted them, and the cameraman trusted the director.

They knew I could give them gold. I knew they would record gold if I could give it to them and hang in there with me. If they saw gold coming, they would stay there for it. I knew we'd get it in one take, and I also knew there wasn't going to be a second chance. So if you had an instinct, you better let it flow fully because there was no take two for John Frankenheimer, especially in timeline process.

In another scene we're in a room where we're surrounded by guns. Well, I got this tremendous overwhelming feeling. I couldn't do it in real life, but I felt I had to tell Marthe Keller that I loved her because of her partnership with me through this movie that we'd done for nine weeks. I couldn't get near her because she was living with Al Pacino. And the character wanted her to know that he loved her for what she'd done for him. I knew the movie would work better if an American audience could understand how frightening a terrorist could be and realize this isn't a joke. These people have real lives. They have love, they have death in their lives just like everybody else. Their hearts beat, and they're out there sitting right across the street from you and right across the table from you.

While we're sitting around all these guns waiting to kill the pilot in the morning and take the blimp, in our last moment together, without ever looking at each other, my character tells her he loves her.

I saw Frankenheimer out of the corner of my eye. Alonzo said to Frankenheimer, "I got him."

Frankenheimer went "No, no, don't cut it because he might do something."

That's when you know you're on a movie where you might have greatness. That's what Gadg would do. Hitch wouldn't do that. Mark Rydell would do that. Sydney would do that with Burt Lancaster. Michael Ritchie would do that. Where you knew that your director knows he's got certain people working with him that have special gifts and you cannot cut a camera on those people. That's the difference between a director and a filmmaker. They are two different folks. I've worked with lots of directors. I've only worked with five filmmakers. I've worked with directors who have been filmmakers three or four days in the course of a movie but not every day. The filmmakers are in Cooperstown. The directors are not. Even though some directors are great directors. I don't know that Bob Altman was a really great director. But I have to give him Hall of Fame status as a filmmaker because he dreamed and pulled off dreams.

The scene with Marthe Keller is the single best moment I've ever had in a movie in my career. It's the most troubling moment the audience has seen in the cinema, and that's exactly what I meant it to be because it's a training ground. Terrorists are human beings, and that's what makes it troubling, because they do love each other. They are zealous. They are you and me and anybody else. They've just sold out for what it is they're gonna do and you can't stop them.

In '76, it seemed okay. I would not make *Black Sunday* today.

That scene with Marthe Keller also demonstrates why one doesn't sleep, court, have sexual relations, or a love relationship with an actress you work alongside in a movie. For example, the weakness of *Eyes Wide Shut* is that Mr. and Mrs. Cruise had an opportunity unseen by me before in the motion picture industry to examine the inner fabric of the most delicate of relationships in the history of the cinema. It was not addressed, it was not taken advantage of, and it was not explored to the nth degree as it could or should have been. Now whether it was because Mr. Kubrick was sick, whether it was because the two actors were too young, or too early in the development of their own marriage or in their education as actors, to have the courage to go there as the couple, I don't know. Maybe it was their beliefs, one being a Scientologist, and one not being a Scientologist. The movie was less than it should have been by a great deal. Yet sitting right there is Sydney Pollack, who, had he been directing it, would have kicked their asses and insisted that they go there. But he couldn't say a word. It wasn't his job. He was hired as an actor.

I'm much more of a psychiatrist as an actor in that I take things too far that way. But it seems to me, it was a chance to tear at the fabric of a relationship and rip at it and come up with what you will with a director who does that; a director who can let a guy sit on the toilet seat with an M-16 in a movie (*Full Metal Jacket*) and end up doing what he does. It seems to me a director could do the same thing with a marriage and end up with the same kind of a result and maybe put it back together again and maybe not. But he would have needed the actors to come forward and say, "Let us help you. You be our psychiatrist. Let your instrument, the camera, examine it and we'll rip our marriage open in front of you." That would have been exciting! That would have been interesting to go to work and do a movie about every day. That didn't happen in *Eyes Wide Shut*. That doesn't happen if you're gonna put a married couple on the screen or a couple that is having a romantic relationship during the course of a movie. That's why I've never messed with the people that I work with in front of a camera on a movie. That's how I got the purity of the "I love you" to Marthe Keller on *Black Sunday*.

I'll go to movies to see one moment. I've seen *The Killing* every time it's on the air because in the locker room when Sterling Hayden takes the Thompson submachine gun out of the flower box and he's tugging the gloves on, finally getting the second rubber glove on, he takes a deep breath. And that deep breath is *it*, because I've stood in the arena. I've been on the Coliseum track with 95,000 people there when they announce your name and they say, "And from the University of Pennsylvania, Bruce Dern." And it's not that they roared for me, they didn't; they didn't have a fucking clue who I was. But that's what that deep breath is all about. Sterling Hayden did it, and my guess is that Kubrick didn't have anything to do with it, it was just Sterling Hayden.

I never met Sterling Hayden, but that moment, to me, is worth seeing the movie, and I'll see it every time just for that moment, but, Jesus, you've got to see every movie Stanley Kubrick makes after that, just because of that. That's why years later—and this is going to rub some people the wrong way—I was quite irritated when I saw a billboard that said, "Cruise, Kidman, Kubrick." That really pissed me off that there was a movie coming out that was no longer a Stanley Kubrick film starring Tom Cruise and Nicole Kidman. It was Cruise, Kidman, Kubrick. I didn't like that. It sounded wrong, it looked bad, and it struck me as a lack of respect and taste. It should have said, "A film by Stanley Kubrick," because that's what it was. It just was wrong.

I eventually caught up seeing the movie, only because I did a movie, *The Glass House*, with Leelee Sobieski, and she asked me to look at her work in the movie, so I saw it. I enjoy Tom Cruise's work to an extent. I've followed his career since *Taps*. I will never get over how truly terrific that collective work of young actors was, and topped by

George C. Scott's performance as the head of the school. I mean, you had Sean Penn, Timothy Hutton, and Tom Cruise, and they were all brilliant. And then they go on and become really good actors in movies.

Ms. Kidman I've never met. She seems to hold her own rather well every time she's out there. She's a fabulous-looking dame, and she tries to push the envelope every now and then, and I commend her for that. And I think Cruise still has tremendous potential as an actor. I question the roles he chooses to play. I don't think he challenges himself enough in walking on the edge.

We had a makeup man on *Black Sunday* named Bob Dawn, who was an old-time makeup man — by old-time he's seventy-two years old, seventy-five maybe, and he's been doing it since he's eighteen. He's made them all up. He looks like Clark Gable, and he's done Clark Gable his whole career. Frankenheimer has a bunch of young guys on the crew, but he's surrounded by warhorses from the Hollywood era of the thirties, forties, and fifties, before he got there.

This reminds me of a beautiful seventy-year-old woman who was our script supervisor on *Marvin Gardens*, Meta Wilde. She was married to a Hollywood publicist named Art Wilde. And Meta Wilde was considered one of the three greatest script supervisors that ever lived. She was from the Delta in Mississippi, a grand dame, and sought after by Curly Bob Rafelson strictly to do this movie because he wanted a class act. Meta Wilde, for twenty-five years, in her heyday in Hollywood, had been William Faulkner's mistress and grew up about a mile down the Delta in Mississippi from Mr. Faulkner. Needless to say, every night, Mr. Nicholson and I would get Ms. Wilde with a little bit of a demitasse, sit her down, and just pick her brain as long as we could for stories about the Mississippi Delta and Mr. Faulkner.

Now, you cut to *Black Sunday*, four years later, and the script supervisor's a lady named Charlsie Cantor, who is Mr. Frankenheimer's Meta Wilde. I don't know about her promiscuity in her day, but she is one of the three great randy dames who have done this for fifty, sixty years in Hollywood, who go back to the silent era, who you don't mess with. Who never come up to you and say, "You said, 'God damn it.'" They just say, "I love the way you did that. You might want to think about doing that again." Rather than saying to you, "You said, 'Hell' instead of 'Damn,'" or you said this or that, they listened for what sounded best, what made the scene work. The directors who understand film, Mr. Rydell, Mr. Pollack, Mr. Hitchcock, Mr. Rafelson, any director I worked with in the seventies; in the eighties, Joe Sargent, Lee Phillips, James Foley; today, David Jacobson, Bob Collector; they all hire script supervisors that are enormously helpful, because they want to hear the movie that they're making, not necessarily the movie that's on the page.

On *Gatsby*, Annabel Davis-Goff was the script supervisor, and she was the only consistent employee on the movie, besides the first assistant, David Tringham. She could work both places because she was an Irish citizen. She was a devotee to the story, but more of a devotee to Jack Clayton, who wanted to see the story evolve in a language that people could understand but that was still true to Fitzgerald. Francis Coppola had literally translated Fitzgerald to the cinema, but without realizing that the actors on the step still had to make it lifelike. Although he did a very credible job of picking the right scenes, we didn't have Francis day to day. He was doing *Godfather II*, so we were left with a book and a script. All those directors that I mentioned were all flexible in their understanding of the fact that the movie was in the now, in the moment-to-moment behavior of the day and the scenes we were shooting. That has seemed to change in the last ten years, not for the better, which is troubling. The written word is not as important as it was before because personality-driven actors have become more prevalent than they were when we were coming up, even though our personalities were more dominant than they are today. For example, when you look at a movie like *Mystic River* and you look at the dominant award-winning movies of the last few years, the personalities of the characters are what make the movies.

After *Black Sunday*'s release, the neatest afternoon I ever had was for the seventy-fifth anniversary of Paramount. They got all the people that had starred in Paramount pictures that were still around together to pose for a picture in front of the studio gate. This is maybe twenty-five, twenty-eight years ago. And they put it on the cover of *Life* magazine. Before they put us in front of the gate, they had a cocktail party for about two and a half hours in a room on a soundstage where all of us were together with no press, no photographers, no press agents, just us. Where we got to mingle around and meet people. Just seventy-five of us. And I met people like A. C. Lyles, who produced a lot of westerns. I got to meet Joel McCrea and Randolph Scott. I met Miss Elizabeth Taylor. I hadn't seen Jimmy Caan in a long time.

Jimmy and I started about the same week on Broadway back in 1958. He was at Michigan State, I was at Penn. He quit the same time I quit. He was an athlete. So we knew each other from that, and then we got into acting about the same time and crossed paths in a couple of TV shows. One was with Mickey Rooney.

I did a one-hour movie for *Bob Hope's Chrysler Theater* that Dick Berg produced. Mickey Rooney was the star, and Jimmy Caan and I were the little guest stars. Jimmy Caan was on his way. Mickey Rooney was the sheriff in this southern town. Brucie was Mickey Rooney's deputy. Jimmy Caan comes whipping through town. He's a surfer from California, he's got a Volkswagen, and he's on his way to New York, where he's going to be an actor. He breaks every law in town, speeds, runs a stoplight. We arrest him, take him into jail, and he and I become buds. Mickey Rooney wants me to take his belt because he collects belts. If you don't have a belt, your pants fall down. If your pants fall down, then Mickey's on him. He wants a little heinie. He wants to show him the heinie maneuver. Not the Heimlich maneuver, but the heinie maneuver.

Mickey's about the funniest man I've met since I've been in show business. We worked about three days, and Jimmy can bring it. Jimmy's a good actor. Jimmy's also funny. This is 1967, so we're not Jimmy Caan and Bruce Dern yet. He's not Jimmy Caan from *The Godfather*. But he'll do *The Rain People* soon and he's already starring in TV shows. I'm not.

We're working one Friday night about eleven. In those days, you'd work on Friday nights, but you'd stop at eleven thirty. When I first came to L.A., you worked until lunch on Saturday. Five-and-a-half-day weeks. So Jimmy was talking about some puss that he'd gotten into, and he'd just gotten divorced. He had good-looking girls who were on him all the time and Jimmy was semiconnected to a lot of guys in Las Vegas. This was way before *The Godfather*. Jimmy was talking to me.

Miss Diane and I were on the outs, and Laura was not born yet. I was in a twilight world. I was sniffing around. I was prowling.

Mickey says, "Hey, you guys. Quit the bullshit. Who are you talking to?" This is Mickey Rooney. Five feet five, if that. And that's with lifts. He says, "Why don't you take a look at this?" He pulls his wallet out. He says, "Jimmy, last night." He flips his wallet open and shows us a picture of Judy Garland at eighteen years old with nothing on, and her hands all over herself in action. He says, "Jimmy, shut the fuck up."

Hadn't seen George Segal in a long time. Met Roddy McDowall. I've never gotten an autograph from anybody, sports or otherwise. I'm just not into that. I'm not a worshipper. I met Gregory Peck. I suppose of all the people I've worked with in the business, he was the most indelibly gracious. If you were to pick an individual like Jerry West as the logo of the NBA, I would say Gregory Peck is the logo of the Motion Picture Academy. Not that his work was better than anybody else's. It's just that he was a dignified person, and we shared a tragedy in that I had lost a child and he had lost his son Jonathan, who I knew and who held the California state record in the half mile when he went to Harvard Prep School in the San Fernando Valley. This is before it was Harvard Westlake. This is when it was just shitty little Harvard down on Coldwater Canyon without a tartan track. He was potentially the greatest half-miler in high school who ever lived. He ran faster times than anybody as a schoolboy in the United States. In 1962, he came out of nowhere and blew everybody away at the state meet in Sacramento. He passed away when he was young.

Mr. Peck and I talked a half hour about it one night, and he never shed a tear. He never batted an eye. He talked with such beautiful reverence about it all. I never forgot that he never lost his dignity when talking about it, yet at the same time, he was full of emotion and full of wonderment. All the time I was looking at him, I was thinking that I'm listening to Captain Ahab talk about his son. I'm also listening to Atticus's speech. You just can't get over those images. Sometimes people come up and talk to me like I'm the guy who walked into the ocean in *Coming Home*. They're saying to me, "It's okay. You don't have to do that. You can stay. You don't have to go."

· 17 ·

I Can't Make It through a Hobbit Movie

In *Coming Home*, Jon Voight was a fabulous partner, as was Jane Fonda, and the partnership between the two of them was wonderful.* In one scene, filmed at the Rancho Los Amigos VA Hospital, in Downey, California, there is a rap session. It's where guys are talking with their psychiatrist, who's the real VA psychiatrist, and Hal Ashby asks if he could film it. Jon has a big speech, which is important to the movie. The topic for the day is, would any one of you go back? Remember the movie takes place in '73 or '74. We shot it in '77, so embers are still burning, but in the movie they're really burning

---

*In this 1978 drama, Dern plays a soldier whose wife, played by Fonda, fell in love with another vet while he was away in Vietnam. The movie drew Academy Award nominations for Dern, Fonda, Voight, Penelope Milford, the director Hal Ashby, the editor, and the writers. It was also nominated for best picture. Fonda, Voight, and the screenwriters Waldo Salt, Robert C. Jones, and Nancy Dowd actually walked off with statues. Unfortunately, it went up against another major Vietnam film that year, *The Deer Hunter*, which beat it out for best picture, best film editing, best director, and best supporting actor (Christopher Walken).

because it's still '73. All these guys in the chairs are limbless at least twice, some three times. Some have no legs. Some have no arms. They are all almost totally damaged amputees.

One guy raises his nub, and says, "Yeah, I'd go back. But before I did, I'd like to grab America and shake it by its ass."

Now, none of this is scripted. The only person that's scripted is Jon, who doesn't say anything until they finish. Jon looks at Hal, and Jon's charged to go. Hal looked at him, smiled. Jon smiled. And Hal and Jon both said basically the same thing without saying a word: Well, you can't beat that. Let's just move on. And they were right. You can't beat that.

Now later that day, same thing. Bobby Carradine's in the little glass room. He takes himself out, kills himself. The same rap session guys are outside in the hall knocking on the glass door as he's killing himself. They can't get in, the door's locked. They see it happening. Jon Voight comes whipping down the hall in his wheelchair, and in the script he says, "What happened? What happened?" He can't raise himself up really to see, but he knows something happened to Bobby Carradine. He's supposed to have a lot of dialogue about it.

Hal says, "Action." The guys pound on the wall.

Jon comes whipping around the corner and says, "What happened?"

And before he can get to the next stuff, this guy Louie in another chair says, "The man went out. He just went out."

"Cut."

Jon and Hal looked at each other, and they just winked. Can't beat that. That's what Hal Ashby was. He was a guy who left it to chance when he wanted to and you couldn't beat it. Extras couldn't have done that. Only vets could have done that. My problem in *Coming Home* was I didn't have that. I had nobody to research. I had nobody to talk to. The best help I had was Max Cleland, who was our tech adviser on the movie. At the time, he was head of the Veterans Administration. He had just been named that, and later he became the United States senator from Georgia, and he just lost his seat in 2004. He was fabulous to me. He was a triple amputee. He was in a chair, and I had one two-hour session with him, and I said, "I just have to take it from my own instincts," and he said, "What I've seen you do so far, you're just dead on. Don't try and talk to anybody. Just let me give you a couple of statistics. So far, of the majority of the guys that have come back that are physically whole, twelve thousand have taken themselves out. That's more than forty percent."

That shocked me. I said, "They don't belong."

He said, "That's all you need. You're right on with what you're doing. You took the words right out of my mouth. They don't belong."

It became obvious to me after watching the men interact with Jon and Hal. I went to the set on three or four work days that I didn't have to work just to see. I stayed away the rest of the time. I was totally disjointed from the movie because I didn't want to be around survivors.

One day I went to visit the set at Rancho Los Amigos, where we shot six weeks. This is February '77, so you're only three years removed from guys unloading off airplanes. There are no extras in the movie that aren't guys who were in Vietnam. In one cut, there was a great deal of wheelchair basketball featured. Those guys could play. This isn't bullshit.

Anyway, they're having a picnic scene with the vets eating lunch with the nurses. I forget how many of these scenes are still in the movie. Nat King Cole's daughter had a part in the movie. I forget which daughter it was, but it wasn't Natalie Cole. She was bitching about something at the time. She was cold and we were shooting outside. Not freezing, but southern California winter. Fifty-five degrees. She was cold, wanted to wear a sweater.

Hal said, "It doesn't match. You didn't have it on this morning."

She said, "Well, I'm not used to cold like this."

He said, "Well, it doesn't match. You can't be in the scene then."

They started arguing, and he just canned her. I got it. She didn't get it. Hal couldn't give a shit. She tried to pull some rank on him and make a stink about it. But nothing happened. She was gone. But it frayed a few nerves because it was Nat King Cole's daughter. Hal couldn't have cared less, and he was right. It didn't match. It was a big deal when they hired her, though, because they made an announcement about it.

So Hal's editing the film, and he calls me one morning. He says, "Derns, come up here. I want you to see something. I want you to look at a scene."

I had told Hal, "Don't fuck me on this movie. Don't make me a bad guy."

And he got very upset with me. He said, "What do you mean a bad guy? How can you be a bad guy? You're the key to the movie. You're the linchpin in the movie. The movie can't have a bad guy. You're not a bad guy. There is no bad guy. The war isn't a bad guy. We're not naming bad guys here. And you're certainly not a bad guy. You wanted to go. You went. That's the way the story is. You came back. And you're the most wounded guy in the film. That's the whole point."

So I go up to his house, way up in Malibu Hills with a long driveway so he can see every person coming up there to fuck with his movie. And if one of the suits is on the way up, he just takes the reels, puts the cans in the back of his car, and goes down the other driveway—he's gone when they get up there. So Hal's there and he puts on the last scene that has just been cut, so I see the cross-cutting. I see Jon enter the high school and the little pimply-faced kid get up and say, "And now, for another perspective, here's Luke Martin." And Jon goes up in the wheelchair with the dress blue Marine sitting behind him in the chair—perfect setting. You have a bunch of seventeen-, eighteen-year-old kids who look like "Yeah, sure, tell us something, little wounded guy. A war we're never going to. We'll be in Canada or Redondo Beach for surf's up. "

Then you cut to me standing with Jane on the beach.

And Jane says, "So I'm going to get us some steaks, and we'll have a barbecue, and we're going to make this marriage work. I love you, Bob."

You cut to Jane, who's on her way to the market in a little sportster, and Hal with Michael Haller, his partner, who is the set designer on the movie, is in another sportster passing her. This is Hal's Hitchcock shot—signature shot. Little did we know he'd never be on film again.

At the end of *Marvin Gardens*, Jack goes up to see our grandfather. He becomes a screen where the home movie—eight millimeter—plays out on his face.

And Jack says, "What are you watching this for?"

The grandfather says, "Because I wanted to see you guys together." Jack closes the door but the movie is still playing on the door when he walks out.

So up in the editing room, Hal shows me the cross-cutting without any sound except Jon's speech. Jane says she loves me and "I'll get steaks." I say nothing, and nothing is said in the market.

Now Hal says, "Now I want you to see the scene again the way they're going to see it in the theater."

He starts the scene again, and I hear chun, chun—a guitar . . . Tim Buckley. And this is what Tim Buckley sings, but he says it. That's what's so haunting about that fucking song—and that whole album. The song is called "No Man Can Find the War." And he says, "Once I was a soldier and I fought . . ." and I've started across the beach by now, and Jon is on the stage, and Jane's in the car.

"Once I was a soldier and I fought on foreign soil for you. Once I was a hunter and I bought home fresh meat for you. And once I was your lover and I looked deep behind your eyes for you. Soon there will be another who will tell you I was just a lie. I wonder, oh, how I wonder, will you ever remember me?" And he sings two choruses of that.

And as he says, "Oh, how I wonder . . . Oh, how I wonder, will you ever remember me?" Jane Fonda walks out the door of the Lucky Market, and what does the door say? "Out," and the film runs out.

And Hal turns to me and says, "That beats fucking Curly Bob, don't it?"

And I say, "That beats it."

He says, "But two pretty good fucking I'm-outta-here shots, aren't they?"

And I say, "Two pretty good fucking last shots."

He says, "Curly and I can make movies, can't we, Dern? Not only that, but on Monday I'm starting *Being There*. Have you read it?"

I say, "No, I can't pronounce the guy's last name. Is it Sozinsky or Kozinsky? What is it?"

Hal says, "Who gives a shit? I've got Peter Sellers."

And yet, years later, on his second-to-last movie, *The Slugger's Wife*, the studio locks him out of his editing room, locks him out of his fucking editing room. It wasn't a very good movie. It certainly wasn't good Hal Ashby. The guy made seven movies in the seventies (*The Landlord, Harold and Maude, The Last Detail, Shampoo, Bound for Glory, Coming Home,* and *Being There*). What a decade of moviemaking, you know?

The Best Years of Our Lives was the best war movie I ever saw. The best war movies are the ones without actual combat in them. I'm not a big *Platoon* fan. I'm not a big *Gone with the Wind* fan. I'm a huge *Lawrence of Arabia* fan. Huge. To me, *Lawrence* is the best movie ever made. David Lean simply went to war to make *Lawrence of Arabia*, which was about a war. I've seen *Lawrence* twenty-five times. *Lawrence* overwhelms me both as a work and as a movie, and I'm thrilled by the business I'm in.

I like movies in which there are actual historical lessons. That's why I can't get through a Hobbit movie, because I've got to walk a long way from my street to see a fucking Hobbit.

When *Coming Home* came out, the only negative criticism was toward me, my character and me personally. Some people thought that my inclusion in a positive way was a mistake. Some industry people, including a few that were stars in their own right, wrote criticism that I wasn't rightly cast because I wasn't a villain. This upset Hal much more than it did me, because Hal said they missed the whole point of the movie if they think that. One star on my street in the Malibu Colony, who made somewhat of a comeback in a popular Christmas movie (*Meet the Fockers*) and whose nose is really prominent, was very unhappy with my selection and thought I ruined the movie with my performance, based on my past image. "Why would they put him in the movie? He ruined it. He's not compassionate. They should have drowned him in the second reel instead of at the end."

I won a People's Choice Award for Best Supporting Actor for *Coming Home*. Florence Henderson gave me my award. Florence was the best, a Cloris Leachman kind of dame, a trouper, a talent, a fox, and she can bring it.

I received the award and said, "I really don't know what to say. I'm embarrassed because I never served. I never put a uniform on for this country, so I guess I'm a little ashamed—not that I won this award, but that I won an award for playing somebody that I never really had the courage to do what they did. So this is really an acceptance for anybody who ever put on a uniform to protect the flag of this country. For all you guys and girls that did that, I'm forever grateful."

I had tears in my eyes. To this day, it's the one performance and the one thing I've done in my life—and only because of the role I played—that I'm glad I did. I'm thrilled I was a part of it. I'm honored to have been in *Coming Home*.

I lost the Oscar to Chris Walken that year, but he deserved it. He's a wonderful actor. I can't say I was better in my movie than he was in his. I'm not strong enough to be George C. Scott. If they invite me for the chicken and peas, I'm going to go. If they want to give me the statue, I'm going to accept it. I don't agree that it's a competition and I don't agree that there should be a final winner. In fact, the Academy Awards are given because the Academy needs the revenue to exist, and the revenue is earned because of the show itself, so they have to have a show. Well, then have a show, and seal it off with the nominations. All the participants will come. They'll all show up. There's no loser then. The nomination is the prize. Everybody will get up and get a certificate. The presenter will say, "You're one of the five that was nominated that year," and that's it. Why pick a winner? I think it's dreadful when you start saying one person is better than another in an artistic forum.

George C. Scott had the courage to stand up and say, "No, thank you."

And when they said, "We'll send it to your house," he said, "Last time I looked we were all speaking English here. I said, 'No, thank you.' Which means don't send it. I don't believe in it. It's not right. It's not a competition."

Richard Sylbert was having a dinner for a bunch of people who were famous for things other than what they had been honored for that year. It was a neat dinner party. It was given for eighteen of us who were recognized for something that year in show business. Oscars. Nominations. Yet we had won awards at a higher level for something else in our lives. I had been second in the world at 1500 meters and 800 meters as a runner for guys over forty in the senior Olympics. Dick Sylbert, who had just been nominated for his fifth Oscar as a set designer—he won three—was the greatest fly fisherman in the world and had beaten Ted Williams three times in a row and his book was now a best seller. George Plimpton had just won the squash championship for men over forty in America. Dennis Connor had just won

the America's Cup. It was a bunch of us who were in the movie business or had written books or in some way had achieved recognition in
other venues that had nothing to do with the reason we were there on
Oscar week. It was neat. Richard Burton was there with his wife, Susan
Jones, who was there representing her ex-husband, race car driver
Sterling Moss. Burton was there because he still held the 200-meter
low hurdle record for Wales before he was eighteen years old. They
don't run that event anymore. They race 400-meter hurdles, but then
it was 200. And he's in the record book, it's R. Burton, Churchill,
Wales. It's kind of neat that he's in there.

His wife was the most beautiful woman I'd ever seen in my life. She
was South African. Burton said, "Bruce, this is Susan. She's enamored
of you."

I said, "She's six feet four. How could she be enamored of anything
less than Wilt Chamberlain?"

He said, "I'm afraid she's probably enamored of him too."

· 18 ·

Briefer's Better

A lifetime achievement award is not something that Bruce Dern would aspire to or applaud. Lifetime achievement awards go to guys who rescue people off mountaintops or carry people out of burning buildings. On stage at the Kennedy Center Honors, it's nice to see entertainers up there, but my God. Two days ago in Pasadena, some lady stuck her kid in a washing machine. Whoever found that kid and pulled him out, that's a lifetime achievement.

My lifetime achievement will be to get to triple digits agewise. That'd be neat. I'd like to go to a hundred. What do they call them, centenarians? If I could run a mile at a hundred, that'd be cool. If I could do an entire scene in a film where I had a normal amount of dialogue at a hundred, that'd be good. If I could pick three or four winners in basketball or football at a hundred, that'd be good. If I could still drive a car and not miss the off-ramp, that'd be good. But most of all, I'd like people to be able to say, and it's a horrible expression, I hate the expression, but it kind of says it: "He could bring it." Not just that he showed up on game day. I grew up with a bunch of guys who had a creed. The creed was you get to the Hall of Fame or you don't. Very few people where I lived ever got to the Hall.

I have a phrase I've used since I was six years old, a Cub Scout, my first year. It's the ultimate compliment from Bruce Dern to anybody, and if somebody could say it about me who was a Musial or a Koufax in their field. Or Uncle Adlai, or President Roosevelt or Mrs. Roosevelt, or my Uncle Archibald or Dr. Oppenheimer. People like that, that I revere, and I'm leaving out a lot. People that mean something in my life. Mr. Nicholson, or Mr. Redford, or Mr. Eastwood, and certainly Mr. Reynolds. If they said the thing that I've always said about people, and if they meant it the way I meant it, the ultimate compliment from Bruce Dern to somebody is, "He could play." If they say that about me, that's a compliment. I'm telling you, Bruce Dern can play. I've been doing it since '71. I couldn't play in the sixties. I was good, but I couldn't bring it every day.

On *The Driver*, I found a surprisingly wonderful set companion in Ryan O'Neal, who was very, very funny.* Almost shockingly so to me. He had a friend named Joe Amsler, who was a bodyguard and took care of Ryan's daughter, Tatum. He was Ryan's best friend in high school and was a celebrity with us because fifteen years earlier, he'd gotten in a shitload of trouble for doing something that was stupid and silly. In 1963, Joe Amsler and his friend decided, on a ploy, to pay off a gambling debt in Tahoe. They needed $37,300, so they kidnapped Frank Sinatra Jr. when he was playing at the Cal-Neva Lodge. They drove around the lake on the California side, and halfway around the lake, they realized they just violated the Lindbergh Law because they had taken Frank Jr. out of the parking lot at the Cal-Neva Lodge on the Nevada side and drove to the California side, and they were fucked. Plus the fact, they asked Frank Jr., "Would you mind getting in the trunk? We gotta call your dad because we need $37,300 and we need it by one tomorrow afternoon or some guys are gonna kill us. Your dad will give us $37,300."

---

*In this slick cops-and-robbers picture, written and directed by Walter Hill (*The Warriors*, *48 Hrs.*), Dern plays a detective trying to catch the best getaway driver in the business, played by Ryan O'Neal, fresh off *Barry Lyndon* and *A Bridge Too Far*.

He said, "I wouldn't bet on it. He's not nuts about me in the first place. He loves Nancy, but he ain't shown me a lot of love."

So they call the dad, and the dad says, "I don't know. It's a little high. How about $32,000?"

They arrange to have the money left in a Dumpster behind the Safeway at Ventura Boulevard and Laurel Canyon in L.A. When they came down Kingsbury Grade on the Nevada side, they saw red lights at a blockade at the bottom. So they left Frank Jr. off and went on driving down the hill figuring, "Fuck it. They'll look for Frank Jr. We don't have Frank Jr. They're not gonna know it's us." The problem was, they were in Frank Jr.'s car!

So Joe Amsler was taking care of Tatum now because Tatum needed somebody. Ryan was constantly working and was the biggest movie star in the world. A funny, good guy. Too wise for that time. Joanna Moore was his first wife. She was a foxy, beautiful-looking dame, who'd starred in a couple of movies with Elvis. She was Tatum and Griffin's mom. Then Ryan married Leigh Taylor-Young, who was a hippie star. She has since moved on to Sedona or one of those places. But God, was she beautiful. And he had not bedded Farrah yet. She was still Mrs. Majors.

The Driver was interesting, because I'd just done a movie with Chabrol, and here I'm with Isabelle Adjani, who was struggling like I had been. She was on an American set and had never been to America. She had been nominated for an Oscar the year before for a movie called *The Story of Adele H.* and was beautiful to look at. She had those little lips, and she was nineteen, and you knew that Ryan, if he wasn't on her, was about to be on her. He was certainly after her. Ryan was a good-looking guy, and he was at the top of his game. He had done *Paper Moon.* He had done *What's Up, Doc?* He was a star. He was the Brad Pitt of his day. He was more well-rounded than Brad Pitt, in that he was funny. He had proved it as a comedian in movies. He was clever, and he was quick.

One night on the set, we're sitting there, and I said, "I gotta tell you something. A couple of years ago, you were walking on the beach with someone. And as I ran by you, I thought you said, 'I'd never have that guy in a movie with me.' Is that true?"

He said, "Oh yeah. I said that."

"And yet here I am. Why?"

"Because we're on equal footing. I figure I can joust with you. You can never be in a movie with someone if the jousting is not on a level field."

"Why'd you feel that way?"

"Because you're the best."

"Well then, how come I don't have a career?"

"Why do you always say that? Every place I read, you always say you don't have a career."

I said, "Well, I don't."

He said, "Well, then how are you above the title with me?"

I said, "Because you don't have one either. It's no big deal. Ryan O'Neal, Bruce Dern, and Isabelle Adjani. If we were anything, why the fuck would she be above the title? Who is she? She doesn't even speak English."

He said, "Not with you. She says all the words I need her to know in English."

"And what might they be?"

"She gets the F-word pretty straight. She's good with the S-word."

"Well how many letters are in those words?"

"Four."

I said, "You know something? We're gonna be friendly for life."

He said, "I think so, but we'll never be friends."

"You know something? I like you. You can bring it."

"I've been bringing it since I was five years old. I've learned two things, and both end with the same word."

"What's that?"

"I learned how to get ahead, and I learned how to get head."

I don't think I ever had a conversation with him since that day. That was near the end of the movie. The Ryan O'Neal I knew on that movie had the potential to be what I thought was the biggest star I worked with since I came to Hollywood. There are scenes that he does in *Barry Lyndon* that are so magnificent. He was in the hands of a director who obviously had magnificent stature and the wherewithal to get that kid to risk things like in the duel in the movie where he toys with a handkerchief in such a way. This fuckin' guy could do anything he wanted to do as an actor. Then he fucks it up later on with other stuff. But you go back and look at some of his scenes in *Love Story*. He is really, really touching. And if you look at *Love Story* carefully, you say, Matt Damon must have looked at *Love Story* twenty times before he shot *Good Will Hunting*, because the knavishness of Ryan O'Neal in *Love Story* is a bit reminiscent of the charm of Matt Damon in *Good Will Hunting*, and they're thirty years apart. Damon is ingrained with a little bit from Ryan O'Neal especially when you look at *Rounders* in the scenes with Edward Norton. At times, I accuse Jack of leaning into the window with a little Brando. Well, you look at Matt Damon and Affleck, particularly, and there's a lot of Ryan O'Neal. You realize that Ryan O'Neal can be proud that he was a guy who was copied by guys who followed him twenty-five or thirty years later. This shows you that Ryan had tremendous potential.

At the end of *The Driver*, at three thirty in the morning, Ryan O'Neal goes into an absolutely empty Union Station, this beautiful Frank Lloyd Wright–type train station in L.A. To this day, it's still worth going in once a year and sitting down when there's not many people there and looking around. Ten minutes later, I go in. Ryan walks over to me. I've got fifty of L.A.'s finest behind me, and Walter had written a line that said, "You're under arrest."

I said, "Briefer is better."

Walter said, "The line is 'You're under arrest.'"

I said, "Briefer's better."

He said, "The line is 'You're under arrest.'"

I looked at Ryan, and Ryan said, "Briefer's better."

Walter said, "Where does it say you say a fuckin' word?"

Phil Lathrop, who was the cameraman on *They Shoot Horses Don't They?*, rolls the camera.

Ryan comes up to me.

I say, "Gotcha." That's the end of the movie.

Walter says, "Cut." And he's got this huge grin on his face. All the policemen, everybody on the crew, applauds. They snap their fingers like that's it. The rest of the movie, four more days to shoot, everybody walks around saying, "Gotcha." It was the best. So when everybody settles down, Walter says to the cameraman, "We'll do a shot on Bruce, a shot on Ryan, but first we're gonna do the scene that's gonna be in my movie where he says, 'You're under arrest.' Because on the screen, it's gonna say, 'A Walter Hill Picture. Written by Walter Hill. Starring Ryan O'Neal, Isabelle Adjani, and Bruce Dern.' Nowhere on the print will it say written by Bruce Dern. The line is 'You're under arrest,' and that's what I need to see in the movie."

· 19 ·

Three Days, Two Million

People ask, "When you're not making a movie, what are your hobbies?" My hobbies are getting ready to bring it every day I work. Some days I'll run longer, but I stress myself every day with some kind of Mickey Mouse time trial, usually six hundred meters to one thousand meters. Nobody knows what I do. Nobody gives a shit except me. I write it down—little chicken scratches in a book—it says, you know, 5:59.7. No one knows what that means, but I know what it means. I know how many RPMs that is. I know what my pulse rate can do. And the only time people get interested or even astounded by what I do is when a guy takes my pulse or I go for my movie physical and the doctor calls the production company and says, "You know what you have going to work for you? You have somebody that has a heart that works two and a half times less than anybody else's heart on your set. His resting pulse is 46. And yet he can boost it to 154, and in two minutes, it drops to 63. His blood pressure is 90 over 58." When they first check you—and I do it on purpose because I get a kick out of it—I don't tell them I'm a runner.

The doctor says, "I'm calling Cedars."

I say, "What are you calling them for?"

"Well, because there's something wrong with your heart. It doesn't beat. You didn't come up the stairs, did you?"

"No, I took the elevator."

"Well, when you get out of your car, do you have trouble walking to the elevator?"

"No, not really. I go real slow, though. I don't run anywhere and I don't stand unless I have to, and walking is out."

"I know. When I walked in, you were sitting. You asked where the chair was immediately. Do you have trouble breathing?"

"No."

This one doctor said, "Could you jump up and down ten times for me?"

I said, "Yeah."

He said, "Let me take your pulse. I can't find your pulse."

I said, "It's there. Trust me. Why don't you feel it right here where everybody else does? How many beats you got in twenty seconds?"

"I got eight."

"Well, that's twenty-four."

"No. No, let's do it again. I'm going to do a half a minute."

"How many beats you got?"

"Twenty-two. You have a pulse rate of forty-four right now and you just jumped up and down? Have you had your heart checked lately?"

"Yeah, about four weeks ago. Why?"

He said, "You do something. What do you do?"

I said, "An O'Henry bar and a Coke every morning."

"Come on. What do you do?"

"I'm an actor. What do you do?" And he just keeps looking at me. I finally said, "I'm a runner."

He said, "Three people could live off your heart."

I wanted to go back to Broadway. Sherman Yellen had written a play, *Strangers*, for me and Vanessa Redgrave. My producers got very afraid because it was in her big anti-Zionist days and they were concerned that the audiences on Broadway would not come and see her and support her in it. In January 1979, Andrea and I flew to New York to do the play. Vanessa wasn't used. Lois Nettleton was in the play with me. Arvin Brown, a guy who ran the Long Wharf Theater in New Haven, directed the play. Sherman Yellen, who had written a couple of other plays, wrote this play about Sinclair Lewis and Dorothy Thompson.

We rehearsed for a month. Then we went to the Colonial Theatre in Boston for three weeks, where we sold out every single day. And I had gross. We were a hit. The Colonial is a big, beautiful fourteen-hundred-seat theater just up from Copley Plaza. Harvard is right there. Boston is a very academic city. They love Sinclair Lewis and they know all about him, so they supported the play big-time. I didn't have much salary, but I was a partner. Manny Azimov was the head of the box office. I would go talk to him every night after the show and ask, "How'd we do tonight?" If it was ten more people, that was $1.40 more for me. So I learned all about the business of Broadway, what it costs to mount a show and where the money goes. Each week it cost $63,000 to run our show before any money went back to the producers—$63,000. It was a Schubert show. And Manny was the guy running it for the Schuberts.

Opening night in Boston, Joan Kennedy, who had just been outed as a drinker and was still married to Ted Kennedy, came to the play and was introduced to me afterward. We sat down together for about half an hour and talked, and she was fabulous.

I said, "How did you like the play?"

She said, "Well, it made me real thirsty."

One day, Michael Cimino, who was a good friend of mine, was having lunch with Joe Levine, and he asked me to come across the street and just say hello to him. Cimino introduced me to Mr. Levine, who I had never met. I remember how he dazzled me with this story of *A Bridge Too Far*.

He had bad eyes and wore those little Mussolini kind of glasses. When you see someone wearing those fabulous sunglasses, you expect them to be speaking Italian.

He said, "I've got this script, and I've got a director, Dickie

Attenborough. I don't have a dime. But I want to do this movie. And I can get Fox as my partner, but they're not going to give me a dime to make the movie until I get the movie made.

"So I go to Gary Hendler and say, 'Look, I need Bob Redford for three days. I'll give you two million dollars.' He says, 'What do you need him for?' I said, 'I need him to row a boat for three days in Holland. I'll give you two million dollars. And I can't promise him top billing because I'm going to bill everybody alphabetically.' He says, 'What kind of movie is it?' I say, 'Read the book. It's called *A Bridge Too Far*. It's about taking the Remagen Bridge in the Second World War . . . a bunch of American soldiers. If they don't take it, Germany wins the war. If they do take it, the Allies win the war. Takes about a day and a half for them to do this. But when you tell it from all angles, it's a movie. I'm going to use international stars. I want Redford to lead the group of commandos that detonated the bridge—the guys that went in the pontoon boats they had to row down the river. I need Redford.' And Hendler says, 'You give me two million dollars for three days?' I say, 'Yeah.' He says, 'Well, Redford doesn't do movies like that.' I say, 'So, what you're saying is you don't want to work for Joe Levine. Is that what you're saying to me, Hendler?' He says, 'No, no, I'm not saying I don't want to work for you.' I say, 'No. You're saying Redford won't work for a Jew. That's what you're saying. Redford won't work for a Jew.' And he says, 'No, I'm not saying that at all.' I say, 'Well, what you're saying to me is you won't work for two million dollars, then. That's what you're saying? You don't want the Jew's two million dollars.' He says, 'Joe, I'm Jewish.' And I say, 'Look, I wrote out a check. Here's a cashier's check made out to Robert Redford for two million dollars. You going to take it or not?' He says, 'Jesus Christ, this is two million dollars! You're not kidding me. That's a cashier's check for two million dollars.' I say, 'Yeah, it's yours. You want it or not?' 'Well, when do you need him?' 'I need him May twelfth through the fourteenth. That's three days. And Hendler says, 'Yeah. God, that's three days for two million dollars.'"

Now, *A Bridge Too Far* came out in 1977. This isn't today. This was a lot of money then for three days work. Guys are just barely getting a million dollars then.

Levine says, "'Okay, let me talk to Bob. Call him now.' Hendler says, 'God, I don't know. I don't know where he is now.' 'You know where he is. You knew where he was ten minutes ago; you know where he is ten minutes from now. You call him up. Go to the phone booth and call him up.' So Hendler goes to the phone, comes back, and says, 'Well, he says in May he's usually in Sundance.' I say, 'What's he in Sundance for in May? There's no skiing. There's no boating. He doesn't play golf. There's no tennis because the snow hasn't all melted yet. So he's just fucking off, right? So let him fuck off in Holland. He can do whatever he wants. He can take his family. I've met him. He's a good guy. He'd like it. There's shopping. He can go look at the dikes. What does he want to do? He likes sports cars and stuff like that. I mean, how far is it to wherever he wants to go? Three days. And if he rows fast, he could do it in two. You want me to call him?' Hendler says, 'No, I think we'll work it out. I think we can do it.' I say, 'Have I got your word on that?' He says, 'We'll work it out. We'll do it. I've got some paperwork, but yeah, you've got my word we'll do it.' So I'm done with him. Now I go and I know I can make my movie because I can call any other actor in the world and I can go back to Fox. Alan Ladd Jr.'s running Fox then, and I can say, 'Laddy, I got Redford to star in *A Bridge Too Far*.' No one else is going to turn me down."

And no one else turned him down because all the other actors said, "Hey, he got Redford."

Levine said, "And I haven't given away the lead position in the movie and I have set a price precedent, but at the same time he's the number-one movie star in the world and he doesn't have top billing and he's bought alphabetically at R so I've got A to R to offer. It was easy after that."

They ended up making the movie for around sixteen million dollars. But, what happened was, as soon as Levine got Redford, before he hired another star, he sold distribution rights in every territory in the world with Redford in the story and Dickie Attenborough directing the movie.

Levine said, "I had—I don't know—thirty-seven million dollars in the till. I had a budget of sixteen. I laid six over, meaning twenty-two million. I took fifteen mil for myself and I gave Fox the rest—twenty-two. They made the movie. I made fifteen mil before we ever rolled a foot of film. Mike, Bruce, that's how you make a movie. I never spend a dime. And furthermore, the check I showed Hendler—the cashier's check—I made it that morning on a machine in my house. It wasn't a real cashier's check. All I needed to do was show him that, you know, I was in earnest. And it worked."

The movie did very well. And actually, as those movies go, it's a pretty good movie. It's interesting and it was cut very well. And Attenborough did a terrific job on it.

· 2 0 ·

Glencoe Asshole

The play doesn't run long on Broadway, and when I get home I get a phone call from Marty Krofft saying, "I want to bring a script to your house. Jon Voight said he won't do my movie. He recommended you."

He brings the *Middle Age Crazy* script.* He also brings his wife, Christa, and introduces Andrea and me. He says, "This is Christa. She was the third Playmate of the Year. She was also Miss World. And she's a Nazi, and I'm a Canadian Jew." Sergei, our dog, is barking at him. And he says, "I'll pay you $350,000. Will you do it?"

I say, "I haven't read it."

---

*Sid and Marty Krofft produced exactly two movies, *Middle Age Crazy* and *Harry Tracy, Desperado*, both Canadian productions starring Bruce Dern. The rest of their extensive careers have been in television, and they're probably best remembered for hallucinatory 1970s kid shows like *Land of the Lost, H. R. Pufnstuf, The Bugaloos*, and *Sigmund and the Sea Monsters*.

He says, "We're going to sit here and talk to Andrea while you read it. I'm not leaving the house until you say you'll do it. I've already talked to Fred Specktor. He knows what you're going to get. He says it's fine. You'll get billing above the title and you get to pick your costar, although we've already offered it to Ann-Margret."

I say, "Well, will I like it?"

He say, "I don't know. Read it."

I read that first scene about where they're doing humpers and she's trying to have a bingo watching Johnny Carson. I read it in about an hour and forty minutes. And I say, "Yeah, I like it. I'll do it. What else do I need to know?"

"Nothing," Krofft says. "You show up June sixth."

"That's two days after my birthday."

"I know. Your cake's in the car."

The producers negotiate with Ann-Margret. I don't know what they pay her. That's not my domain. Even though I could be allowed to get in it, I don't. And I shouldn't be. An actor shouldn't be involved in what they pay the other actor even if it's twice as much. One of her demands was that she have a dressing room the same size as mine.

The provisions of the joint Canadian-American ventures in those days were that you could shoot a third of your movie outside of Canada, and the other two-thirds had to be shot within Canadian provincial territory. So we shoot two of the six weeks in Houston and the other four in Toronto.

We get to Toronto, and about the third day I'm coming down the steps of my motorhome to go to the set. I see Roger Smith, in the back of my motorhome, pacing off the length. I don't say anything. I go around the front of it to make sure he's not playing "Teacher, may I" by himself. He's taking little baby steps. About an hour later Marty Krofft comes up to me. Marty Krofft's really a fabulous guy, but he's different.

He says, "We've got a problem. Your dressing room's two feet longer than Ann-Margret's. They're pissed off."

I say, "Well, fuck it. Then give Ann-Margret mine."

"You'd do that?"

"Yeah."

"Well, I won't do it."

"What's the difference?"

He says, "Fuck 'em. I'm not going to do that. That'd make him happy. I don't want him to be happy."

I say, "But forget him. It's Ann-Margret you want to be happy."

He says, "Not as long as she's married to him."

I say, "Marty, don't do this. You do this on every goddamn thing. Don't do this."

I went over to Roger right away and I said, "Did you play 'Teacher, may I' growing up?"

He said, "No, why?"

"Well, I saw you practicing this morning. I saw you taking baby steps in the back of the trailer."

"You know Ann-Margret's trailer is supposed to be as big as yours."

"It's two feet bigger now."

"What do you mean?"

"Because tomorrow morning you're in my trailer."

"Oh, come on. I just told Marty that he made a mistake."

"No, you can have my trailer."

"No no, Marty didn't live up to his part of the bargain. I'm going to make him get another trailer that's the same size so you both have the same trailer."

"Roger, don't do that. Just have my trailer."

"No. He's a goniff. And he's a Canadian goniff, which makes it worse."

I said, "They're just Jews from Quebec, Bud."

Smith said, "No. Canadian goniffs are bad. I'm an Australian goniff."

"God, there's no getting away from you guys. Why can't you just be American goniffs? I know how to deal with that."

"No, you don't have a clue. Canadian goniffs are the worst. Because they'll tell you they're Quebecois. They'll tell you they're from England. They'll tell you anything, but they won't tell you the truth. We'll tell the truth."

Ann-Margret kept the trailer she had. Roger Smith's point was the principle that Marty had lied. Those are the kinds of things that make movies fun to me.

The first scene in the movie, Ann-Margret and I are lying in bed watching Johnny Carson with the swami hat on predicting things, and she's trying to have five bingos on my fortieth birthday. So we're getting ready to shoot and Ann-Margret's already under the covers. The camera's behind the TV set. We're looking at the TV set. They have the tape on of Johnny Carson so we can do it again and again and again. Roger Smith is standing right behind the TV set behind the camera laughing with this big grin on his face. I have my little shorts on, and I get in bed. Ann-Margret's got nothing on.

I say, "Whoa."

John Trent, the director, says, "Now get on top of her, Bruce."

Now we're under the covers. And I hear, "What the hell is the matter with you?"

I say, "What do you mean?"

"Get those goddamn shorts off."

Whoof. Now what goes through my mind immediately is, well, if I take them off and don't get a boner, she's going to hate me the rest of my life. And if I take them off and do get a boner, her husband's going to rip the covers off and kill me. Or she's going to say, "You sick fuck!" The covers are going to come off. She's gone back to California and the movie's over. What do you do?

I say, "Well, I'm just trying to be polite."

And she says, "Oh, you Glencoe asshole. No wonder you were offering us money when we were freshmen in high school, because none of you Glencoe guys ever got laid."

In *Middle Age Crazy*, they give me a fortieth birthday party, which is what the movie's about. They make a videotape of everybody saying "Happy birthday, Bobby Lee." My family is sitting there. It's a very well-constructed scene. Ann-Margret is sitting next to me, and it's tough because I don't know Ann-Margret that well at the time. I know a little bit about her through high school at New Trier and a little bit about her when she was a freshman at Northwestern where she bailed after three months because she was plucked out and immediately put in *State Fair* with Bobby Darin and she was an instant movie star. We had some people in common like Jack. She had a rough time with Jack because *Carnal Knowledge* was a rough period of time for him.

He was just emerging, and Garfunkel wasn't an actor. So we're doing the scene, and they're all Canadian actors except Ann-Margret and me, because they have to be. We're in Toronto. They've made this documentary that I had not been shown, on purpose. Everybody's coming on with a personal zinger at Brucie as well as the zinger that's in the script. John Trent did an interesting thing. He had every actor introduce himself by saying "Happy birthday, Bobby Lee," and then going, "And Bruce, working with you has been . . ." and then they give this personal zinger that was designed for me. The zinger was just in case I didn't know how to act. So it got nothing but hostility out of me at the director. Not at the actors, because the director put them up to that.

So after the first one, I said, "This sucks, stop it. Cut all this fucking shit out. I don't need this."

Marty Krofft said, "Aw, shit! We thought it'd be funny."

I said, "Fuck you. I don't need that shit. Get it out of there. Just cut it all out."

He said, "Well, we have a reel without it."

"Fine, take it out of the fucking video and put in the real one. Come on, I'm Bobby Lee, I'm not Bruce Dern."

Now the videos are funny, and we know what the movie's about. My son, who's seventeen in the movie, has got this nasty little girlfriend. You can see some gnarly little hair underneath her bathing suit, and she's hanging around the pool at our house. I notice it, and my dad, who's played by Eric Christmas, notices it and asks, "What are you looking at, son?" I say, "The same thing you're looking at." Now the birthday video comes on. Everybody says a nice greeting. My dad's the last one to talk before my wife. He's a cheery little guy, Eric Christmas. He's like a little Santa's elf.

He's saying, "Happy birthday Bobby Lee. Forty years old, huh? Boy oh boy. Who'd have thought that I would ever have a son that would turn into such a sick bastard. Taking shots at your son's girlfriend because she's got some nasty little curls under that bathing suit. Lord almighty. Shame on you, son."

Then Ann-Margret comes on and she says, "Happy birthday, darling," and with the cameras on me in the shot, I just started to cry.

She's sitting next to me and my arm's around her, and the tears started coming down my face and she was stunned.

Ann-Margret said, "My god, he's crying. Oh my god."

It went on maybe ten seconds, then Trent cut the camera, and that's what you see on the screen. Everybody applauded. The crew went on to set up outside by the hot tub for the next shot. I sat there, I couldn't move, and John Trent sat down next to me and put his arm around me.

He saw the look on my face and said, "You're appalled, aren't you?"

I said, "Yeah, shocked."

He said, "I know." He took his hand, and he patted my leg, and he had tears in his eyes. "That's why I moved from England to Canada. But they don't get it here, either."

He grabbed my knee and squeezed it real hard.

He said, "I want to thank you for this. I'm just a Brit, trying to get something said. Couldn't do it there. Came here, this is my tenth film here. Today I had what I think is my career moment. You gave it to me. I'll love you till the day I die. I got a moment in a movie I directed, and goddammit I hung in there until I got it. It's the purest moment I've seen on screen, and I got it on one of my movies. They didn't get it. Maybe an audience will get it, but they didn't get it."

Ann-Margret said, "He's crying," like it wasn't acted. That it really happened, that it can happen, that human beings can behave in front of a camera after the gun's gone off and the race is on that people can actually be relaxed, and it's part of the craft and yet it doesn't look like it's part of the craft. They're so shocked that they say, "He's crying" instead of "You're crying."

He got it and was thrilled that I got it in his movie, and he had something to do with it. It was in no way a knock on Ann-Margret. It's just that sometimes I'm harder on other actors because they don't want to get as personal as I get in front of the camera. There's a few of us— Jack included—that take things a little more personally than others when we act. Some people don't agree that it goes as deep into the soul as it does. Well, for me, I have to take it there. Jack has to take it there. And that was an example of someone who doesn't have to take it there to get the same result. I have to. And when she said, "Look, he's cry-ing," that's as far as she could see herself going. Whereas both John Trent and I knew that if she had gone that extra inch, she would have said, "You're crying." But she could never see the depth of her being mine and me being hers, so she could say, "You're crying," meaning she and I were really together and a couple. That would have meant Roger was out of the picture and it wasn't playacting anymore. She and I were a couple for just that instant. That's why actors sometimes hook up on sets.

There was a scene at the very end of the movie in which Ann-Margret comes home and gets in the hot tub with me. She's gone off and had her little affair because I've had my affair, and the last line in the movie is, "Well, I'm home, Bobby Lee, and I love you and I'm gonna stay with you and we'll make the marriage work."

And I say, "Well, I'm just gonna settle for this. I'm forty years old and I've got hot water shooting up my ass, and I guess I'm just an Oldsmobile man," which is a line from a Jerry Lee Lewis song, and I get teary-eyed. I start to cry and she hugs me and it's just Ann-Margret and me. A picture of me holding Ann-Margret became the logo of *Echoes Magazine*, the New Trier magazine, and it replaced the picture of Charlton Heston as Moses parting the sea, which replaced Rock Hudson in *Giant*. They take something for every decade and we were later replaced by somebody from *The Breakfast Club* because it was shot at New Trier.

Now, one day on *Middle Age Crazy*, there was a notation. The most outraged moment I've ever had in movies. On the call sheet it said we had to finish up the hot tub scene, and under props, next to my name, it said, "For Mr. Dern: Tears." That's the one day in my career I lost it. I went to Marty Krofft and said, "I want you to find out who made up this fucking call sheet and who put down, under props, spe-cial effects, Mr. Dern has to have tears ready." It was props and makeup. They had to have tears ready for me to do this scene in the hot tub in case I wouldn't be able to cry. It was the only time in my career when I found the person who was responsible for it. It wasn't the makeup person. It was the guy who made up the call sheet, the second assistant director. He was brought in front of me, in front of 112 people at lunch, and I fired him. I paid him off myself, $862. I counted it out, and I said, "You sir, are done. If I work in Canada again, and I ever see your fucking name on any piece of paper to do with any movie I'm in, you will never work for me as long as you live and this mistake that you've made has embarrassed me beyond belief. I just showed you last week and I showed you last night."

He said, "Look, I was just covering my ass."

"Of course, that's your job. In your world, your job is to cover your ass. In my world, you're persona non grata. As long as you breathe. You're done here. Good day, sir."

In that cafeteria, 112 people got up and gave me a hand. They liked the guy, but they gave me a fucking hand. This is August 27, 1979. We're in a public arena in Brantford, Ontario, outside of Toronto.

As our crew finished the hand, we all sit down, the guy says, "I'm sorry to everybody." They gave him a hand. As he walks out, suddenly eleven thousand people give the loudest roar I've ever heard in my life from another place in the building. It's two thirty in the afternoon.

The place erupts and people come running through where we are out in the streets, screaming, "He did it! It's unbelievable! The fuckin' kid did it! He did it!"

We don't understand what's going on. A guy runs through and says, "This fuckin' kid, he's only fifteen years old, but he did it. He's unbelievable."

These people are running in the streets, and they're saying he's put this fucking place on the map, he did it. He's the best that ever lived. He absolutely did it. Wayne Gretzky, at fifteen, had just scored at another end of the building, his one hundredth goal in the Canadian Junior Hockey League. Four years later, he won the Stanley Cup as most valuable player.

In the early seventies, Steve Blauner, Jim McBride, and I were in Calgary, at the Calgary Inn, having our famous meeting, with marijuana smoke floating around the room, about building an interior set so we could make *Gone Beaver*. It was a very down meeting, because I knew the movie wasn't going to be made. We walked out of the meeting at two in the afternoon. There wasn't a soul on the street. There wasn't a car moving. It was October. There wasn't anyone in the bank building. It was a weekday. There was nobody anywhere. Calgary's a big city and nothing moved. There wasn't a sign of human life. It was like the end of the world.

Steve put his arm around me and said, "We'll make this movie. You and I. We'll go back, and we'll make the movie."

Suddenly doors started flying open, people started coming out of windows, and confetti started flying out of buildings. Furniture got thrown in the streets. Suddenly, Calgary, instead of having 165,000 people somewhere else, exploded onto the streets like Hiroshima. The population was all out there. It was the most joyous, most positive explosion I've ever seen in my life. "We did it!" Paul Henderson had just hit the goal in the World Cup Hockey Championship where Canada beat Russia for the first time.

So I was there for those two things: the Calgary celebration and Gretzky's breaking the record, the day that the AD put tears on the fuckin' call sheet. I had to have tears.

· 21 ·

It's a Maud, Maud, Maud, Maud World

I did *Tattoo* because I didn't get a movie I wanted to do, which was *Four Seasons*, an Alan Alda movie with Carol Burnett and Jack Weston. Alan Alda saw *Middle Age Crazy* and, according to the people that watched it with him, laughed his ass off and loved it and called Fred Specktor about it. But the producer thought I wasn't able to be funny. So they cast Len Cariou. I don't know Len Cariou. I've not seen him in a movie. I sure as hell didn't see *Four Seasons*. But I didn't get the role, and I wanted it because there was a good script that worked well. I thought Alan Alda was quite good, and I wanted to work with him, and I liked the other people. Miss Burnett, I never got to work with her. I've never even met her. But I didn't get it, so along came *Tattoo*.*

---

*These two early eighties films couldn't be more different. Alan Alda wrote, directed, and starred in *Four Seasons*, a bittersweet comedy about a circle of well-off middle-aged couples that falls apart when Len Cariou's character gets divorced. In the poor man's version of *The Collector*, *Tattoo*, Dern is again an exploitation-style psycho, though this time the character at least gets to have it with a Swedish model.

My marriage to Andrea has never been threatened by a costar. Never. Certainly never emotionally. The closest it came to being tested was the physicalization of the relationship with Maud Adams on *Tattoo*. The very first day, Maud and I made a pact that we would never take the physicalization or any romantic part of our relationship off the set. We would never, ever, for the eleven weeks of the movie, be alone together off the set. If we had dinner, it would always be with her boyfriend, Reed Smith, and Andrea. We would never be alone. After work, we just wouldn't go there. I had a driver; she had a driver. I never knew where she lived. She had an apartment somewhere in Greenwich Village. She knew the hotel that I lived in. We never went there, not when you're that close to somebody who was naked for fifty of sixty-six shooting days, in front of a crew of sixty-five people, and then, the last twenty-two of those days, we're both naked. We couldn't even put robes on because we had a full body of silk-screen tattoos, and it would have smudged the stuff. So we would just walk around naked all day long. During the day, between shots, we'd sit in a small bedroom they gave us and anything could have happened. They closed the door. They'd lock it on us, so no one could fuck with us. And we could have done anything, but we didn't. I have more respect for her than any woman I've ever worked with in my career in terms of violation or chance to violate, and vice versa. Now I'm talking about off-camera in the privacy of a room. On camera, what you see is what you get. In other words, if you believe it looks like something happened, it happened. Anything that went on with Maud and me is recorded on film and is onscreen in the movie. There's nothing to delete from the movie that didn't happen. And there's nothing not in the movie that did happen. Any pledges I made to her verbally or physically are in the movie, and never were carried beyond that. Was there some kind of intercourse? Maybe. Was it unavoidable? Yeah. You lie on top of somebody for six hours a day for ten days and rub against each other, there's no place for things to go except where they belong. And there's just nothing you can do about it. Now do people get off in those circumstances? No. But things go into areas where they go. And the sex act of it—the grinding and all that—does go on, but it looks like humpers. And it's unavoidable. We're on top of each other. You've got a camera here. You've got a camera here. You've got a camera here. You've got a camera here. It's going to see something. And yet it can't see something because then you've got an X-rated movie.

When that movie was over, it was a tremendous relief. Within a week of that movie being over, which was probably the fifteenth of June, 1980, I have not said a word to Maud Adams, nor have I seen her. It's not intentional. It's just our relationship at that time went as far as it could go without consummating something. There was an opportunity for what might have been ultimately an unbelievable relationship between Maud and me. I don't know where she was in her life in her relationship. She was surrounded by guys and girls that she loved. I know that she had consummated relationships on both sides of the street and was into both sides of the street, but the other side comes basically with modeling. That's just where they go. She's basically a heterosexual dame. We didn't pursue it, because we pursued it every day in front of the camera. And if we had consummated it, we knew it was dangerous to us and to our partners. She made a classy, classy, classy statement to me when it came time to decide whether we would ever cross the line. And I've told Andrea this. Maud and I flew home from New York after Memorial Day weekend. The movie was over for us. I still had to fly to Tokyo on my own to do the stuff at the beginning of the movie where I see the guys actually tattooing. The Japanese tattooing was interesting because I'd never seen that done. That's downtown tattooing. It's a lot different than on the Sunset Strip, and a whole lot different than silk screening because that's for real there. It's an eighth of an inch beneath the skin—big-time, downtown. It's like they do in Clovis, New Mexico. There's a guy and his wife that tattoo bikers in that part of the country, and they're absolutely fabulous, and they do it the Japanese way. People come from all over America to get tattoos there. They do fabulous, fabulous work. Like the people in *Whale Rider*—that's Maori tattooing. It's funny. I did a movie later on called *Mulholland Falls*, and the guy who directed, Lee Tamahori, did a movie called *Once Were Warriors*. I don't want to talk much about *Mulholland Falls*, but I can talk about *Once Were Warriors* for a long time.

Anyway, we were flying home, just Maud and I—it's the only time we were alone in public—and realizing that the twelve weeks were over. We'd done it, pulled it off, stuck to our guns, stuck to our word, had fallen in love as the characters but knew that it was doomed from the beginning because we were lucky enough to read the script, and we knew that I would be destroyed at the end, though she realizes that she destroyed the only thing that ever really loved her in her life. I don't think Maud had been married when we'd done that movie. Since then, I think she's been married a couple times. The whole package considered was about as pretty a total package as I had ever seen, much less worked with, plus a class act. Plus she's big. She's a tall woman. And she had these incredible cheekbones. She was the first L'Oreal girl, with the water dripping down the face. She ran with all these other models that were just racehorse dames. So we rode on the plane, and as we started dropping down from Vegas heading toward the L.A. Basin, it became apparent that one of two things had to happen. We either went for it or we didn't go for it. And an arrangement had to be made or not be made. I broached the subject and so did she, aiming for the negative end of it. "I guess we're never going to do anything about this," hoping the other one would say yes or no. She didn't say anything, and we both cried. I had my arm around her, and she had her arm around me. It was very, very sad. I felt I loved someone I could never touch, and she felt she loved someone she could never touch. Whenever I really want to talk to a girl and get her attention, I always hold her face in my hands. As we were coming down, she turned to me and she held my face in her hands.

She said, "You know, I never want to be the woman in the place I'd be putting Andrea in by us doing that."

It's the classiest thing anybody's ever said to me in my life, and I've told Andrea and Laura this. That really, really touched me and made me love my wife that much more. But it also made me love Maud that much more, because she had enough class to say that. What made it okay for me to not see her again after that was being the pathetic soul that I am, I realized that I got a big-time Dear John, you know?

I don't have the ability to carry on two relationships at one time, so if I was having a good sexual relationship with a girl, I would leave home. I would say, "Hey, I love this girl, and I don't love what I have here"—and I would leave. When the new relationship wore out, I wouldn't have either one. I'd have to go back home, and that's terrible. It's awful for the person you're married to. I treated Diane, my second wife, like a complete shit, really poorly. With Andrea, I made up my mind: in this marriage there's no way I'm gonna blow it.

I've always been fascinated by what makes people do what they do, particularly in times of crises. Why do we make the choices we make under pressure? Why do we do A instead of B? Letterman once asked me, "How do you describe these people that you play?" He probably has gone to a public perception of me being damaged goods a little more than anybody else. He always likes to have me on because he says he's one of the first guys that discovered me as damaged goods and promoted it. It was nice to have a guy like that. Johnny Carson was a big, big booster of mine early and so was Jay Leno when he took over, and Conan O'Brien's been a big booster. All those guys have been very good to me because they watched my movies early on. Johnny Carson was a devotee of *Silent Running*.

So Letterman said, "Why do you take those roles all the time? Why are you drawn to that? And who are these people?"

And I said, "Well, I enjoy playing people that live just beyond where the buses run."

The biggest salary I ever made on a movie was on *Tattoo*, and I got half a million dollars. The most money I ever made was on *Coming Home*. We all did the movie for $100,000 and then took pieces of the profits. The movie made quite a bit of money, and my piece took me over half a million dollars. $660,000, I think, is the total. Never made close to a million. No bullshit. Those are the facts.

If an actor can now get twenty million dollars for a film then let him go get it. If he can get one million dollars for a film, shit, I never got it. If producers want to pay them that, that's fine. I just think if you're paying an actor twenty million bucks, that's five four-million-dollar movies that didn't get made. The budget on *Monster* was four million dollars. Writer-director James Brooks paid Adam Sandler twenty million for *Spanglish*? I mean, they're only going to give it to him if they think he's worth it, if he can open a movie. He didn't open *Spanglish*, did he?

Andrea and I drove up to Santa Barbara one day on our anniversary in October. Coming home, we stopped in this little place to have a Coca-Cola about three thirty in the afternoon, and sitting out on this little patio was Jonathan Winters. I sat down next to him, and he went on and on about me and my career. I went on and on about him and his career. And he's a big sports fan.

We were talking about sports, and I said, "You know, the first time I met you, Paul Newman and I were in the parlor car of a train going from Philadelphia to New York after we'd finished doing the out-of-town run of *Sweet Bird of Youth*. You had just finished doing an engagement in Philadelphia."

He said, "I remember you because you were a runner and you'd just become an actor and people were kind of dubious about the play and it was Tennessee Williams and I was entertaining Paul Newman and I tried to get him to sing with me and he was from Ohio and I'm from Ohio. And then I followed your career."

He was quoting lines of mine from movies. He was very impressed with *Coming Home*. I just remember it was a fun hour and a half. Andrea loved it.

In October 1986, there was a very young film festival called the Mill Valley Film Festival, where they honored Stanley Kramer and Bruce Dern. I felt very put off that I should even be honored, number one. Number two, that I would be honored with Stanley Kramer. I was embarrassed. I mean, Stanley Kramer is an institution. Bruce Dern is an actor who in 1986 had done a few things including *On the Edge*, which was the closing-night movie. So it was kind of like a homey thing. Stanley Kramer was big stuff. I got to meet Stanley Kramer, and we were talking that night during supper before the ceremony, and I told him about having met Jonathan Winters five years earlier.

Mr. Kramer said, "I'll tell you about Jonathan Winters. When we were doing *It's A Mad, Mad, Mad, Mad World*, you get about twenty people when you direct Jonathan Winters. You get Jonathan Winters who is the most voluntarily genius personality you will ever get in show business at any level. He is without question a genius."

And this is before the emergence of Robin Williams, who is the self-proclaimed genius of the last twenty years. To me, he's not genius. He's clever. Extremely witty. And a personable guy. A little too fired up for me on a consistent basis. But he's a good guy. He's got a particularly gifted big soul. I would never want to go on record saying anything negative about Robin Williams. He's an enormously gifted being. He is a big fan of the movie *On the Edge* and that whole Mount Tam culture up there. His performance in *Good Morning, Vietnam* is about as good as it gets. He's quite a gifted actor. More gifted, I think, than anyone I've seen in quite a while. Unlimited potential. He just has no governor on his motor.

So I said to Stanley Kramer, "Well, what's it like working with Winters?"

He said, "Well, you say 'Okay Johnny, we're ready for you now.' And he'll come and give you anything you want at any level you want all-out. One hundred percent. Or the AD will come to you and say, 'I went to get Jonathan and he won't come out.' And I say, 'What do you mean he won't come out?' He says, 'Well, he's busy.' I say, 'Would you tell him he's the only thing in the shot and we can't shoot without him?' 'Yes sir, I did, Mr. Kramer, but he won't come.' I say, 'Did you tell him that I needed him? That it's personal for me?' And he says, 'Yes. He doesn't care. He says he's busy.' So I would go over and knock on his door. And then he'd say, 'It's open.' And I'd open it, and he'd be there, drawing or painting something. I say, 'Johnny, come on. We're all lined up. We've been waiting on you now for about fifteen minutes and we've got to shoot the shot. We're losing the light. You're the key to the shot.' And he'd say, 'Do you mind? I'm drawring an owl. Close the door.' And that was it. And he would stay until he'd finished drawring an owl. Not drawing . . . drawring."

"He was gone. His mind was just drying out."

I said, "Did you talk to doctors about it?"

"He is a doctor."

"What do you mean he is a doctor?"

"At that moment in time, he's his own analyst. He can tell you at another time he was drawing an owl because it was time to draw an owl. It was not time to come onto the set. Because there was no set to go to. It was time to draw an owl. He would get into a chamber in his mind, and he was locked into it. And until the owl was complete, he couldn't leave that chamber."

Kramer had never seen anything like it.

· 22 ·

Cycle Savage Meets Gumby

I hosted *Saturday Night Live* twice—in February 1982 and March 1983. Fred called me up and said, "I've got a phone call from a producer, Dick Ebersol. Lorne Michaels isn't with the show this year, and Ebersol wants to know if you want to host *Saturday Night Live*."

I said, "Absolutely out of the question. I'm not a host. Tell him that."

He said, "He wants to talk to you."

I said, "Put him on."

Ebersol started with how when he was in high school or grade school he saw me run. He gave me the whole history of the Penn relays, New Trier track, and he greased me a little bit. He said, "How many guys have you known in Hollywood who have actually won letters in sports in college? If I told you there's only five that are stars, would you believe me?"

I said, "How do you get five?"

He went through Gary Lockwood who was a big athlete at Southern

Cal, great football player. But they all changed their names—Lockwood had a different name. Lockwood was running under some Czech name when he went to USC in the backfield with Mike Garrett.

I liked Ebersol on the phone.

I said, "Okay, I'll do it, but what'll I do?"

He said, "It's a piece of cake. Come back, you meet the people. We'll write skits around what you want to do."

When I got there, the writers showed me sketches based on what they thought I like to do in my career, which are bikers, nasty sickos. They had nothing to do with the movies I was proud of. They had some lame skit from *Drive, He Said*. It was a takeoff on a basketball coach who berates his players. They took the coach from *Drive, He Said* and made him into the guy who killed John Wayne. They took a biker and had him be a guy who read the Bhagavad-Gita. I got all the Chicago people—Mary Gross, Tim Kazurinsky, and Bob Tischler, who was head of the writers.

My first skit was with Joe Piscopo, and I couldn't get the fucking word *Bhagavad* out. I didn't know what it was or what it meant, and they had me saying it five times.

They give you five grand.

I said, "I want it in cash."

They said, "Hey, it's Saturday."

I said, "I don't give a damn."

I came in Monday night to have a meeting with these pathetic people—not one of them made me laugh.

Tischler said, "No, it'll get funny during the week."

I said, "No, Bud, there's not a laugh at this table. Your black guy is funny, but he seems bored shitless."

I looked at Eddie Murphy and said, "Black Guy, you're funny. Why don't they give you more to do?"

He said, "I like that. He called me Black Guy."

I said, "You'd have to be blind not to know that you're funny."

He said, "No, but you didn't say that. You said, 'The black guy, he's funny!'"

I said, "Well, how come I can't have a scene with you?"

Eddie said, "Yeah, put me in a scene with the white guy."

I said, "No, everybody's white but you. Can't we give you something to do that's not token?"

Ebersol was fabulous. Tischler was good. I liked him. Al Franken was there, and his partner, Tom Davis. My wife loves him. I never got behind him. He was like a poor man's Art Metrano. The kids—Christine Ebersole, Mary Gross, Tim Kazurinsky—were wonderful. Piscopo I liked. He was fun. I was always surprised that he had the career he had so suddenly and then it didn't go on, because he worked the hardest to be who he was. I'm surprised it didn't last much longer than it did, because in certain kinds of comedy, he'd have been wonderful if they'd have hung in there with him. But they didn't. He certainly was as clever as John Belushi. These guys were just after the Aykroyds and those guys. They were good. Robert Downey Jr. hadn't come yet. It was just before his group. Mary Gross was good, nice, tall, innocent, and very sweet. Again, she was Chicago. I think she'd been with the nuns a little too long. She seemed like she had the strictest Sisters of Notre Dame education I'd ever seen in my life.

The week was fun. Saturday was tough because you're doing a matinee and an evening show. And they're both recorded. One goes live, and one doesn't. The audiences don't know that sometimes they'll use a piece from the first show if the live one doesn't go well. They'll play that piece for the West Coast feed instead of the one that was shown on the East Coast.

So Ebersol called me at the beginning of the season in '82 and asked if I would do it again. I heard that Eddie was leaving. I said, "I don't want to do one unless Eddie is there."

He said, "Eddie owes us so many shows this year. He will do the one you do because Eddie wants to work with you."

Dick Ebersol would walk me to my hotel from 30 Rock. NBC has their people stay in a nice hotel, but very different from the Sherry Netherland. It was like a Santa Ana kind of night—a March night—in New York City.

I said, "You've been real good to me. I didn't want to do it, but you gave me Eddie. And Eddie seems enthusiastic. I like the idea for the show."

They were going to assassinate Buckwheat. I couldn't believe Ebersol was going to get all those people, including Dr. Christiaan Barnard and Jarvik, the guy that made the artificial heart, Ted Koppel, and President Reagan. It wasn't going to be filmed. They were live.

I said, "How are you going to get a camera in the White House?"

He said, "We're going to do it."

Buckwheat is shot coming up the steps of 30 Rock. They interrupt for a live news show. They had Dan Rather.

Rather said, "Buckwheat's been shot on the steps of 30 Rockefeller Center. Now he's in surgery."

Jarvik is putting the plastic heart in, and Dr. Christiaan Barnard is performing the surgery to save Buckwheat's life. They're hooking the heart up, and the monitor is starting to not flatline. They're going to save Buckwheat's life. Jarvik's holding the two wires with his pliers and it's Mickey Mouse, and a newsperson asks them, "Doctors, have you seen the footage?"

They turn to look at the footage because they've never seen it. And Buckwheat dies because they don't make the connection in time. Reagan is reading the funnies in the Sunday morning paper and says, "Nancy, oh, my God! Did you see Buckwheat's been shot?"

He puts down "Dick Tracy" or whatever he's reading, "Look, oh my God, Buckwheat!"

She turns to him and says, "Ronnie, remember."

He says, "Otay," because that's what Buckwheat always said—otay.

Ebersol and I were walking, and I said, "I can't insist on it, but I want you to do me a favor. I've got a monologue to start the show. I'll do it for you tomorrow, but I'm not going to write it out, and I don't want it on cue cards because I don't know just how I'm going to say it."

He said, "How long will it run? No more than a hundred and twenty seconds—two minutes?"

I said, "It'll be within that."

He asked, "Is it hilarious?"

"No, but it's Dern—pure Dern. That's why you have me hosting, right?"

"Will it suck 'em in?"

"It sucks them in, then it cuts their throat. The only time you'll know what it is is when I do it for the first time in the dress rehearsal show that you'll record."

"Oh, that's dangerous," Ebersol said. "If Lorne Michaels were here, he'd never let you do it."

I said, "That's why I wouldn't be here for Lorne."

So I did it, I came out and got surprisingly shocking applause. I was amazed because I didn't know the audience knew who the hell I was. I always thought of myself as a second-banana guy from the 1970s. I wasn't comfortable yet because the guys and girls I grew up with in the business became synonymous with being leads in films. I played the guy who did a bad deed and became known as the bad guy—not as a particularly good actor. I didn't realize that in doing those deeds, the audience gave me credit for being quite a good actor because of the way I did those deeds. I had a lack of confidence in my ability because I thought they just remembered my performance because of the deed that was done. So I came out and they gave me warm applause. I cut it off.

I said, "What are you doing?"

They stopped.

I said, "What the hell are you doing? I come three thousand miles, I walk on a stage, and you start applauding for what? For me? No, no. I look out there. I see your faces—that guy right there. How many O'Henry bars have you scrunched all over your face to get that many pimples, huh? You put them in your mouth, and when you haven't fin-ished them, you just smear them all over your face, don't you?"

Of course, they're laughing their asses off. This poor kid wasn't a plant. I saw chocolate all over his face since he was six, you know? I mean, he's laughing at himself.

I said, "I look out there and I see you. You're not the first ones I think about. I turn to my agent, Fred Specktor, and I think, it's him. I blame it on him. I go back and I think about Mom, and I start blam-ing it on Mom. I blame it on my sister and my brother. Wait a minute. What about Andrea, my wife? She's the one. How about Gordon Phillips and Gadg and the nasty little bastard Lee Strasberg? They're the ones."

I named about five or six other people, getting nastier and nastier as I'm going along.

"I finally realized this week as I got on that goddamned airplane to come back here to New York City again to host this pathetic, rotten show, exactly who it is—exactly. I figured it out. You know who it is that insists that I play these filthy, rotten bastards every time I get a part in a movie?"

I look straight at the audience.

"It's you. Every goddamned one of you. You." There's a big, fat girl there. "You, fatty. You're the one who gets up on the edge of your chair and who wants me to squeeze every ounce of life out of every god-damned Palestinian that ever lived. Or you, cowboy-looking bastard, you're the one who makes me kill John Wayne. It's you people. You're the ones who insist Dern can't be funny. He can't cry. He can't have a kid. No one'll believe him as a father. He's Dr. Death. So, you want to know something? Next time out, I'm going to give it to you. But in the meantime, it's going to be 'Live from New York, it's Saturday Night.'" Ebersol loved it. It was a great tip-off to the show.

Eddie and I came out as twin Gumbys. We each had cigars. Eddie was fun. I've never seen him since then.

During *Wild Bill*, I asked Walter Hill, "Did you see Eddie lately?"

He said, "No, but when I do see him, he always says, 'Say hello to Bruce Dern if you see him,'" because we had Walter Hill in common. Eddie's a genuinely gifted guy. If Eddie wanted me to do a movie where I had scenes with him, I would go in a second. I feel quite sad about what happened to Dick Ebersol's family.* I sent him a card letting him know I was quite touched by what happened to his boy. It was really tragic. Ebersol is one of the princes in a business in which there are no princes. He has to make hard calls and tough decisions, but he's an hon-orable man. I know his wife a little bit from before he knew her. She's from Rock Island, Illinois—Susan Saint James. She's a good actress, and a great dame. They're girls that get it, go with the flow. She was destined to be whatever she wanted to be. She's always been a class act.

---

*In November 2004, Dick Ebersol was involved in a private plane crash, and his son, Teddy, was killed. Ebersol himself was seriously injured but survived with another of his sons.

· 23 ·

A Manilow for All Seasons

That Championship Season began shooting with George C. Scott.* I don't know who was playing my part. But then, George C. Scott was out, and the film fell apart. When the producers came back with Robert Mitchum, they offered a role to me. In the play, Richard Dysart played my role, but he was not involved in the movie. Paul Sorvino's the only actor who was in the play and the movie. It was a wonderful experience for me. I really liked Jason Miller. He was like a coach, a Vince Lombardi for me. He was there for me every day. He encouraged me, and he said, "Look, you can do this role. You are this role. I need your emotion as the linchpin for this movie because I wrote this guy to be much more emotional than he's ever been played.

---

*The movie was written and directed by Jason Miller, based on his own Pulitzer Prize–winning play. Miller's first and last directorial effort, it had many of the typical failings of a play put on the big screen. The excellent cast, of a basketball team and their coach reunited in middle age, included Bruce Dern, Martin Sheen, Robert Mitchum, Paul Sorvino, and Stacy Keach.

Nobody has come forward with that because we never drove it in that area. I want you to drive it."

The movie takes place in a seven-hour period of time—from five thirty till midnight. It's quite a wonderful setup. What they can do in the movie that they can't do in the play is walk through the old neighborhood at twilight where they walk past the houses and you see where these kids came from and what they did. What you don't know in the play is who these guys were in real life—that George Raveling was the center on this team, that Jason Miller was the guard on this team, and that these kids were all from an industrial, Catholic boys high school in downtown Scranton, Pennsylvania, that went on to upset the reigning state champions. They broke a guy's nose on the orders of their coach, who was a Jesuit priest and also ran the high school. George Raveling was quite a gifted high school athlete, and Jason wasn't that good a basketball player, but he knew the game. He knew exactly what the system should be and where everybody should be on the court. So, they pulled off a miracle. Then their lives fall apart. They go back to the coach's house for a twenty-fifth anniversary.

I had a wonderful relationship with Jason's sons, Jordan and Jason Patric, the actor. Linda Miller, who was Jason Sr.'s ex-wife, turned out to be a wonderful, wonderful girl, an actress, who, as trivia will tell you, is one of Jackie Gleason's two daughters. So Jason Patric's grandfather is Jackie Gleason. The ensemble acting is as good as it gets in movies. Sorvino was good. Marty Sheen was good. Stacy was wonderful. I was good. Mitchum was good. When the poetry comes out of Mitchum in that speech in the gym, "The credit belongs to the man who actually stood in the arena," it's fabulous. To be with Robert Mitchum, who actually did it for a number of years on a high level, a big, bona fide, legendary movie star, for ten weeks was great for all of us.

It was like camp in Scranton. There was Jason Patric, who was in charge of getting Cokes for me. There was Laura. They were sixteen. There was Mira Sorvino, who was running around helping out her dad. All three of these kids became movie stars. Mira won an Oscar (*Mighty Aphrodite*), Laura was nominated for an Oscar (*Rambling Rose*) and her acting work is as courageous and fine as it gets, and

Jason Patric's certainly done good enough work to be nominated for a couple of Oscars. Those three kids did pretty good—all working on a film in which their dads were involved.

Mitchum called Paul Sorvino "Cochon" during the filming. Sorvino didn't know he was being talked to. Mitchum's a guy who lays it out there. You bite or you don't bite. He gets an audience or he doesn't. "Cochon" finally became Sorvino's name. He didn't realize what was going on until Mira came up and said, "Daddy, why do you let Robert Mitchum call you a pig?" But Paul didn't go up to Mitchum and say, "Why did you call me a pig?" So he left it alone. Naturally, we called him "Cochon" all day long. He's a good guy. He can be a very good actor when he wants to be. The singing is out for me. I don't get it, and I don't like it. "Break into song for us, Paul!" No. Go in the men's room and sing.

I did a scene in the movie where I talk about our child who was born to us, a tubular pregnancy baby—ectopic pregnancy—and the child obviously didn't make it. The baby was in a jar, and we kept the jar in our house. I have to tell that story, and it's a very, very emotional story because of what I'd been through in real life. I'm on the porch telling the story to Stacy and Marty's sitting inside, half shit-faced, listening because the window is open. When the shot is over, Marty Sheen leans through the window and gives me the nicest compliment any actor has ever paid me.

He said, "That was brave work, brother, brave work. I'll never see anything quite as good as that again."

I appreciated the comment. And that was before he was president of the United States. He was great in *Badlands* and *The Subject Was Roses* with Jack Albertson.

We were in a restaurant in Scranton. I'm in the men's room and Barry Manilow comes in wearing a white suit, and he says, "Hey, Bruce, how are you doing?"

I say, "Hey, how are you?"

He leans toward me and is very interested in my mechanism I'm using to go number one with.

I say, "Did you get a good peek?"

He says, "Yeah, nice machinery."

I say, "Yeah, it works." I zip up and walk out. I sit down at the table and Jason Sr. says to me, "So Barry Manilow hit on you, right?"

"Right."

"He's hit on a couple of us. He can't keep his eyes off my kid."

"I'll bet." Jason Patric gets all embarrassed.

Jason Sr. says, "How about I give you a little hint?"

I say, "What's that?"

"It's not Barry Manilow."

"Bullshit! That's Barry Manilow."

"No, this guy lives in Scranton. All his life, he's made out that he's Barry Manilow. He looks just like him. We'll have a Polaroid taken with him."

So we had a Polaroid taken. And, by God, this son of a bitch looks exactly like Barry Manilow.

I said, "You mean, I can't go home and say that Barry Manilow hit on me?"

He said, "Not *the* Barry Manilow, but Scranton's Barry Manilow."

A dead ringer. After the Polaroid, I said, "Barr, you going to knock off a couple bars for us?"

"What do you want?" He sat down at the piano.

"How about a little 'People'?"

He sang it . . . didn't miss a note. Sounded like the guy. I said, "Come on, what are you? Twin brothers?"

"No, sir, I'm Barry Manilow. Get it together. And you, Mr. Miller, you'd better stop telling people I'm not Barry Manilow."

He pulled it off. We were convinced. But no way in the world was it Barry Manilow.

Jason Miller and the producers made a mistake with Robert Mitchum, which was misjudging his greatness. He had his sixty-fifth birthday while shooting *Championship Season*, and at the wrap, Miller and producers Menahem Golan and Yoram Globus gave him a present. They bought him a cake with a stripper. I didn't know about it. I was embarrassed for him. Mitchum was ashamed of it. He was very pissed off and told them, "You didn't respect me. You were disrespectful to my wife, who was there. She went along with it. My kids were there. My niece was there working on the movie. Just because I played the roles I played and I'm an open-book guy and tell it like it is, I'm also somebody else. Most of all, to you fucking people, I'm Robert Mitchum. I'm not Bob. You don't treat me like that because you don't know who Robert Mitchum is, was, and will be." We're not Robert Mitchum. Clint's not. I'm not. Redford's not. Jack's not. Dustin's not. We never will be.

We went to New York to open *That Championship Season*. We posed for a picture for *Time* or *Sports Illustrated*, and a female photographer from the magazine gave Mitchum a basketball. He was a little smashed. The photographer got down with the camera. Immediately, Mitchum threw the ball right back at the camera and broke the photographer's eye socket. I couldn't believe it. Mitchum stood there. Nobody went after him.

I said to him, "What was that?"

He said, "I wonder if she'll get the picture now?" Everybody was intimidated. I went out on him a little. The girl was obviously hurt— her eye was cut. Mitchum didn't care. That was a fuck-you to the producers for what they did to him on his birthday. He went back into the bar.

The review in *Sports Illustrated* was damaging to me because Frank Deford, who wrote it, was not nuts about the movie. He didn't consider it a sports movie, therefore, he shouldn't have been reviewing it for a sports magazine. He found it couldn't have happened, even though it did happen. He wrote that everyone was a real athlete except for Bruce Dern, who showed no semblance of any athletic ability whatsoever.

Frank Deford had a script for a long time that he'd written about Bill Tilden, that he wanted me to do, and I wanted to do it, but he refused to tackle Bill Tilden's homosexuality. I said, "It's got to be part of it. It's part of what drove him." Deford wouldn't change the script, and it never got made.

That Championship Season came out, and it didn't do well, and I put it to bed.

In February of 1983, I'm in my beddy about eleven thirty in the morning and my phone rings. I pick it up and get a drunk Jason Miller, which is not unusual, on the phone with Jason Patric, and they're laughing. They said, "Dernser . . ."

I said, "Where the hell are you guys?"

"We're in Berlin. We brought *Championship Season* over here and it won an award."

"You're kidding. I thought nobody went to see it."

"You wouldn't believe it. You won Best Actor, *Besten Darstellar*. Jason went up and accepted it for you. It was given by Jeanne Moreau, and it's called a Silver Bear, Best Actor at the Berlin Film Festival."

I'd won the People's Choice Award for *Coming Home*, and I'd been nominated for an Oscar and a Canadian Oscar (Genie) twice, but I'd never actually won a film festival award. *Championship Season* was a movie I'd forgotten about in terms of being down the pike. I never thought anyone would ever catch up with it. I never thought anyone would see *Harry Tracy*,* and I got nominated for a Genie Award, best actor in Canada. I was also nominated in Canada for Best Actor for *Middle Age Crazy*. Twice in England for *Gatsby* and *Black Sunday* for best supporting actor.

Two days later, I picked up a trade paper, and my press agent called and said, "Why'd you spend all that money putting the ad in the trade about your Silver Bear? We didn't know you won the award. You're supposed to tell us this."

I said, "I didn't take out an ad."

It was Yoram and Menachem who took out an ad congratulating me on winning the best actor at the Berlin Film Festival. That afternoon Jason and his son got home and they brought the award by and just left it in my mailbox. When Andrea brought the mail in, there was a paper sack with this silver thing in it—no note. The next morning, I pick up a trade paper and it says, "Menahem Golan and Yoram Globus flee America to Israel. Cannon Films goes under."

I never heard a word from them since. They're in Israel now and they make movies, but they got caught up in the war and a bunch of

---

*This well-acted 1982 Canadian production that had limited release starred Bruce Dern, Helen Shaver, and pop star Gordon Lightfoot. The film, with Dern in the title role of the last surviving member of Butch and Sundance's Hole-in-the-Wall gang, ran up against the similarly themed *The Grey Fox*, which garnered a best actor Academy Award nomination for its star, Richard Farnsworth.

other stuff. Here I get involved in something that works, and suddenly I get guys fleeing the country and I'm holding the silver bowl. Jason Miller has since passed away, and his son is my dear little guy. I love him. He can act.

Next I did a movie called *On the Edge*, which is about running. It was produced by Roy Kissin, who once won the Dipsea race. The director, Rob Nilsson, came to L.A. to convince me to do the movie. Somehow my brother, Jack, got involved with it through a lawyer in San Francisco named John Stout, and got a lot of San Francisco money involved, and got a bunch of guys who I'd grown up with and gone to high school with to put money in the movie. The producers promised me $400,000. I ended up getting only $100,000, and a couple of times I said, "Hey, you promised this," and they kept scaling it back to three hundred then two hundred, then they said, "Look, we only have a hundred thousand, and if you don't want to make it, we'll get Kris Kristofferson." Kristofferson couldn't run like I could, but he could run. He certainly could run better than Dustin ran in *Marathon Man*. I saw Dustin training once at the reservoir in New York City, and once at UCLA's track. The movie's called *Marathon Man*. The shots are of him running all-out. This is not correct. He'd run all-out for that take for about twenty seconds. That looks good if you're trying to catch Maurice Greene who runs the 100 and 200 meters. The marathon's 26.2 miles, Dustin. I never talked to him about it. I don't know Dustin Hoffman. I've only met him a couple of times. His mom is in the business. Some stars don't want you to know that. Teri Garr's mom, Phyllis, was my wardrobe lady on *Family Plot*. David Janssen was cool with it, his mother was an extra on *The Fugitive* all the time, and he was the Fugitive. What's the big deal? His mother was absolutely beautiful. David Janssen was a city pole vault champion when he was at Fairfax High School.

With *On the Edge*, I met the Marin film community. These people can make movies, but they make a different kind of movie. It's guerrilla filmmaking and they know what they're doing. They know how to move fast, they know how to move well. I got a cinematographer named Stefan Czapsky, who was in America a year, a year and a half at the most. He had fabulous ideas, could do things with no light,

or a little bit of light, or natural light, and, amazingly, was not threatened at all by another cameraman working side by side with him who
shot the running stuff, running with me at six miles an hour. We
worked out a little drill and did it all on the fly.

I liked Pam Grier. There were two versions of *On the Edge*. There
was the Pam Grier/Bruce Dern version and the Bruce Dern version,
which is the same movie with the love story removed. The version that
was released in the theaters was without the love story. The video version is with Pam Grier, an interracial love story. You can also get the
version that was released in theaters on video. John Marley wasn't feeling well when we did the movie, but he was wonderful in it. We made
the film in 1983, but it wasn't released until '85, when Skouras Films
bought it and released it, but then went out of business.

So *On the Edge* was over. *Championship Season* had come out
and died. *Middle Age Crazy* didn't do anything, *Tattoo* didn't do anything, *Coming Home* had come and gone by now. I was wallowing.
I did a movie that shot for two weeks until the producers ran out of
money. Jackie Cooper directed, and Katherine Ross and I were the
stars.

I was upset. I wasn't panicked, but the guys in my age group who
were doing well were doing very well, and they were making a good living. I had started to get up in price and was being paid well for what I
was doing, yet being careful not to be paid so well that I kept myself out
of being cast. I wasn't being offered sensational things. I did turn down
a role in *Gandhi* that Martin Sheen ended up playing, the Lowell
Thomas role. I'd been gone so long and I was exhausted, and I had a
phobia. I was terrified of snakes. Sir Richard Attenborough wanted me
in Calcutta or Delhi for six to eight weeks, because he didn't know
when he'd get to my three days. I said to him, "You've been wonderful to me. I really appreciate the offer, but I want to ask you a question:
when I get up in the morning and I go out with my wife and I walk
down the stairs of the best hotel there is, is there going to be a guy playing a flute on the steps, standing near a woven basket? And what's
going to be in the basket? Will there be a rope coming out of the basket that could kill me?"

Sir Richard said, "There might be a cobra or two."

I asked, "If I go for a run six or seven miles out in the woods, will there be a tiger there?"

He said, "Oh no, no, that's way out in the country."

I said, "If I go into the river to cool off afterwards, will there be nine thousand people washing?"

He said, "No, no, you're not going in the river."

I said, "Then when I come back and go up the steps, will the same guy be there with the basket?"

He said, "No, it'll be a different guy."

I said, "God, I'm so afraid of snakes."

Anyway, I passed. Sir Richard wanted to pay me wonderfully, but it was a long time and there wasn't much to do and I didn't feel I could make a statement in the role. I wasn't sure I saw his vision of the movie. It hit me at the wrong time. I should have done it, but I didn't, and that's a mistake I made.

· 2 4 ·

The Final Frontier,
for Now

S*pace*, based on James Michener's book about the history of the
NASA program, was a miniseries—thirteen hours, five nights, a
very ambitious project. I was excited about it because there were
good people involved. James Michener, even though he was in his late
eighties, was a live wire. His Hawaiian wife was really a spitfire. He was
still actively teaching at the University of Texas when we were shooting *Space*. We started in May and finished in October. We had two
crews shooting simultaneously: one crew was directed by Joe Sargent,
the other by Lee Phillips. Joe Sargent had directed wonderful things
in television for years and was an Actors Studio kind of director much
like Sean Penn's dad, Leo Penn. They were good friends. Phillips had
been an actor who had a big lead in the original *Peyton Place* movie.

The stars of the miniseries were Jim Garner, Bruce Dern, Harry
Hamlin, Blair Brown, and Michael York. I played a prototype of
the first guy who ran NASA when it was created in the 1950s, Chris
Kraft.

We filmed a month in England, then we came back and did the rest of *Space* all around America. On certain days, the two companies actually were shooting side-by-side because actors were going from 1950 to the late '60s and early '70s. I'd be shooting as Dr. Stanley Mott in the '50s with the Mercury astronauts, and then change my wardrobe and jump into the Apollo program in the late '60s and do a scene with Pete Conrad or Neil Armstrong and Dick Gordon. That became tough. We filmed in L.A. It was the year of the '84 Summer Olympics. Then we shot in San Diego. Melinda Dillon played my wife. By the end of the '80s, Melinda had more nominations than anybody else in our age group, four or five nominations.* She was nominated for *Close Encounters*. I'd always forgotten. You just accept that she's the vague one because she's so wonderful at it, so sweet and so nice. She was a terrific partner, and she's a dame who's survived it.

So the day-to-day acting relationships were good. What was tough was jumping years as fast as we had to jump them. Our liaison was Dick Gordon, who, unfortunately, never got to walk on the moon, but he flew six missions. His guys walked on the moon, while he was in the orbiter flying around.

In the story, my son decides that he's going to lead a gay lifestyle, and it's during Vietnam, so he goes to Canada to beat the draft. It's tough on me, being the head of NASA, that my son goes to another country, but I embrace his lifestyle with his friend. I go to Canada, not to get him and bring him back, but to let him know he's always got a place in our house, he's always going to be my son. We were shooting in Griffith Park in L.A., which was supposed to be Stanley Park in Vancouver.

I asked Mr. Michener before we shot the scene, "Would it be okay if the dialogue I'd like to say isn't in the book?"

And Mr. Michener said, "Be my guest, Mr. Dern. You have been right on the whole time. Say what you want to say, and we can always go back to the text if we don't like it."

My son and I are walking. Clearly I'm upset that he's done what he's done. But I still say, "You can come home."

---

*She was nominated for a Best Performance by a Featured Actress in a Play Tony Award, a Best Female Acting Debut Golden Globe, and two Supporting Actress Oscars.

He says, "You know, Dad, my problem with you is, you just said to me, 'Why don't you come back from Canada and do something worthwhile in your life beside run away from everything?' I don't condemn what you do, even though your life hasn't been worthwhile as far as I'm concerned. What contribution have you made? You send one up; the Russians send one up. You sent a monkey into space. Big deal. A guy walked on the moon four years ago. Who cares?" There's no real end to that scene. I said, "Let the scene go a little further. Let's see what might happen." I don't know what came over me that night. It might have been the moon. It might have been feeling bad for Dick Gordon because he was up there six times and he never got to walk on it. I grabbed my son by the neck—the actor who played my kid was much bigger than I was, about six-three—and I said, "Don't you ever talk to me like that. Look. What is that?"

He said, "It's the moon, Dad, and it's full. So what?"

And this was off the top of my head. I said, "Before you ever tell me that my life or what we're doing here hasn't been worthwhile, might I remind you that six guys have walked on that and come home to talk about it. So fuck you."

Joe Sargent says, "Cut." Mr. Michener walked up to me. The eighty-eight-year-old man took his glasses off, put both his hands on my shoulders, and looked me in the eye. He had tears in his eyes. He looked over his shoulder at Dick Berg and Joe Sargent, pointed to me, and said, "That, gentlemen, is exactly why I wrote *Space*." He got all choked up. "That is what they did. And nobody has bought it to this day. They don't get it. Goddamn it, this country is not going to ever understand it. But this guy just got it. And you know what? I failed to have the courage to write it down on the page because I felt somehow somebody would exclude it in the editorial process. And, therefore, I failed." He put his arm around me and said, "But Mr. Dern saved the day. I don't want to see this on the cutting room floor, even though he used the F-word."

That night when I finished, Dick Gordon told me how beautiful that was, and he said, "That'll go down in space history as a key phrase that'll be used again and again and again. Six guys walked on that and came home to talk about it. So F-you. That says it just about as specifically as you can say it. That's a halftime speech if I ever heard one."

Then he said, "You know, *Silent Running* was mandatory viewing at the Air Force Academy when I was there."

I said, "How could that be? You were there in the fifties."

"No, when I was instructing there."

"When was that?"

"1977 through 1980."

I said, "What do you mean mandatory?"

He said, "Well, every cadet saw it because we snuck it in somehow to the program. We even had Freeman Lowell patches." He pointed to the stars and asked, "How long do you think it would take to get to one of those?"

I said, "I have no idea."

He said, "Take a guess."

I said, "No idea."

He said, "Alpha Centauri is the closest star. If you and I left right now, traveling at the speed of light, 186,000 miles per second, it would take us seventy-three years to reach it. Got your attention, didn't I?"

I said, "Bruce Dern has been rendered speechless."

The next February on President's Day weekend, the show's scheduled to go on the air. Chevrolet is going to introduce the AstroVan. I went on a publicity tour and ended up in Dearborn, Michigan, at the auto plant where they showed a ninety-minute version of the movie to the press. Had a big dinner and I had to get up and say something. Pete Conrad, Dick Gordon, and five guys who walked on the moon were there. It was kind of neat, and *Space* was going to start airing the next Sunday, then Tuesday through Friday. Five nights, thirteen hours. A miniseries had never been that long except for *Centennial*. On Tuesday the shuttle went down. During the filming of *Space*, I had a chance to meet both Christa McAuliffe and Judith Resnik, and they were just super folks. I got a phone call Tuesday afternoon about two o'clock from Dick Berg.

He said, "You're the only person who I know would be feeling like I do. I just wanted to talk to you. We're going to pull the show."

They had to go with the AstroVan, so it came out, no advance publicity. They ran *Space* a year later in April. I don't know how it did. I watched a couple of the nights. I never saw the whole thing. I couldn't watch it after that because these women were a big part of it and they were on the shuttle. All these people we'd worked so closely with were on the *Challenger*, and they barely got off the ground. It was just never the same to me.

Mr. Michener wrote me a letter, and in it he said, "I don't deal in the past. I write about it, but I don't deal in it. I'm a forward-looking person. But as I told my students the day after the shuttle disaster, I'll always be left with a memory, and I told them to look at episode four of *Space* and look at the last half hour when you give your son the speech about what six people had done. I thank you for that, because, if nothing else, that's the accomplishment I remember the most. We did do that."

· 2 5 ·

The Encyclopedia
Brucetannica

I played a blind man in *Big Town*. I liked the role. Laura had played a blind girl in *Mask*, and I asked her how tough it was.

She said, "Well, you're the one who told me what to do."

So I got dark glasses with blacked-out Coke-bottle lenses.

The prop person said, "Don't you want it to look like you can't see, but you can see?"

I said, "No, black them out. I don't want to have my eyes sealed shut. Just make black glasses that I can't see out of."

It was hard, but it was fun. I got the part very quickly, but I didn't get time to practice or go to training camp. I got the job on a Friday, and my first day working in Canada was on Tuesday. I only worked three days, and they paid me well. Lee Grant played my wife, and the producers had gotten rid of Harold Becker, who had hired me, and hired the British guy. I forget his name. I'd know it if I heard it.*

Big Town marks the beginning of a period in Dern's career where Hollywood didn't know

230

Matt Dillon was a good kid, a non–Brat Pack kid, who came along at the same time as the Brat Pack did. He was in a way a Brat Packer because he was in those Francis Coppola movies they did in Oklahoma, *The Outsiders* and *Rumblefish,* with Emilio Estevez and the others. Anyway, Lee Grant was great. I like her because she was an acting teacher. She and her husband, Joe Feury, had been together a long time and they ran a school together. He was from Philly, an Actors Studio guy, though he didn't act much anymore. He'd been a dancer and an actor, a *West Side Story* kind of guy. Never had a lot of luck as an actor. I tried to get him work a couple of times. Lee Grant is a fabulous actress. Anytime she works it's a blessing you have her in your movie. Tommy Lee Jones was good. I didn't have but one or two lines with him. He was only in one scene, and I tried to talk to him a couple of times. The best acting work I have ever seen was the work that he and Bobby Duvall did in *Lonesome Dove.* It's the best communal work with two guys I've ever seen, certainly on television. I've never been able to do work like that with another actor, consistently day after day after day.

Diane Lane was in *Big Town,* and I have an affection toward her because she was very good to Laura when Laura was just twelve years old. It was like Laura having an older sister, and she's been in Laura's life on and off ever since.

The film *1969* interested me because the director, Ernest Thompson, couldn't pay a lot of money, but he could pay decent money for decent people. Thompson was a young man who had written and won an Academy Award for *On Golden Pond.* He wanted to do this movie, *1969,* which was about an experience that he had gone through in the town he grew up in, where the townspeople had too many local kids die in Vietnam. They got together and marched from Maryland to Washington, D.C., to protest the fact that their town was losing so many kids in Vietnam. It seemed disproportionate and not right. I met Thompson, and he wanted to make sure that I was the guy that he was

---

quite what to do with him. Like many other actors in their fifties, he was too old to play a young guy, and too young to play an old guy. Directed by TV director Ben Bolt, Dern costarred with one of his rivals for all-time great villain portrayer, Tommy Lee Jones. A young Matt Dillon and Diane Lane anchor the film.

seeing in movies. He wanted to make sure I understood the role he'd written, and the point of the movie.

We got down to Savannah, where we shot it, and a kid named Dan Grodnik, who was a little hairy, but a sweet guy, was producing it. The cameraman was Jeff Jur, who had just photographed *Dirty Dancing*. Nobody bothered to ask how long it took to shoot *Dirty Dancing*. They just liked the look of it. Ernest only had a certain amount of money, and a certain amount of days, and in the cast he had two sets of parents. Mariette Hartley and I were Kiefer Sutherland's parents, Joanna Cassidy was Bob Downey Jr.'s mother, and Winona Ryder had no real parents. The kids were all in high school. Kiefer's older brother in the movie was a soldier in Vietnam, and he was going to come home in a body bag. The movie revolved around Kiefer, his buddy Downey, and Winona, who was sixteen then. Her real mom and dad were around most of the time; they were activists from Petaluma in northern California.

When I got to location, they had shot four days, and they were four days behind schedule. Jeff was not good at moving fast, and Ernest, as bright as he was, was a first-time director. Producers give first-timers a budget and a schedule, but AFI doesn't teach them how to deal with that. They know they've got twenty-four days, but they've got twenty-four days with every abuse there is. They think they're going to shoot twenty-hour days. In the second day, they start at 6 A.M. and they're still shooting at 11:30 P.M. They think you're going to come back and shoot at 6 A.M. the next day and do it again. You can't do that because in SAG you've got twelve-hour turnarounds. They think they can stagger their actors and come to somebody like me who'll play ball, and I'll go to the other actors and get them to play ball. The other actors would look at me and say, "No, fuck you. I've got a twelve-hour turnaround." Then, the crew starts to drop, because they're all non-union anyway, and there's a lack of discipline and a lack of leadership.

That's what happened on *1969*, so they got rid of a bunch of people and brought in a guy named Bill Badalato, who's absolutely fantastic, has wonderful producing credits, and he's what you call a production doctor. He comes in and saves a movie; produces it, line produces it, and production manages it. He puts it on its feet, gets the finances straight, gets rid of people who can't do it, brings in people who can do it. The first thing he did was bring in Jules Brenner, who's a cameraman. He's a little over-hippied. In 1986, he's still wearing Santa Fe Indian jewelry, but he was the cameraman on *Posse* for Kirk Douglas, and he just gets it. He's fast, and he wants to get everything right and make a good movie. *1969* was the hippie era, so he was right for hippie stuff. He's not a mechanic, but he's good and he's got a wonderful personality.

I bury my son, and the town, sixteen hundred people, actually walk the forty-six miles to Washington, D.C. That's the way the movie ends. It's ironic the way things come back to other movies I've done. There's a scene where I'm sitting in the living room and I'm watching TV and it's July 1969, and Kiefer and Downey and Winona are there, she's sleeping with both of them, and Kiefer's got a knapsack on. They've got an old Volks bus, and he says, "Dad, I'm out of here."

"Where are you going?"

"We're driving all night. We're going to Canada."

"You want to watch a little of this?"

"No, I don't want to watch TV, I'm on my way to Canada, Dad. I'm going to see the sights."

They're really going to avoid the draft because their draft number's coming up since they graduated from high school.

I say, "You might want to look at this, a guy's walking on the moon."

Kiefer says, "Yeah, sure he is, Dad. Sure he is," and he walks out.

Ernest actually told that to his dad. He said, "What a schmuck I was. I got in my car and we turned on the radio for some music and somebody was saying, 'One small step for man, one . . .' and my girlfriend said, 'Turn that shit off. Put on Sly Stone.' The next day we picked up the paper, and it read, 'Man walks on the moon.'"

We had a scene in which Downey goes berserk because he's on drugs. Neither Kiefer nor Downey were behaving themselves. They were not resting when work was over the night before. So they were coming in the next morning without a game face. They had a face, but it was last evening's face. Both are extremely talented actors so it's not a question of me saying, "What a waste." I just didn't get the best Downey or the best Kiefer, and that disappointed me. I'm not going to make a comment. I'm not the director; Ernest is the director. And he had now had it with them. He was pissed off. He wasn't that much older, probably thirty-five, and they were twenty and both were established; Kiefer hadn't done *Young Guns* yet, but he was close, Downey had already done *Saturday Night Live*. We had to do a scene where Downey goes a little crazy and they chase him around the gym. He's in his underpants, and he should be confined to a mental hospital. He grabs the gym rope—I have never even tried to attempt the rope-climbing event in school because I have no strength in my arms, little tiny arms, rope, climb, fuck that—he's swinging on this rope, and he swings up onto the balcony and then he leaps down, missing the stage and landing on the gym floor. In the rehearsal, they put a stepladder for him to climb on. He's running around loosey-goosey, and it's about nine fifteen in the morning and we're getting ready to do the shot, and he's doing it all-out each time. He's not with it, you know what I mean? We have to break his fall when he jumps from the balcony to the gym floor, because otherwise he'd kill himself. He climbs up the ladder. I'm on the gym floor, and they've moved the ladder closer to the edge of the stage, but still he has to climb on it to jump. He leaps from the top of the ladder to the gym floor, avoiding the stage. I reach out to break his fall. If I don't, he's dead. In doing it, he ripped my right shoulder out of its socket. He got up laughing hysterically, and I looked like the Elephant Man. My arm was to the ground. I didn't tell anybody; it's rehearsal, there's no camera there.

I had a guy that stood in for me for twenty years named Jim Sparkman, and he said, "Ooh, it looks like that hurts."

When he first came to L.A., Sparkman roomed with Jerry Bruckheimer and Don Simpson, because he grew up with Simpson in Alaska. He played at Anchorage High School in basketball and was pretty good. He was one of these acerbic guys, like Simpson and Bruckheimer, who owned the world. We stopped being around each other about eight years ago, because he drank too much. He was part Eskimo, part Indian, and it's not a good mix alcohol-wise. But he was great standing-in, and he was a good guy, a good companion, and extremely bright.

He looked at my arm and said, "That's not good."

I said, "Well, we're going to have to fake it for the next fifteen days. I'm not going to let anybody know that it hurts."

So at lunchtime, we went to a local doctor, unbeknownst to anybody except Badalato.

The doctor said, "Your rotator cuff is torn."

I said, "I'm not having surgery, because I'm not Tommy John. I don't have to pitch 250 innings next year."

He said, "The prognosis is a lot of codeine, a lot of pain, and it'll take three or four years for it to heal with an enormous amount of atrophy. And because of your age, you're going to get a lot of adhesions, and your shoulder is never going to be the same. You're going to have no strength in it."

Anyway, I let it go ten years, it eventually healed up, and I got hung up on codeine bad, and I couldn't lift my arm above my head. No one was going to cut on it. I can't do anything that I used to do. I can't shoot a basketball. I used to swing a golf club, I shot 91, 92, on an eighteen-hole course. I used to play tennis. I got a game off Bob Redford. I could play Ping-Pong. I could play baseball, but I can't get a full swing now. Everything is shortened because my right shoulder has atrophied. I'm not going to have an operation, for Christ's sake. Who gives a shit? I can still carry a baton in a relay, I can hand off, I can give it down, I can pump my arm. I never brought it up to Downey. I haven't seen him now in probably twelve years, but I told his dad, Robert Downey Sr., about it. His dad gave up on the kid a long time ago. I liked the dad. I don't know what the kid's demons are, but the kid is an enormous talent. Kiefer's an enormous talent, and very funny. I have a lot of hope for Kiefer. He's got enough power and fame now that, when he gets a chance to get away from the little box, he'll do extraordinary stuff as an actor in the movies. He's been on the road as an actor since he was three years old. I got to know Winona a little bit, I knew her a little before, and I know a great deal after. So I feel a kinship with her, and I try and watch out for her a little bit when I see her around.

One night, at one thirty in the morning, I got a call from Robert Downey Sr. Hal Ashby was dying. He was living two doors from me in the Colony. Downey Sr. said, "Get over here. Your friend is not doing well and wants to see you." So I went over to Hal's house, and there was Downey's girlfriend, Diane Schroeder, and this girl named Griff, who Hal was living with at the time who was terrific. When he died a week later, she took care of all the funeral arrangements. She was a tremendous gal. It was Downey Sr., myself, and Al Schwartz, who was a writer, very, very funny guy. Hal was really fading, and he'd lapse in and out of consciousness and he came awake while I was there. He just wanted to have us talk. Tell stories. Then he'd laugh, and then he'd pitch in and tell a couple of things. He asked Schwartz to tell a story and it's the funniest show business story I've ever heard. God, Hal was just so feeble and weak and it was so sad to see because he was a shell of a person. If you knew Hal, he wasn't a big man. He was more like a long-haired, leaping gnome.

The story was about Walter Matthau, Myron McCormick, who was a big Broadway actor, an Irish red-faced guy, a hard drinker, comedy writer Pat McCormick, and Al Schwartz. They were in their box at Hollywood Park on a weekday. They were all horse players. They had bet the races, and Myron McCormick had the three horse in the first race and the six horse in the second race and had bet like ten thousand dollars on the Daily Double. The three horse came in in the first race. By the second race, Myron was really drunk. What is it now, one twenty in the afternoon, and the first race was at twelve thirty? Second race, they're around the eighth pole and they're coming down the stretch and the six horse has about a four-length lead. Myron's on his way to making quite a bit of money for a ten-thousand-dollar Daily Double bet, maybe a couple hundred thousand dollars. Myron has a heart attack, a bona fide heart attack, which he was vulnerable to anyway because he was about seventy years old. He was overweight and a gnarly angry Irishman—they weren't drinking wine and beer, they were drinking hard stuff and he'd done it for fifty-five years. He has this massive heart attack. Matthau is the first one to get to him. He's two rows back in the box, and Myron's down at the rail. Myron goes down like a rock, and Matthau runs down to him. Schwartz and Pat McCormick are running down, and the horse is now three hundred feet from the finish line. Matthau's picking Myron up.

He says, "Myron. Myron."

Myron's gone. He's dead. But only Matthau knows it at this moment. And now the horse is 150 feet from the finish. Clearly, he's got the race.

Schwartz says, "Walter, is he alive?"

And Matthau looks up and says, "Only in the double."

Hal laughed so hard I thought he was going to die right there.

I'll never forget that as long as I live.

Hal Ashby's memorial was very hard for me. I'd never been to one. I don't think I could ever go to another one. At the memorial, it's open, anybody can come. The Director's Guild holds 500 people? And there were maybe 250 people. The usual suspects were there. I was quite upset by who wasn't there. Jack wasn't there. Jane wasn't there. Voight wasn't there. I didn't like that, particularly for those three. They could have all come. They had a little program, and on the program was written, "These are the movies that Hal Ashby made." Each movie was represented by a person who was going to get up and talk. It was moderated by Jeff Bridges, who was in *Eight Million Ways to Die*. On the screen behind him is a picture of Hal Ashby in a little Porsche as he goes past Jane Fonda in another car at the end of *Coming Home*. It's the last time anybody ever saw Hal on film. That's the shot that's on the screen, frozen. One by one, everybody went up. I was the spokesman for *Coming Home*. After my turn, Andy Garcia, from *Eight Million Ways to Die*, got up. And then they just threw the floor open for anybody to speak. Lester Persky got up because he was Hal's partner, manager, agent. Sean Penn got up, which really shocked me. He had never worked with Hal. Sean had just come back from doing his sixty days up in Bridgeport for breaking the law. You can only break so many of Madonna's teeth. Bud Cort represented *Harold and Maude*. He walked up onstage, looked at the picture of Hal, then out at the audience. He simply said, "Well, I was Hal's favorite."

My next job was *World Gone Wild*, which had Lee Katzin as director, who was the assistant director on *Stoney Burke*. Bob Rosen was the producer, who was Mr. Frankenheimer's producer on *Black Sunday*. It was a futuristic movie where I played the old sage. We shot it outside of Tucson. I had two costars who were absolutely the most fun guys I ever worked with: Michael Paré, who was a fabulous guy, should have been a major movie star. He starred in a movie for Walter Hill called *Streets of Fire*, with Diane Lane, in which he was pretty good, a good-looking, big physical guy; and Adam Ant, who had just broken up the rock band, Adam and the Ants. I had no idea how big a star he was until we walked in the hotel one night and girls just descended on this guy. He's a little black-haired kid from Brighton, England. Adam and the Ants were huge. They were as big as Freddy Mercury and Queen. My wife and her mom were there, and Adam Ant was with these Druid-looking, black-haired girls, who looked like tiny, thin vampires. They were white-skinned, nasty-looking little girls, and they were pledged to him, and he said, "Whatever you want, Bruce."

I said, "Well, my wife and my mother-in-law . . ."

"Whatever you want, whatever they want."

There was a big lightning storm one night. All the lights went out, and we were in the huge hotel lobby, much like the Ahwahnee in Yosemite with high ceilings and a rock fireplace. It was like musical chairs. Everybody was running for the chairs to sit on, and my mother-in-law, Violet Rose, runs for a chair, sits down, and starts squirming because she's sitting on someone.

She gets up and says, "Oh my God, I'm sorry," because she's sitting on Wynonna Judd. Adam Ant sits down on Naomi Judd.

She says, "Wynonna, Adam Ant is sitting on my lap! Can you believe it? If only it was the other way around!"

We had a lot of fun. Filming was arduous, because the story was apocalyptic. The bad guys are pursuing us, we're defending our little gas station, which is nothing—a rubble of tires—and these fifty bikers dressed in white sheets are attacking. We're staving them off. There's fires, burning tires, and all kinds of shit. In the middle of it, Michael Paré and I are back to back. He's got a zip gun, and I have a cane that shoots lightning rods. He says, "Are we going to go down? You think this is what it was like at the Alamo?" And I say, "Well, we'll always have Paris." The whole movie was like that. The script writer, Jorge Zamacona, wrote funny shit. His mom was a biker from Milwaukee, a leather chick, who was tough, and into guys. She ran off with a crew member. Jorge wasn't a biker. He had a wife and lived in Hollywood and was just trying to be a writer. The script, Katzin, and Rosen were the reasons I did *World Gone Wild*.

When it came to *The 'burbs*, I got the role because Joe Dante, who directed it, was a Roger Corman guy and had always liked me. He grew up in Roger's stable. *Piranha* was Joe's first movie for Roger. Joe had girlfriends who were great-looking dames—quiet, wan, and strange, and they'd play with the L.A. Philharmonic. One was a violinist, and one was a cellist, and they were in different worlds than I was in. Carrie Fisher, who I didn't really know, was part of the film. There was the Corey Feldman kid, and he was really odd, different. I didn't realize he was a drugger and all screwed up at that time. He was a big star at that point. There was Tom Hanks, and I didn't know him. I met him on that movie, and he was wonderful. My wife in the film was Dick Schaal's daughter, and she was fabulous. Gale Gordon was in it. He was a good guy. Rick Ducommun was a big Canadian kid who everybody thought was going to be a big star. He was a funny kid. A nice kid. Henry Gibson was about as sweet a guy as you'll ever meet. Brother Theodore, who was the weird little Mr. Klopek character, had a one-man show in the Village in New York City. When I went to meet the producers, Joe laughed at my stuff. Larry Brezner, who was the manager of Rick Ducommun, was a writer on the script with Dana Olsen, who was the real writer, basically on his own. Brezner was a comedy producer who produced a show about six comediennes— Paula Poundstone, Lizz Winstead, among others—for HBO. Larry thought he knew comedy real well, and he did.

He came up to me afterward and said, "You're funny."

Olsen came up to me with a Cubs hat on and said, "You're a Chicago guy."

Chicago guys are like the Belushi Brothers. I'm not a Chicago guy. I'm eighteen to twenty miles north of Chicago. It's like saying, "Are you a Claremont guy or are you an L.A. guy?" I'm not a Chicago guy. Dana lives four blocks from Wrigley Field. He's a Chicago guy. It turns out Dana's roommate and writing partner is Robert Collector, who wrote and directed a movie I would do, *Believe in Me*.

The first day on *The 'burbs* I wasn't good, because I misunderstood the broadness of the comedy they were making. I saw nothing but pratfalls and fart jokes, and I thought, Oh God, I'm in the wrong fucking movie. I can't do that. I can't do fart jokes. The first thing I had to do was come out of my house and raise a flag. So I did and they laughed and they loved it, and I hated it.

I said, "It's cartoonish, it's not real."

Joe Dante printed it and said, "You know why I loved it? Nobody'd ever expect Bruce Dern to do that."

Larry Brezner came over to me, and I said, "I hated that. It's a cartoon. These other people are making a cartoon, and I don't want to be in a cartoon. I want to do it again."

Brezner said, "Let me talk to him."

I said, "No, I don't want a mouthpiece. I'll talk to him. Who are you anyway?"

He said, "I'm producing the movie."

I said, "What does Opie do?"

He said, "Who's Opie?"

"The red-haired kid there, Ron Howard, with the spiky-haired guy, Brian Grazer, what do they do?"

"Well, they're the executive producers. That's the company that's making it, Imagine."

"Brian Grazer lives three doors from me. They're miracle workers. They have something to do with this movie?"

"Yeah, they're the producers."

"Well, what do you do?"

"Well, I'm the producer of the movie. I brought the material to them."

I said, "Jesus, how many of you guys are there?"

He said, "I produce the funny stuff, they produce the movie. The movie got made because of them, but I brought the material to them."

I said, "I'll go talk to Joe Dante. Maybe Joe and I have something to say about what goes on in the movie. Or maybe I should talk to Tom Hanks. Oh, here's Rita Wilson. Maybe I should talk to her. She's Mrs. Tom Hanks. She's got a sister, Lily. Maybe I should talk to Lily Ibrahimoff."

He said, "Who's that?"

"That's Rita Wilson's real name, Rita Ibrahimoff."

"Ibrahimoff? That's not her name."

"Sure it is. John Ibrahimoff is the bartender at Hollywood Park. That's their father, in case you didn't know."

"Wait a fucking minute, Ibrahimoff? How do you get from Ibrahimoff to Wilson?"

"I don't know, they met on *Volunteers*."

"*Volunteers*? That movie with John Candy?"

"Tom Hanks, Rita Ibrahimoff, John Candy, they were all in the movie."

Larry said, "Jesus, you know all these things about these people. What are you, an encyclopedia?"

I said, "No. What I am is not funny in that scene we just did, and I want to do it again."

So the next morning, we came out. I did it again. I did it totally different, and it was correct.

Joe said, "I've just realized how the scene opens for you and what you're going to play in the movie now. When you come out of your front door and you raise that flag, I realized what you're trying to do in the movie. I realized the music for you, the opening theme from *Patton*. I couldn't have played that with what you did yesterday, but the way you did that today . . ."

I put my hand on my heart and I said, "That's why I'm here for Joe Dante, because Joe Dante fucking gets it."

I developed a relationship with Tom Hanks. I had more fun with him. He rented a home in the Malibu Colony that summer, and Laura was going with Renny Harlin, who was renting a home there. Hanks rented Frankenheimer's house, so he lived two doors from me, and we'd drive back and forth to work some days. He had a little yellow Volkswagen then. I was off one day, and *Big* opened while we were doing *The 'burbs*, and I went to see it. I was quite enamored of his work while we were filming together. I saw tremendous potential in him. I saw *Big* and called the set. He was working, but I didn't want to wait until I saw him the next day. I got him on the phone.

I said, "Hey, Bud, make no mistake, usually I use this in a threatening way, but not today, make no mistake about who's making this phone call to you. I've not seen a talent as unique as yours since I've been here. Go for it. Just choose differently. Your performance in *Big* is unparalleled to what I've seen, period."

He was very gracious and thanked me for taking him out of a scene to take the phone call.

He said, "I thought you were going to tell me to take Cleveland in the second game." He's a big Cleveland Indians fan.

I said, "Whatever you're thinking about doing, no small screen, stay on the big screen; you belong there, and do courageous things and don't make the safe choice. This certainly wasn't a safe choice. You did good with the little girl from New Trier [Elizabeth Perkins]."

I liked Carrie Fisher, who played Tom's wife in *The 'burbs*. I'll go on record as saying this: she's damaged goods, and it's all over her, but she's the only person I ever worked with who has the ability to work through being damaged. Heroically. But, goddamm it, she needs an arm around her every day, all day long. She is so fragile. She is beyond bright. You realize she could be as fabulous as anyone you'll meet in your life, but is right on the edge of taking herself to the other side. Nobody's going to get her but herself because of her lack of confidence. Something absolutely brilliant will come out of her mouth, and before the sentence is finished, she questions whether what she said was brilliant. She's a complex, complex girl, but she's fetching, and I wish I had had more time to spend around her.

· 2 6 ·

Hitting the Wall

The eighties died out for me. At the end of that decade, my career was trickling down into an area of not knowing what was going to happen next. The eighties ended up in what I felt was an unsuccessful, unfulfilled period for me. I didn't know where I fit in or what was going to happen next in my acting career, or in my running career, or in my life. I really didn't know what was going on. Andrea was just starting to get into her painting and becoming a little bit of an entity. People were starting to buy her work. Barbra Streisand bought one of her first paintings. Heather Locklear bought a painting. Pierce Brosnan bought one. People in the industry were starting to be aware of who she was. She was tentative about what was going to happen with her. She had painted for ten years and never showed anybody her work. I hadn't had a lot of success with the movies I really felt I'd put a lot into, like *On the Edge* or *Smile* or *Space*. They'd all had funny things befall them, so I was kind of in limbo.

243

Jason Patric had a lot to do with my being in *After Dark, My Sweet*, because I got a call out of the blue to come in and meet for it.* He never copped to it, but I thanked him anyway.

Tommy Signorelli, who I'd known since 1958, had just read before me and was coming out when I was going in for my interview. I thought, well shit, he's perfect. Why am I even going in? You know, they don't have any money. They can't pay much. And Tommy Signorelli doesn't go for much money and he's a good actor. He was in *Bang the Drum Slowly*. Even though that was seventeen years earlier. He's a good actor. He's everybody's buddy and he's a good athlete and a good sports fan and a good guy.

So I went in figuring they'll give the role to Tommy Signorelli. And I sit down and I talk to them and I don't read. I can't perform reading. I never will be able to, so I don't do it. I sat down, and I talked to them about the role and told them what I thought about it. I had a very strong lock on it and I understood what the movie was and I absolutely loved it.

In *After Dark, My Sweet*, I worked with Rachel Ward. She was a great trouper. And her husband, Bryan Brown, is a great guy. I hope they're still married.† He's a fabulous actor. *TV Guide* asked a bunch of us what our favorite movies of the seventies were. Mine is *Breaker Morant*. They asked "What about *Coming Home*?" *Breaker Morant* said the same things that all the Vietnam war films said, but from an Australian standpoint, about a British Vietnam. Britain didn't want to send their guys to South Africa. So they sent the children of the prisoners that had been sent to Australia, to Gallipoli and to the Transvaal. I was touched by that film. *Breaker Morant* is better than *The Deer Hunter, Coming Home*, and *Platoon* put together because it had no war, no pyrotechnics. It took place in a courtroom and held our attention by going back to the scene of the crime four times. But the crime wasn't war. The crime was a religious Bible salesman who had rifles in

---

*This modern-day noir was based on a novel by Jim Thompson, the writer behind *The Getaway, The Grifters*, and *This World, Then the Fireworks*. In the movie, Dern, Patric, and Rachel Ward plan to kidnap a kid to get a hefty ransom.

†They are.

the Bible boxes and fought under the guise of something else. It was Europe in Africa, defended by England, marked by Australians doing England's dirty work. Edward Woodward and Bryan Brown were fabulous playing two stalwart guys that faced up to it and were executed. You always think of Walter Huston in *Treasure of Sierra Madre*, talking about the wonderful way Mexicans have of executing bandits. "They have you dig your own hole and put your shovel down. They give you a cigarette. They let you say a little something to your friends, then put your hat back on. They blindfold you and you stand in front of the hole and they shoot you." It brings back moments in movies that make me proud to be an actor. Unfortunately, they're not movies that I was in but they're reasons that I continue to act and hope I get to have moments like that.

In my days working on *After Dark*, I became incredibly impressed with the gifts of the director, James Foley. When you realize that in a two-and-a-half-year period of time this man back-to-back directed *At Close Range*, *After Dark*, and *Glengarry Glen Ross*. I'll go to the mat for him any time he wants me to work for him. And look at the cast he put together in those three movies. Look at the actors who are willing to work for him. And look at the work that came out of those movies.

I had a good time on *After Dark*. The only time it wasn't good was at Thanksgiving. We worked Thanksgiving Day, and it pissed Andrea off because Thanksgiving dinner's a big deal to her. Not the celebration of the event, but the meal: the turkey, the stuffing, mashed potatoes, sweet potatoes, pumpkin pie, two kinds of gravy. She wants that. And we were staying at La Quinta and they had a feast. The crew elected to work Thanksgiving Day because then they got Friday, Saturday, and Sunday off. So I didn't get back to the hotel. We had the evening meal on the set, but that's not a Thanksgiving meal. So she went bonkers. Andrea's tough. She missed her Thanksgiving turkey. I called her.

And she said, "I'm not going to go in the dining room and get cranberries by myself."

I said, "Well, I'll call them. I'll have them bring you—"

"Oh, yeah, sure. I'm going to eat my Thanksgiving dinner in front of the TV watching *Starsky & Hutch* or some grim, goddamn TV show."

Oh my God. She was unhappy. And every Thanksgiving, it always comes up. "Maybe we should drive to La Quinta and I should eat my dinner by myself." Oh God.

I'm very proud of *After Dark, My Sweet*. In the movie I do one of the better scenes I've done in my career, where Jason Patric and I have an actual three-minute scene of one hundred percent moment-to-moment behavior. I felt that I was reaching Jason and I felt it was the best work he'd done in his career. I thought that was a platform and that he would go up from there. As I watch his career, the closest he's gotten to that is in *Your Friends & Neighbors*, when he tells that story in the locker room, the Timmy story. But when he tells the story, he embroiders a little bit. And I think to this day, Ben Stiller thinks that there was a Timmy in Jason's life. When I met Ben, I said, "I don't know if you know this but Jason's bisexual. And there have been several Timmys in Jason's life. He wasn't bullshitting when he told you that story." Jason and I had planned all this. He's a good kid, Ben Stiller. I thought, at one time, I was going to do a movie with him, *Dodgeball*, but the director, Rawson Marshall Thurber, didn't think I was funny. I met with him and Vince Vaughn. I like Vince. I didn't know much about him. He said he went to Highland Park High School, which is a rival of New Trier. It's the next town. I was shocked because he's so big. I had no idea he was that big, six feet six or seven. And he's funny. I thought I had an inside track on the movie, but Thurber didn't want me. Rip Torn got the part.

These kids today cannot tell the truth to your face. They have so much respect for you because they grew up watching your movies that they would rather talk about the admiration they have for you than tell you you're one of nine for a role. They love all nine guys so they tell all nine they've got the part. Well, with Frankenheimer, Ashby, and all those guys, you came in and you knew, not this time, maybe next time. It's not going to happen. Or Gadg, "Love your work, I just don't see you playing the part of Nick or Tim."

There are a couple of things that bother me about the younger guys I've worked with. I see a lack of discipline from take one to take two to take three. And I see that more often than not. I see a lack of training and ability to get through the day without the mind wandering. I don't see excitement about coming to work every day. It excites me when I see forty people excited to come to work behind the camera. There is a mentality in front of the camera that, from the minute we arrive, we're getting screwed somehow. The actor is getting screwed. That wasn't there before the independent film. The crew is getting their money. Are they getting screwed? Yeah. But they're volunteering to get screwed because they're working outside the union and they know those are the rules. They signed on to do that before the movie was made. There's no need for the actor to be screwed because the producer who owns the movie is going to make his money down the road. The actor generally is not a participant in that so he's working for scale.* SAG allows the actors to get screwed so they'll have more actors working. In other words, the union is involved in solving the problems of 120,000 of its constituents, which I guess is its job.

Last year they said 3,100 actors made a living wage. That's 3 percent. We have got to work that out. You can't do a movie where one guy gets twenty-five million and everybody else works for scale. It's just not right. Nobody has the guts to take on the guy who gets twenty-five million. Why can't he get twenty-two million so the other ten people in the movie don't have to work for scale? I've been in movies like that, and it conveys a sense that isn't healthy from the very beginning. The stars that allow that to happen have to examine themselves real carefully before they go forward. It's on them. Any actor who's in a movie that allows that to happen has his head in the sand. The star that says, "I don't worry about what the other actors get" should know about it. You don't need to know individually what they get. But are they being taken care of? And if your producer won't tell you that and you find out during the course of the movie that there are ten people in the movie getting a thousand a week while you're getting fifteen million,

---

*Scale means the union minimum, which is a few hundred dollars a day. Actors with more clout can not only draw a larger salary but get a percentage of the total take. Dern's friend Jack Nicholson is considered the modern master, having made a rumored $50 million for playing the Joker in Tim Burton's *Batman*, when all was said and done. A person can also participate in the profits by arranging to get a share of the net—the revenue minus the costs—but Hollywood is famous for making every movie, even the biggest blockbusters, look like a loser in the accounting books.

it's not right. If you've got Kris Kristofferson, Elliott Gould, Bruce Dern, George Segal, Jimmy Caan, Donald Sutherland, and some hot kid, and we're working for a thousand a week, and the star's getting twenty million, that's not right. It's not ethical, and if he doesn't correct that, then it's on him. Now if the group is good enough, they will level the playing field while the switch is on, but we still have to go home and maintain a lifestyle.

In our business, the studios give it to them because they can open a movie. Did Ben Affleck open *Gigli*? I guess Tom Cruise must be worth it because he can open a brown paper bag. I think you're worth what you can get. But I'm not doing the paying. We're just limping along trying to get whatever we can get for doing a movie.

I did a TV movie called *Carolina Skeletons* starring Lou Gossett, where I got to work with director John Erman, who had been the casting director on *Stoney Burke* thirty years earlier. He was a Chicago guy and had been an actor in *Blackboard Jungle*. I got to stay in Buckhead, near Atlanta. I'd never been to Buckhead. I met Julia Roberts's mom, who is an acting teacher and was around the set for a day. She lives in Alpharetta, and I realized that Julia didn't walk in from a pumpkin patch. She knew how to hit before she ever came to Hollywood. She didn't fall off the turnip truck. That was consoling.

On a Friday night before Labor Day in '91, I got a phone call from a CAA agent, who said, "Bruce, they're sending you a script. It's called *Diggstown*."

I said, "I don't know anything about it."

She said, "They start shooting on Monday."

I said, "No, they're not. Monday's Labor Day."

"Bruce, don't argue with me. They start shooting in Sacramento, Monday, on a movie called *Diggstown*."

"No, they're not. Nobody shoots on Labor Day."

"Don't argue with me. You're going to get the script. You have to accept it or not tonight."

"What do you mean?"

"They're going to give you a hundred thousand dollars. They need you for eight weeks. At eleven tomorrow morning, you have to be at

MGM, because they're having a reading. Michael Ritchie's the director, Lou Gossett's the star, and James Woods is the costar. You're the third star, but you're not above the title. It's Lou Gossett and James Woods."

"I'm not above the title? Is it an equal part?"

"Yeah, it's an equal part."

"Is it a good part?"

"Yeah. You're the heavy."

"What's it about?"

"Boxing."

"I don't box."

"You don't have to box."

"Is it good?"

"Yeah, it's good."

"Where's Fred on this?"

"He's not here. It's Labor Day weekend."

I said, "Well, where are my other agents?"

She said, "You don't have one right now. It's just me."

"Why are you there?"

"Because Pam Prince is away."

Pam Prince was my real agent. I said, "She's the best agent I have except for Fred."

"She's not feeling well, and blah, blah, blah. So you have to take it. So do you want to do it or not?"

"Why?"

"Because it's five minutes of eight and they want an answer and if they don't have one in five minutes they're going to go to another actor."

"I haven't read the script."

"Take it or leave it."

"I can't do that. I haven't read the script. What if it's awful?"

She said, "Take my word for it, it's not awful."

"Can I call Michael Ritchie? He and I speak the same language. I did *Smile*."

"Take it or leave it. You don't have time to call Michael Ritchie."

I said, "Well, I'd like to call Michael Ritchie."

She said, "If you call Michael Ritchie, you won't get the role."

I said, "Why don't I just gamble that I'll get the role and I'll call Michael Ritchie."

"Mark my words, you won't get the role."

"Why do I think somehow that you know something that I don't know?"

"Because I handle the actor that they're going to next."

"Then you have two offers at one time."

"Maybe."

So I said, "Okay, I'll do it."

And she said, "You really want to do it?"

"Yeah, I'll take the role. I'll do it for a hundred thousand, no billing."

"What do you mean no billing?"

"I want to go uncredited. No billing."

"Well, you can't take no billing as the third lead in the movie. You're in every scene."

"I want no billing. Just give me the hundred thousand. Give me Michael Ritchie's number. I'll take it."

The next morning at eleven, I go to the meeting. On that Saturday, Southern Cal was playing its first game of the year against Memphis State. They weren't playing until one, and it was one of those foggy September days where the whole city's fogged in and it's not going to burn off. The meeting was in a new MGM office building, all that was left of MGM. Sony had taken over the MGM lot. Michael Ritchie was waiting outside on the steps for me, and he said, "Big Bob, I know, I know," as I walked up. Big Bob's the guy I played in *Smile*.

Ritchie said, "You were in the movie from day one, but I had to go through all the shenanigans. Lou Gossett and I wanted you from day one. And it's Lou's movie, so to speak. James Woods is going to be in it, but we had to fight for him, and then I had to fight for you. The studio wanted a bunch of other people above you in the pecking order. But you're here."

I said, "The agent stuck it to me."

"But you're here. So come up. Have you read the script?"

I said, "It never got to me. She didn't call me until eight last night."

He said, "What do you mean? She had the offer at noon yesterday."

I asked, "Who else did you offer it to?"

"What do you mean who else did I offer it to? We didn't offer it to anybody. We offered it to you."

"She said if I didn't take it you were going to go to somebody else."

"No. She's been pitching Donald Sutherland for three days to us. And we kept insisting on you. We weren't going to use Donald Sutherland. He can't play the part the way you can."

I said, "I see what's going on."

He said, "When Fred gets back after Labor Day weekend, you better sit down and have a talk about this girl."

Well, she was gone about a week or two after this incident. I suddenly became aware that there were certain teammates in the building that were not teammates for everybody else. She wasn't even my agent. But she was the only one minding the store Labor Day weekend. So, when the call finally got passed down the ranks, they gave it to her. She tried to avoid calling me until the last minute, hoping I would pass and she could get the part for Donald Sutherland. Anyway, we did the movie, and I had a wonderful time. *Diggstown* was a good movie. I had my buddy Ritchie back. I had a scene where I had to get all my fighters together and give them a pep talk before fight night. I didn't remember that Jim Caviezel was one of those ten fighters. I forgot that he was in *Diggstown* until I went to do *Madison* in 1999, and Jim Caviezel was the star of it.

He said, "I'll never forget that locker room speech you gave us because I got punished when I started laughing. I couldn't believe that an actor could come up with anything like what you said. You turned on me because I was laughing in the shot. And you said, 'You think that's funny?' because you knew that shot would be cut if you didn't make a comment on it, and your stuff wouldn't be used and we'd have to do it again. And so you turned on me, incorporating what I was doing into the shot so they wouldn't cut it. Michael Ritchie let it go because he knew what you were doing to save the shot. I've never seen anyone move that fast in my life to be able to think like that."

I said, "On that day I laughed because I said to Ritchie, 'Now look, I'm going to do this scene the way it's written. But at the end of it, keep the camera running because I want to do a Dernser.' And Ritchie said to me, 'I'm going to get a Dernser?' I said, 'Yeah.' He said, 'God, I need three or four every movie I do. On *Smile* you gave me four,'" and he named them off: One is "Who's been fooling with my thermostat?" Another one is when I'm selling the pregnant couple the motor home and I pat the little girl on the stomach and I say, "God, how wonderful. You're going to own this thing. And just imagine how wonderful you'll feel sitting on top of five hundred gallons of gasoline with a little bun in the oven on the open road. That's got to make you feel comfortable." And then when I walk into the jail to see Nicholas Pryor, who's in there because he shot his wife. The inmates are whistling at me and humming. These are real inmates because we shot it in the Santa Rosa jail. They're not actors. One guy yells at me, "Hold your head up high when you walk down that goddamn corridor. You're amongst real prisoners here, Bud." Somebody else yells something as I go by. Nobody told them to. They just did it. The camera's been on me all the way as I get to Nick Pryor's cell. As I go into his cell I ad-libbed, "Sounds of the Big House." The fourth one is when I'm talking to the two Marines at the end of the movie, and I say, "You guys are in the second division, huh?" They say, "Yes sir." I say, "Yeah. I was in the second division. We held the Chosin reservoir." And they don't know what the fuck the Chosin reservoir is. Anybody who'd been to Korea would know because that's the reservoir where 2,100 Marines fought, and only 64 guys survived it, but they held the reservoir, which turned the tide of the Korean War. I wasn't in it, but I pretended that I was. They ignore me and one says to the other, "Did you see the tits on Miss Anaheim?" It's just the incongruity of it.

I said to Michael, "Just tell the other actors the camera's going to keep rolling and Dern might add a little something, and not to start cutting out or start talking or break the action of the scene." So, when I get done with the scene, I continue, "Now I want us all to grab hands in a circle here. Come on. You, Robbie, let's grab hands. Yes, hold hands." Everybody grabs hands. "Now get down on your knees. Dear God, please give us the strength to rip this black man limb from limb."

Ritchie said, "Cut. Print. We're out of here." All of them burst out laughing and applauded, including the black guys.

Nine years later, Caviezel says to me, "I can't believe that a guy would have the ability to look at me, turn on me, and say what you did and it stays in. But to make that up right on the spot, get away with it. Not having it be off-color. Have it work perfectly. I'm religious and it didn't offend me and it's so perfect for the movie. It's that moment that made me decide I wanted to be an actor and pursue it and that it wasn't a game."

I'm not going to volunteer things to actors unless I find them floundering. It's not my job. You never know what's in their heads, and sometimes they think you're fucking with them — is he trying to screw me up so I'll be bad and he'll be better in the scene than me? They're very cautious and wary of you, depending on who you are, so you've got to be careful. If they're bigger stars, they think you're trying to steal the movie. I never understood that kind of thinking, stealing movies, stealing scenes.

I saw an actor struggling on *Diggstown* and I gave him some help, and he got better from it, but he has not been courteous in his treatment of me in interviews. We'll meet up again one time soon. He gets a great deal of work and ascended to starring in two TV series. Neither one lasted more than a season. I don't know why he doesn't entertain me; he's good, he just wasn't very good in *Diggstown*. I gave him hints and he used them, and they were effective, but Oliver Platt bores the shit out of me.

On *Diggstown*, I was very enamored of James Woods and his work. He's got tremendous abilities. He's inventive, he's creative. Puzzling in a positive way and a great partner. As a teammate, you'd pick him every time. He's in your first group.

The role I played in *Diggstown* is one of those characters least like Bruce Dern. The nasty guys with no compassion. *The Cowboys, The Driver*. The enraged guys. The bikers. Kinsky in *Tattoo*. The sadistic bastard. The motherfuckers are the guys most removed from me and the hardest to play.

Michael Ritchie passed away in 2004. I miss him a lot. He was a terrific guy. Very talented. Funny. Witty. Wonderful guy. Laughed openly. His wife was the superintendent of schools for Marin County. His parents were both Stanford professors.

Tom Hanks's sister is some kind of superintendent of schools for the Sacramento School District. Tom's got an interesting family, too. They're all nurses at high levels or academic, particularly interested in kids.

When I did the Amelia Earhart movie for TV, I thought Diane Keaton was very peculiar. She has a sexuality about her, but she's puzzling to me. Of all the actresses I've worked with, she's the one actress I got to know the least but wanted to know the most. I wanted to have some kind of relationship. I didn't feel she let me in. Keaton and I, left alone, could have raised the bar a little bit. The problem was, we only had two or three scenes together, and then she vanished on me. What I miss in my relationship with her is the same relationship portrayed in the movie, and I'm not sure I don't get the two confused. In other words, I started to fall for Diane Keaton just like George Putnam fell for Amelia Earhart, and then she was taken away from him because she went off and never came back. He spent the rest of his life wondering if she was still out there. I see Diane Keaton still out there, but I've never seen her since the last day of shooting. Yet, she left me an absolutely beautiful message after she saw the cut of the film about how wonderful she thought my work was. I was so grateful to hear that from her because she's got game. She can bring it.

· 27 ·

Apocalypse Marriage, Redux

M rs. *Munck* was tough, because Diane wrote and directed it.* Diane was playing herself as an elderly lady, and Kelly Preston was playing Diane as a young lady. Diane and I were dealing with a tragedy in our own life, and Kelly was playing Diane going through that tragedy. Laura was in Toronto at the same time doing a movie with Vanessa Redgrave and Raul Julia, who was not feeling well.[†]

---

*Based on a novel by Ella Leffland, this 1995 movie by Diane Ladd was her only directorial effort. Ladd and Dern had two children together, one of whom died in a tragic accident, and they divorced almost three decades before this movie was filmed. In the movie, Ladd plays a woman who had an affair in her youth with a cruel man, which led to a child who died in a tragic accident. Three decades later, she takes a job caring for the cruel man, now blind and in a wheelchair, and she tortures him. For the cruel ex-lover, she cast Dern. Method acting indeed.

†Julia knew that he had cancer but continued to act, and he died from a cancer-related stroke before *Down Came a Blackbird* was released.

Diane cast Shelley Winters, who was also not feeling well, in the movie. She happens to be Laura's godmother.* Travolta came to the location in Toronto having just finished shooting the Quentin Tarantino movie *Pulp Fiction*. He knew he had something in the can that was going to revive his career. He's a good guy. When I was in *Sweet Bird of Youth* on Broadway, Diana Hyland was the ingénue star of the play. She was the girl who went with Travolta when Travolta broke out, even though she was about twelve years older than he was. She died of cancer in her early thirties. She was a good friend of mine. So I knew John before John was John. I knew Diana pretty well while she was with John. There's a history there. He's a little uncomfortable around me.

Anyway, Diane's wonderful to work with. She's a very good actress, but I felt, who gives a shit? Who's going to see a movie about Diane and me? Why are Diane Ladd and Bruce Dern interesting? It's not us, it's a couple, it's a story, but is the story really that strong? It was a Showtime movie. I don't know if it did well or didn't do well or belonged in the marketplace at all. The film was not easy to make, because we were a divorced couple. But throughout the course of the acrimonious years came this magical little wunderkind who bound us together. To try and recapture that thirty years later for two months in a movie somehow was worth it, only because the treasure was in town with us making another movie, and we all got to see each other at supper. That was fun. But I'm living with a wife who I'd been married to, at that time, twenty-five years, and down the hall in the next suite is my ex-wife and across the hall is my kid's boyfriend's brother and sister making a documentary about us. It was tough. Every day we're dredging up stuff from our lives. I always got the feeling that everybody was looking at Diane and me to see, well, is there something going on there? Every night I'm going in the hotel room and there's Andrea. And Andrea couldn't give a fuck who laughs about

*It's not uncommon for Diane Ladd to make a film a family affair. She costarred with Laura Dern in five movies, including *Rambling Rose*, for which they both earned Academy Award nominations.

Diane and me. She knew how I felt about the relationship. Diane got me paid well and everything was fair.

I'm doing a scene in a car with Kelly where she tells me she's pregnant. She gives me a little present. It's a little lamb in a box. This is a no-no to me. I'm not married to her. She's my secretary and I've fallen in love with her. I don't want her to have a kid, so I tell her to get rid of it. So we shoot the scene.

Diane says to Kelly, "When you give him the box, honey, you can't do it thataway. This is Bruce Dern. This motherfucker. You've got to be tough to work for this motherfucker. But you've got to do it sweetly, hon. You've got to present it like this. You can't anticipate he's going to cut your fucking heart out."

Then she comes around the car to me. She says, "Bruce, honey, you've got to do me a favor in this scene. This ain't *Black Sunday*. You're not killing John Wayne. Have a little compassion. The girl is crying her eyes out. She's giving this to you. You don't have to cut her fucking gut out. Don't tear this girl's heart out, for Christ's sake, you dirty rotten filthy bastard! What the fuck is the matter with you?"

There's sixty people standing there, and Diane's trying to get me to be sweet and nice, and she's dragging up eight years of a bad marriage and how much she hates me. And I'm trying to do take two! This little girl is giving me a lamb in a box, telling me she's carrying my baby, and I don't want her to have the goddamn baby.

I say, "Diane, we're getting ready to make a shot here. We're not doing history. We're halfway through a movie. The sun's going to set in about nine minutes."

She says, "I'm a priestess. I can make sun. I've got an arc right there. All I need to do is light the sum'bitch and we'll have sun 'til nine thirty, you prick."

This is the movie, day after day after day. I've got a scene in a house with Shelley Winters. She's been nominated for about seven Oscars and won two or three. She was Lee Strasberg's confidant. She was, in her day, quite an outstanding-looking girl. Gives a performance in the Montgomery Clift movie (*A Place in the Sun*) where she's very, very good. She's always good playing a girl with a nasty edge to her. She can act. She was the first of the Lee Strasberg–trained actors or actresses that he allowed to teach at the Actors Studio in New York City.

When we did *Bloody Mama*, she was the only one that had Bobby DeNiro's ear. She would turn in the middle of a scene and say, "Don't you do that." He would freeze when Shelley would say anything, because she was like his mom as far as his career went at that time. She vouched for him and put up with anything he did up to a point, and when she decided to stop it, he'd stop it. She's twenty-seven years beyond that, and she's not feeling well. She doesn't breathe particularly well. She's only got one scene, and it's about this old English tea set that she has. She's a sister of Diane's in the movie. I play this cantankerous guy who used to be married to Diane and who's now coming back into her life at seventy. I'm dependent on her because I'm so incorrigible no one wants to take care of me anymore. She comes back after almost forty years of being out of my life, as the member of the ex-family, and says, "I don't love him anymore, but I'll take care of him."

My family leaves me off at her house in my wheelchair, and they all say, "We got rid of him. He's such a cantankerous prick. She'll take care of him."

I get in the house, she closes the door, and says, "Hey old man, remember me?"

I say, "Yeah, I remember you, you fucking cunt. What are you going to do?"

She says, "Watch this, you prick." She goes to the toilet and dumps all my pills in it. She takes my needles and breaks them.

I say, "You can't do that. I'm a diabetic."

She says, "Sugar, you ain't gonna have no sugar. You like Coca-Cola and you like to bet on sports, don't you? Well, there's two things that don't happen in my house. When we were together, you loved anything that had to do with balls. You liked to swing them balls and bat them balls and let me carry them balls around in my hand and put them balls in my mouth. Ain't no balls anymore. Ain't gonna be no ball games, ain't gonna be no betting on balls. But I play a game with a ball. I hit golf balls. I'm going to put you in a moving walker and I'm going to tote you around behind my golf cart and you're going to watch me hit balls because I play thirty-six holes of golf every day. You motherfucking cocksucker."

It's an outrageous script, funny and devilish and very, very sad at times, particularly for me, because we rehash stuff.

At one point, Diane says, "We're going to resurrect our marriage in this scene. You always wanted to do something real. You always wanted to do something for posterity. We're going to make people remember what our marriage was, and we're going to preserve it on film."

I say, "Roll the fucking camera."

She says, "Don't you mess with me once this camera's rolling. I'm still the director. I can cut it any way I want."

I say, "You could never cut it."

The cameraman, Jim Glennon, who shot Alexander Payne's films and later shot *Madison* with me, is rolling two cameras. He's on the B camera with sound and the A camera is an Arriflex without sound. We're sitting at the bottom of a stairway.

She says, "You've been with me how long? A year and a half?"

I say, "Something like that."

She says, "You're out of the chair. You're well."

I say, "A well's a hole in the ground."

She says, "There you go. You just can't behave yourself, can you?"

I say, "Well, what's behavior?"

She says, "You just won't stick to text," and we were off because now we're not on the page, but she knows I'm going to go where she's going to take me, and she's going to go where I'm going to take her. And at the end of the scene, we're going to be together. We know it can't be more than two and a half pages because it'll clutter the end of the movie. I see Diane starting to maneuver her way, heading for one of her classic breakdowns. An emotional breakdown for Miss Diane is pre-Nagasaki, where everybody's going to die, and whoever doesn't is going to be a Baco-Bit. She's running around, and I'm saying, "Getting ready for a big one, aren't you?"

She says, "Maybe. Why shouldn't I? You took everything I had. You left me with no career. No life. Nothing."

I say, "You ended up doing pretty well. Married a guy whose dad built a ballpark.* The kid was a fuck-up so he ended up with no money. You then got a career. Won all kinds of awards." We never made her an actress. "Then you took an old geezer back in your life. Got every ounce of livelihood out of his body so he ended up with a bunch of dead ends, and threw him a bone which he had to share with you."

She says, "What have you got to offer a woman for the next five years of her life?"

I say, "Don't go there. You came to me once and you said, 'How can I be better? They've offered me an opportunity to do something. You can make me better if you give me some advice.' And I gave you the advice. And what did that advice do for you?"

She says, "It gave me a chance to be famous. It launched my career."[†]

I say, "Exactly right. We have no further discussion, Madame. This discussion is over. You know what I'm going to do? I'm going to wheel myself out of this house and I'm never going to see you again. This discussion is over and, ladies and gentlemen," and I look right into Jim's lens, "this film is over. This film never had a chance because it's about nobody and it's about nothing. Our lives are really nothing."

I wheel out the door of the house, and Jim Glennon cuts back to Diane and she says, "You know what? He may be right." That's the way the movie ends.

It was tough working with her. The incongruity of what I lived with for eight years was the incongruity of what I went through for eight weeks on that movie. Sometimes she brings it; sometimes she doesn't.

Miss Diane and I had a rough time, but Andrea and I have a magical existence. I could not imagine waking up in bed without her next to me. Or going to sleep at night without her next to me. Nor could she. But she does not want me by her side the fourteen hours of daylight. And vice versa. It's not that I don't want her there or she doesn't

---

*After Bruce Dern, Ladd married William A. Shea Jr.

†Bruce gave Diane some funny lines to ad-lib as Flo the waitress in *Alice Doesn't Live Here Anymore,* for which she was nominated for an Academy Award and won a BAFTA for Best Supporting Actress.

want me there. She's got an agenda, I've got an agenda. I'm not a guy who can stay home during the day. I like to go out, do my thing, and come back to my house. My thing is very simple. I live in a house in Pasadena, and I keep my mailbox in Santa Monica so I don't have to wean myself off the Westside.

By the end of our time in Malibu, I felt cut off from the rest of the world. After making that drive, after having the mountain come down, after being hit by the ocean. The ocean's not your friend. The ocean hates you. The ocean wants your home. The state doesn't want you to have beach. They want the public to have your beach and the public's entitled to it. Below the mean high tideline. So you're in a constant battle there. The siren goes off and the bells on the abbey go off to let you know fire is coming. The fire can only go one place, to your house because it starts in the Valley and can only go one way. To the ocean. The fires occur during the Santa Anas, and the Santa Anas come from the east, and they're going to burn to the sea. No matter how you cut it. You're going to get cut off at Topanga and you're going to get cut off at Point Dume. So you're trapped. Twenty-seven years in the Colony was enough. I'd had it. I had to get out. For me, it was time to go.

I felt isolated, I felt cut off, and I felt that I wasn't sure in the late nineties if the industry, number one, remembered who I was, knew who I was, gave a shit about who I was. I knew I did but I knew that I wasn't working. I didn't know what the reason was. I thought that somehow, once the phone started ringing, that it was going to ring forever. No. Once an actor turns fifty, he's got to almost annually reinvent himself.

I then went back to work for Walter Hill on *Last Man Standing.**
I have a good time with him. Not everybody does. I love him. He's creative. He gets me. I get him. I know where he's going. I like Bruce Willis. A pretty gifted gambler, and a big-time bettor. He did something that's quite amazing. He comes from Penn's Grove, which is

---

*This 1996 Bruce Willis vehicle is essentially a remake of Sergio Leone's 1964 *A Fistful of Dollars* (which was itself a remake of Akira Kurosawa's 1961 film, *Yojimbo*) in Depression-era America, starring Dern and Christopher Walken. Dern and Hill had previously worked together on *The Driver* and *Wild Bill*.

south of Camden in New Jersey. It's right across from Philadelphia. They have a pier like the Santa Monica Pier. It was a big part of his youth and the place went in the toilet. He took four million dollars and revived it and put his dad in charge of it. He put his money where his mouth was. He's a good guy. He travels with an entourage, not to mention all the kids with the different names. They're good kids. He's got a cook and a masseuse and a driver. He's got an organized group of people that are disorganized. He never flaunts it. He has a good time. He is good with the suggestions he makes to you while shooting a scene. He's a good listener to ideas. He's a guy I would like to do a whole movie with where I'm on equal footing with him.[*] He totally respected me, and I had total respect for him. He could do a great many more things than they ask him to do in movies. He is not cast as well as he could be. He wants to do challenging roles, but the industry doesn't permit him to be cast in those projects. It's not his fault. He was so enormously successful financially to studios in the *Die Hard* films he doesn't get some of the roles he should get that other people get. He's certainly on the same level with the best actors in his age group.

We shot *Last Man Standing* at the Gene Autry Ranch across from Master's College in Santa Clarita, California.

One day on the set, Walter says, "I've got a guy coming here to visit me. He loves you. He loves all your work and everything about you, and he's the next you." It was Bill Paxton, who later played my son in HBO's *Big Love* series.

I said to Paxton, "Walter says you're me."

He said, "No, you have it wrong. My dad is you. My dad knows every movie you made, every line you said. He's in Texas."

I said, "Let's all get up and go to Texas. Shut the movie down, Walter, who gives a shit?"

I was surprised more people didn't go see the movie. My theory was Bruce Willis is one of those guys that audiences will go to see if he's a

---

*Dern got his wish in the Polish brothers' film, *The Astronaut Farmer*, costarring Bruce Willis, Billy Bob Thornton, and Virginia Madsen.

victim and kills. But if he's a gun for hire, the audience doesn't like to see him kill indiscriminately for money. Everybody dies in the movie except me and little William Sanderson, a very unheralded actor who's very good. I'm glad he has a part in *Deadwood*, where he gets a chance to show things. That's a Walter guy.

I did the voice of a toy for the film, *Small Soldiers*. The movie made a lot of money. So the residuals were good. The guy that voiced the bad marauding soldier in the movie was Clint Walker. I don't know that he's ever played a bad guy. He's one of the biggest men I've ever seen in my life. He's like six feet seven and weighs about 260. Oh my God. He did the TV series called *Cheyenne*. One summer he did a movie where he got shot with a real arrow. He broke it in half and pulled it through his chest.

The Haunting was fun because the size and enormity of the production was big. I'd never been in a $100 million movie. We went to England on it. I got to work with my girl from New Trier, Lili Taylor, and Catherine Zeta-Jones, whom I'd never met. It was nice to meet Liam Neeson. We were doing a scene in this big greenhouse when, halfway through the first take, Liam started laughing and had to stop.

The director, Jan de Bont, said, "Liam? Wrong is what?" Instead of saying, "What is wrong?"

They got their fingers in dikes all day long.

Liam said, "I just can't believe it. I'm acting with Bruce Dern. The guy blew up the Super Bowl. I'm acting with Bruce Dern and on the first take he made me laugh."

De Bont said, "You're not supposed to laugh."

Liam said, "Well, he does that to you. He's the caretaker. He's warning me. But it's the way he warned me. The line on the page looks so flat but it's obviously not."

Marian Seldes, who played my wife in the movie, is another great dame. This was a woman who was a friend and confidante of Garson Kanin and Ruth Gordon during their entire marriage. When Miss Gordon died, Miss Seldes married Garson Kanin and took care of him the last fifteen years of his life. She starred on Broadway her entire career, made occasional movies, and ran Juilliard. She taught every kid that came out of the school since 1962. She's got the best moment in *The Haunting*. Liam Neeson, Catherine Zeta-Jones, and Lili Taylor are there, and Miss Seldes says, "Now, I'm leaving. My husband and I leave every night at five thirty. We'll be back at eight o'clock in the morning. If you need anything during the nighttime, there is a telephone. Don't bother to use it because in the night, in the dark, no one will come." And she leaves. Now you realize, this will be a good movie. Too bad it never quite got there.

When I was right at the end of the worst part of my slump in the nineties in moviemaking, where I had nothing going on, I did a movie in Mexico called *If . . . Dog . . . Rabbit* that was written and directed by Matthew Modine. It was shot in Rosarito Beach four weeks after *Titanic* had left. Well, the Rosarito Beach folks were spoiled. We only had an $800,000 budget.

Modine, who had never directed anything, was a sensational kid. David Keith was in it, and he's a really good actor. I just didn't know much about him. I do remember him in *Lords of Discipline*, and I thought, whew, who is this kid? He worked for Franc Roddam, who can direct. People forget that that was a very good movie. Twenty years ahead of its time. It was twisted. It was southern. Race was in it. Pat Conroy–like, but many more layers of stuff. Then I saw him in *An Officer and a Gentleman* and he was good, but he turned out to be a pathetic Tennessee Vols fan.

Anyway, I refuse to stay in Mexico because I realize what the populace of Rosarito Beach, which is only thirty miles below Tijuana, must be feeling after the withdrawal of the gazillion-dollar *Titanic* where everybody got paid for a year and a half. Now an $800,000 movie that has no budget comes in and the populace isn't gonna understand why there's no work for anybody. It's a little tiny movie, and those that do work are gonna work for twelve cents an hour, so I stay in San Diego. I have my driver who's a girl who was fired off *Titanic* because she was American. They were all San Diego State girls or Point Loma girls or Nazarene girls who used to say, "We'll drop out." They had rings in every hole they had. They were great dames. They were my kind of chicks. I love girls like that. They were foxes, and they were nasty and they were everything else, but they could drive. They knew every place in the city. They knew every route in and out of Mexico. They knew all the border guards. They knew everything. They were tough, and they knew how to handle it, but they got fed up after the first few weeks on *Titanic* because they were not getting paid well and they were being taken advantage of, so they quit or were fired or laid off. They were naturally made for Matthew Modine.

So I get to the set, which was a gas station on top of a hill above Rosarito Beach where you could see 360 degrees and not see a sign of the twentieth century. In the movie, I owned that gas station where I employed Matthew Modine, who was just out of jail. The theme of the movie was that El Cordobas was fighting a bull-fight in two weeks in Tijuana, and these kids that had all grown up together in San Diego decided that because El Cordobas had come from Spain, which was a big deal, they were going to rob the gate receipts while he was fighting. They were going to hit the box office, take all the receipts, and split. They had it very well organized, and they were going to pull this off and they do. Modine worked with me at the gas station. I didn't know anything. I was just an old-timer, a wise old sage, and had done my thing in my lifetime.

The first day on the set, I'm kind of the honorary veteran to these guys. Matthew's flying around. He and I have this long scene, we shoot the master, and then he shoots all my coverage. He says, "That's great. Now, we'll move over here." Matthew's a good kid and he's been an extraordinarily good actor sometimes. He makes good choices and has boundless energy. He was just flying all day long, in and out, up and down, just couldn't be better.

He said, "Now we're making movies, this is fucking movies, man. I mean this is a movie."

We're getting near the end of the day and we're losing the sun. There was a great deal of respect for me about the scene and what I did and how I worked. It was the beginning of the movie, but I had to ask, "Matthew, have you got it together here?"

He said, "What do you mean? That's a weird statement."

I said, "You know the scene that we did this morning and most of the afternoon, you never shot yourself."

"Oh my God, oh my God. I never did my close-up."

"No. So you gotta be on me except in the master."

"Oh my God. Oh my God. You're right. You think we need it? It wouldn't just play on you?"

I said, "Don't fuck me like that man. I'm not Mount Rushmore. I mean, shit, you're the scene; you're the star of the movie. Now you're not gonna be in every shot. You can cut to a tree or the gas pump or David Keith can drive his car up and we could just stay on his hood. You gotta do something, Bud."

He said, "Well, we can just go back, and I can spit the words out and we can do it in eight or nine minutes. We'd better do that."

He saved it, he was cool, he was just whipping around so much, he forgot it. But the enthusiasm was just fabulous to see. I mean every one of these guys had it. I've not seen that kind of energy since Kazan, and it was exciting, and I don't give a shit if it was real or chemical. I'm sure it was a little of both. But that's fine. I'd seen it thirty years earlier, a little of both. Whatever works. It gets them through the day. As long as the work's there. It only bothers me when the work suffers. Like in *1969*, the work suffered because of it, and I got injured because of it.

All the honey wagons and my trailer are way the hell down, hidden between the hills because we're shooting 360 degrees so we can't see anything but the gas station. While they're lighting the next shot, I go behind the gas station where nobody can see me, and I take a number one. I'm fairly cool at it, I got it down pretty good so I can pretend like I haven't done it.

I'm walking back to the set and I'm maybe fifty yards from the gas station, and there's a local standing there, and he says, "Señor! You just pissed on my country."

He walks up to me. He's got a Polaroid camera around his neck, and he shows me a picture.

He says, "You just pissed on Mexico."

"Yeah . . ."

He says, "In my country, when you piss on it, you could die."

He's got a Polaroid and it's me. And I don't know whether he saw me peeing or not, but he knew I was by myself standing over a bunch of burning tires, and I was looking down for a second. Outside the gas station is the local federale who's with us.

So I say, "Capitán!" That's the extent of my Spanish.

He walks over. He says, "Señor Bruce, problema?"

I say, "Him."

He says, "Qué?"

"He's got a Polaroid picture of me taking a piss."

The capitán looks at the guy and says, "How'd you get past the barricade, hombre?"

The man says, "I didn't see a barricade. I came up the long way and walked around from the back."

The capitán says, "You're trespassing, hombre. My watch says twelve minutes after three. In three minutes, it will be three fifteen. If I see you at three fifteen, I'm gonna put you under arrest."

The guys says, "It's a mile and a quarter down to town."

The capitán says, "Then you're gonna break a world record."

The man asks, "Where's your badge?"

The capitán, right out of fucking *Treasure of the Sierra Madre*, says, "I don't carry a badge. I don't need no badge."

I say, "You saw the movie, Bud. Now get moving."

Now, I'm as bad an ass as I've ever been. The cop is right there with me.

He says, "I won't take your camera, but I'll take the picture."

The man says, "No, the picture's mine. Furthermore, you're not a cop, you're a fucking extra in a movie."

The capitán says, "Well, if I'm a fucking extra in a movie," and pulls out a big fucking gun.

He fires three shots right at the guy's foot.

"How come they give me live ammunition? Now start walking."

The man says, "Okay, jefe. Why don't you take the picture *and* the camera? By the way, I think I just pissed my pants."

He was gone. But for thirty seconds, it was the most frightened I've ever been in my career.

I was reminded of that story when I was doing *All the Pretty Horses*, which I took for one reason, for one line that was said to me by Matt Damon.* In take after take, he was struggling with the emotion of the scene and wasn't quite getting there. He can be a wonderful actor when he wants to and he's shown it, movie after movie. His bravery and courage in *Geronimo* being the adjutant to Jason Patric are as good initial pioneering attempts by an actor as I've seen, his initial first-time-out instincts. That was his first big exposure role. People will tell you that it was *Good Will Hunting*, but *Geronimo* was two or three years before that. A really sensational attempt. Every choice is the right choice. He will endure as an actor a long, long time if he keeps making courageous choices. If he "Bourne Identities" himself out and gets to number eight or nine, then it's not going to be quite the same. But he's a courageous kid and I like him a great deal.

Matt Damon can bring it, and he's got game. His work was quite lovely in the movie. On this particular night, we did this scene where he's very upset, and he says, "I didn't do anything and I told my friend not to do anything. We didn't move a muscle. We didn't say anything, we didn't do anything."

So I say to him, "Do you really think it would have done any good?"

And this is the line that I did the movie for. He says, "No, sir. Probably not. But that still don't make it right."

That's why I did the movie.

One of the more frustrating things that actors have to deal with in movies—whether you work on inexpensive films or $100 million films—one of the most horrendous phrases an actor hears is "short ends." You get in a scene, and eventually the assistant cameraperson will throw a short-end reel in the camera and say, "Well, I've got 180 feet here. Let's try to use it up." You get in a close-up where you finally find what you want to do, and they run out of fuckin' film. Oh my God. I don't think I've ever been in a movie with a budget more than

---

*This movie, debuting in 2000, marked Dern's resurgence as an éminence grise. Directed by Billy Bob Thornton, from a novel by Cormac McCarthy, the movie starred Matt Damon, Penelope Cruz, and Henry Thomas, alongside Robert Patrick, Bruce Dern, and Sam Shepard.

$8 million. Oh no, *The Haunting*. $90 million I think that was. Except for that one. Oh, and *The 'burbs*. That was $20 million maybe. Oh, yeah, and *All the Pretty Horses*. That movie should have been an $8 million budget, but ended up costing $44 million. Billy Bob Thornton, who directed it, wanted to make it for $8 million.

When Kazan received his special Oscar a few years ago, three-quarters of the room did not stand up, including Billy Bob Thornton and my own daughter, Laura. I was extremely upset. I wasn't appalled, because I saw it coming, but I didn't like it. If you're going to give an honorary Oscar for a lifetime of work, and you're a member of an academy where your board of directors is elected by the populace of that academy, back it or get out of the academy.

The awards themselves are not a joke, but it shouldn't be a competition in the first place. The guts of the academy is George C. Scott. He's the only one that called it like he saw it. What Mr. Brando did when he finally chose to make a different stand was much more reprehensible to me than what George Scott did.* If you don't want it, pass. Don't send somebody up to make a speech about something you're not willing to make a speech about in the same forum. If you don't want it, you don't want it. But that was an F-you to not only the academy but to Francis Coppola. Why, I don't know. And then Brando turns around and goes to work for Coppola again on *Apocalypse Now*. That's his agenda. I never did know him. He was quite a distant actor. But that's his choice. I would not have the courage to do what George C. Scott did, but George C. Scott was right, because it's not a competition. Movies are teamwork. In front of the camera and behind the camera. You are only as good in front of the camera as your teammates are.

If you look at what Mr. Kazan was faced with—how do we know what choice we would have made under the same circumstances? We'd like to be able to say, yeah, we'd have told Darryl Zanuck to go fuck himself and we wouldn't have gone back to Washington. Well, we'd have been incarcerated immediately. That was the first thing. If

---

*While Scott turned down his Academy Award, Brando skipped the ceremony and sent an actress, Sacheen Littlefeather, to the podium to turn it down and decry the way Hollywood depicts Native Americans.

you're subpoenaed, you go. Kazan was subpoenaed. When they slap you with that piece of paper, you're not going to China on them and coming back to play against the Bears next Sunday. You're gone. You come back and you're going in front of the twelve in the box. There's no question about it. And that's just the way it works. Well, they did that to Mr. Kazan.*

He went to Mr. Zanuck and said, "What do I do?"

And Mr. Zanuck said, "You go back there and you answer the questions. I don't care what they ask you. You're under oath; you answer them honestly."

And Gadg said, "Well, I've been advised this and that and I feel that I don't want to do that."

Mr. Zanuck said, "Sir, may I remind you, you're a landed immigrant. You're a naturalized American citizen. You went to Ellis Island. You come from Istanbul. You're not a privileged citizen. And you're under contract to me at Twentieth Century Fox and you're preparing a movie called *Viva Zapata*. Now you go back and you answer their questions if you want to work here."

Now Gadg could have said F-you to Zanuck, and most people said that's what he should have done. He still would have to go back to Washington, or he'd have gone to Terminal Island or Lompoc (prison) because it would have been a federal offense. So he went back and they asked him the questions and he answered them.

And the questions were basically, were you at party A, were you at party B.

"Yes, I was."

"I'm going to read you a list of names. I want you to tell me the names that were at Party A. Ring Lardner Jr. Yes or no." And that's what he did. Now the people in the room that night at the Oscars, how many of the ones who didn't stand up know what the actual questions were and why he answered them? I don't think probably a third.

---

*Kazan, a committed liberal, and a former member of the Communist Party, was one of the few to "name names" in front of McCarthy's committee on Un-American Activities. Disillusioned with, and offended by, the Communist Party, he later said he felt he had done the right thing, and not just the safe thing, in naming names.

What were Kazan's choices? He hadn't done *On the Waterfront*. Hadn't done *East of Eden* or any of that. What would his fate have been had he not cooperated? He'd have gone down. I never talked to Gadg about this. When I became a member of the Actors Studio, I really wasn't aware of Kazan's political dealings.

So as far as that night at the Oscars, no one who stayed seated ever had an answer. They never bothered to go one way or another on it. They just went with the flow. That's what was disturbing about it. It wasn't an individual thing, it was a group thing. That was the danger of the whole blacklist. Joseph McCarthy was going with the flow. The flow was, get 'em out. Weed 'em out. McCarthy was a horror that should never have been allowed to emerge.

· 2 8 ·

Making a Monster

In 2001, I filmed *The Glass House*.* I didn't have much to do in it, but I thought I was good. I liked the director, Dan Sackheim. *Glass House* was the first feature he ever directed. He was good. I liked Leelee a great deal. When Leelee was twelve, she came to Hollywood. She's already a bit of a dame, but she's the whole package; sexy, sweet, funny, and incredibly bright. She's got a lot of principles. But she's out there. Has some ability though very little training as an actress. When Leelee was fourteen, she played Joan of Arc on television. After *Glass House*, she quit acting and went to college for four years. She's back now having a career.

Although I fell in the swimming pool on the set and broke some teeth, shooting *Glass House* was fun. I got to know Stellan Skarsgard. There was a scene in *Good Will Hunting* containing no dialogue where he and Matt Damon solve the math problem on the chalkboard

---

*A thriller starring Leelee Sobieski, Diane Lane, Stellan Skarsgard, and Bruce Dern.

together. They both sit down and look at the problem they've solved. Stellan puts his arm around Damon. It's not gay; it's not homosexual at all. He just puts his arm around him. You've got two guys that just won the Super Bowl. No dialogue. They did something no one else in the world can do. It wasn't just Matt Damon; they did it together. It's one of those sweet moments. I told Stellan that. He got a kick out of it. Those are the moments that I look forward to. I'll watch *Good Will Hunting* every time it's on TV.

Speaking of brilliant, I got a chance to work with Bob Dylan, who is one of the more extraordinary people that I've met in my life. I'd never met him and knew nothing about him except through history until I appeared in his movie, *Masked and Anonymous*.* We really hit it off well and had a nice time. I got to know him in the couple of days that I was around him. I liked him. I also liked Larry Charles. I got to meet Val Kilmer. I'd never met him. I got to meet John Goodman. Got to spend some time with Jeff Bridges who I hadn't seen since *Wild Bill*. He's always fun and a good actor. I like to work with him. I wasn't fond of the movie. I thought it missed a chance to be something other than what it was.

But I got to meet Miss Lange. I never worked with her, but I was on the set for ninety minutes when she was there and I spent maybe fifteen minutes speaking alone with her. It was worth every minute. She's a great dame. She's someone I would look forward to working with if I could. She's an independent thinker. I'd put her up there in women who can bring it. Top five. If I put a dream cast together, I'd put her in because she's interested in examination of self and people, the human fabric. Burstyn would be in there. I'd like to think Ann-Margret would be in there, but I don't know whether day to day she'd want to go through that. She has the ability. It's just where she is in her head, in her life. Would she want to dig that deep every day? I think

---

*Written by Bob Dylan with Larry Charles, who also directed it, this symbolic (or convoluted, depending on your point of view) movie about a singer in a country on the verge of a revolution managed to squeeze in all of the following entertaining performers: Bob Dylan, Jeff Bridges, Penelope Cruz, John Goodman, Jessica Lange, Luke Wilson, Angela Bassett, Bruce Dern, Ed Harris, Val Kilmer, Cheech Marin, Chris Penn, Giovanni Ribisi, Mickey Rourke, Christian Slater, and Fred Ward.

Miss Sally Field would do that. Miss Rowlands obviously would do that. I'd like to think Miss Hawn would do that. I've only met her once. I've always felt that she has potential way beyond what she's ever attempted. Miss Keaton would do it. I refer to them as Miss because I mean it. Not as a joke. It is a deference that I give to them because they've earned it in my eyes. Goldie Hawn is an actress who has earned respect and privilege. I want to see her spend the next decade daring to go beyond the level of work that she set up for herself and not rest where she's at. I want her to take another step into a gray area where I haven't seen her go except earlier in her career. I'd like to see Miss Bening do that. She's a good deal younger than us, but she's got potential.

Keaton will do her thing. You can always count on her to take risks. It's the risks. Those are the fun ones. My kid takes risks all the time. You see a lot of risks taken by the younger girls. Chloe Sevigny is a risk taker. Tripplehorn's a bit of a risk taker. Grace Zabriskie is certainly a risk taker. It's a risk just to show up to work for David Lynch, because he will abuse you. He will put you through the ringer. He will ask you to do things that no other director that lives will ask you to do, thinking it's normal or okay.

Burt Reynolds is a dear friend of mine. We've had a mutual understanding from almost fifty years ago. We never really cemented our friendship, though, until we did a movie for the Hallmark Channel, *Hard Ground*.* It was magical. Burt and I were the two stars of this western set in 1906, where two old-time bad guys who'd had a long friendship have to go back and do their bad-guy thing together one more time to bring in the real bad guys. We're on horseback the whole time. Mr. Reynolds can ride. I fell off my horse and broke my collarbone and seven ribs. Got up like a schmuck, did the close-up, and then worked all afternoon. And Mr. Reynolds just rides on.

---

*A western with the two leads tracking down an evil, killing desperado. Standard Hallmark Channel fare. Or not.

He asked, "Are you going to have an X-ray?"

I said, "Not until lunch. I'm certainly not going to let you have the only close-up out of this scene."

The producers asked Burt, "Will you work all afternoon?"

He said, "Yeah."

They said, "We're going to have to invent some stuff for you to do with the other people this afternoon because we can't ask Bruce to work."

He said, "What do you mean you can't ask him to work? He'll be back by the time lunch is over."

They said, "No, we think it's going to be broken."

He said, "So what? He plays hurt."

They said, "Well, he didn't play football."

And Burt said, "He did the triathlon. Does that give you any idea how sick the fuckin' guy is? He'll play hurt, trust me."

I was back at two. They never taped my ribs. They were just broken. Taping them doesn't do any good. The doctor set my collarbone. It hurt. I finished filming that movie on the next Thursday.

Saturday I arrived in Orlando to do *Monster*,* and, on my first day, they put me on a motorcycle, because I'm a motorcycle guy in the film.

I went to Patty Jenkins and Charlize and said, "Hey guys, when I'm done with this shot, I've got to go to the nurse to have my physical for the movie."

I was completely purple everywhere. The way I read the script there's no fucking way I can ride in on a motorcycle.

So I said, "Let me tell you what I'm not going to do. I'm not going to start the bike because the vibrations will make me pass out."

Charlize goes, "That's cool."

So we shoot the scene. Charlize has seen it all. She's a great dame, and she gave a performance we may never see the likes of again.

---

*Written and directed by Patty Jenkins, and based on a true story. Charlize Theron plays serial killer Aileen Wuornos, and Christina Ricci her lover. Dern is possibly the only sympathetic character in the movie, for a change. Theron won the Academy Award for her portrayal of, or really her transformation into, Wuornos.

So we're finishing the scene and she says, "Hey, Thomas . . ." That's the name of my character.

And the broken collarbone hurts like hell. Charlize's character says, "So take care of yourself and thanks for what you did for me."

I say, "Hey, it's cool."

She goes, "Yeah, man, it's cool," and then she punches me in the fucking shoulder.

Patty says, "Cut, that's it. That was all. Bruce, now you go get your exam and come back at four and we'll start with the coverage."

I look at Charlize, and she looks at me. Completely oblivious to what she did. Goes on doing her thing.

I say to Patty, "I'll let it go today. But did you see that?"

Patty says, "Oh yeah. I get that every day."

I say, "That's Aileen Wuornos, right? No wonder they fried her ass."

Patty Jenkins was just flying around all day long, but I never saw anything in her nose.

I said, "Hey, Babe. I'm not into it. I did all the movies about it. I was surrounded by people that were into it. I still don't know the difference between cocaine and flour. When people are sniffing, I don't know what they're doing. I never see you do that. So what are you on?"

And she said, "I drink nineteen lattes a day, and I put three table-spoons of sugar in each one. I sleep three hours a night during shooting, and then afterwards, I'm a wreck."

Patty was an inline skater and a pretty well-known one before she got hurt about a year before *Monster*. A car ran over her in Griffith Park. She's quite a good-looking girl. She's got hair way down to her waist. Unbelievably bright. She talked real fast all the time. You just can't keep up with her.

Before I got the role, she said, "Bruce, you've got to be in my movie because Kazan's my idol and you worked with Kazan."

I said, "Then why are you so interested in Tom Waits?"

She said, "It wasn't me. It wasn't Charlize. Somebody else wanted Tom Waits because he was going to do all the music and sing a song for the movie."

I said, "You're worried about a song for *Monster*? Why don't you just hire Lurch and let him sing a song called "Monster." What the hell do you need Tom Waits for? I mean, he's a good actor but he was in *Ironweed*, babe. That's 108 years ago. Don't let me lose the part. I can help your movie."

And I feel I did end up helping the movie.

After I finished *Monster*, somebody asked me, "How did you get along with Charlize?"

I never saw Charlize. I never met her on the set. I met her later when we came back and started promoting the movie. The Charlize I met on the set was one angry dame in complete control of herself as an actress. Complete control. Almost so one would think she had been acting and studying acting for thirty-five or forty years. She was that far ahead of the game and with what she wanted to do with that role. She had a game plan and Patty had a game plan that was so far ahead of what I'd ever seen for that age that I thought I was working with Geraldine Page or Kim Stanley or Uta Hagen. It was that extraordinary.

As the movie got closer to the end of when I worked, it faded a little bit because they were getting tired. They were getting stressed and they were getting pushed and squeezed to do it faster. To print less. But, as I look back on *Monster*, the most remarkable thing about the work of those two gals—and I will never put one ahead of the other, I can't push Charlize above Patty or Patty above Charlize, one made a map and the other followed it, one gave a performance and the other one fed it—is the fact that they were two people that met each other at the perfect second in each other's lives for the desperate need to do something as artists, as people, and as women crying out to get something said. They knew it was necessary for them to do the movie. I don't think either one had a dream it would be successful. I just knew they had to make the movie.

I don't see many movies at the theater. I have trouble going out to see a movie. Just finding a place to park. That's the first thing. I went and saw *Monster*. I went the day after Christmas when it opened at the little Laemmle Theatre on Sunset Boulevard in Hollywood. I came out, and they had towed my fucking car, so that pissed me off. But I was pleased because I went in at five in the afternoon, and it was packed. At the Laemmle, there's really no place to park because I don't like underground parking because, in the L.A. earthquake in 1994, I had friends whose cars were demolished in Santa Monica in a parking structure up by the church at Nineteenth Street. Santa Monica got whacked big-time in that earthquake, and their cars were pancaked. So I always thought, God, I don't want to be in an underground parking garage if an earthquake comes. And that's why I don't ride the metro rail because it goes underground. I mean there's no alternative, you can't get out. I love that people ride it, and I think it's a good thing to have it. But why can't it be a monorail? Why can't it be aboveground? Isn't it bad enough to walk on Hollywood Boulevard much less ride underneath it in a subway car? So after the movie, I had to go way the hell down on West Larson to get the car and it cost me $280. That was a drag.

· 29 ·

Going Right for the Jugular

We are our moments. And the inspired ones have those moments. I got a lot of them. Robards had a lot of them. Jack's got a lot of them. Brando's got one fabulous moment in a terrible movie called *The Chase*. He plays a sheriff and he's chasing Redford. Angie Dickinson plays Brando's wife. He's sitting in the sheriff's office. She's sitting across from him. They're alone. He's overweight in this movie. I think it was made in '66. It's the beginning of the scene. He's thinking of how to catch this rich man's son, Redford. He needs his wife's attention and he's not getting it. He just wants to hold her hand. He's not even looking at her. He's looking out. He reaches out and she doesn't take his hand right away. He just snaps his fingers. She takes his hand. I mean, it's Brando. I never met the guy, but goddammit, I don't know why I never met him. Circumstances.

After Jack did *Missouri Breaks** with Brando, we were in the hey-day of our popularity with each other. He called me up and he said, "Better go see it. I ain't had a call yet. You better go see it. Pretty good fuckin' work."

"I'll see it when it comes to Malibu, if it comes to Malibu." I go to see it. Jack pulls up in his limo at my house. The guy drives himself in his own limo, and wears a chauffeur's cap sometimes. It's either the limo or this grim little fucking yellow Volkswagen that's so fucking horrible-looking. Oh my God.

Anyway, on the way out to my house in the limo, he drives over the yellow line coming out of the tunnel through Malibu Canyon. He gets a ticket and says, "Christ, these fucking guys, don't they know who I am? So, what did you think?"

I said, "Well, the first thing I think is the Lakers didn't cover last night. They're playing Walton and they're supposed to cover by seven fucking points."

He said, "We're not here to talk about this shit. We're here to talk about me and Brando."

I said, "As far as you and Bud, you didn't cover either."

He said, "Really?"

I said, "Harry Dean's got the best line in the movie. What else do you want?"

He said, "It's just one fucking line. All you can do is sit in the theater for two hours and twenty minutes and come out and tell me some ignorant asshole from the American Boys' Chorus comes up with a line 'I shot him through the brainpan' and that's all you got from that?"

I said, "No, that and the fact you obviously fucked the Lloyd girl who will never do another movie. What do you want from me?"

And he said, "The work, asshole. I want the work."

I said, "What work? It's a western. Arthur Penn. He directed two other westerns."

Jack said, "Actually he only directed one other western. *Little Big Man.*"

---

*Considering this film was the only onscreen collaboration between the two titans, audiences and critics were completely underwhelmed.

I said, "No, he directed two other westerns. I'm not going to go on until you tell me what the other western was."

He said, "He never directed another western."

I said, "Yes, he did."

The conversation basically boiled down to the fact that Arthur Penn directed a movie with Paul Newman called *The Left-Handed Gun*, which was about Billy the Kid. The little guy who follows Billy the Kid around, the part that little Bob Dylan played in *Pat Garrett and Billy the Kid* was played by Hurd Hatfield, who was also in *The Picture of Dorian Gray*.

So Jack said, "Well, what about it?"

I said, "You never pressed the whole game. You rebounded poorly. And when you had a chance to fast break on him, you never did it. So, I'd give the score about 91 to 77."

He said, "What are you talking about fucking 91 to 77? Give me a fucking break. The guy's in the bathtub. What the fuck could he do?"

I said, "What do you mean he's in the bathtub?"

He said, "He's in the bathtub. He could have anything under the water. He could have a gun. He could have anything else."

I said, "You're coming in this scene. Who's hunting who in the movie? Who's got the drop in this scene?"

He said, "He's a hired gunman. The first day I come to work he's got all this Irish bullshit going on. How do I know where that comes from? I go to a set in Montana, I got one friend, Harry Dean, they give one fucking line to, and this asshole's telling me he steals the fucking movie. You're telling me I'm no fucking good in a movie I lose by fourteen fucking points. Well, how's about I tell you I got a million fucking bucks for the movie and you're working on a fucking TV show. So how about that fourteen points, Mister Glencoe asshole. How would you have done the fucking scene, Mr. Senile at thirty-nine years old?"

I said, "Well, I come to the door. And I knock on the wall before I even let them know who's out there. Instead, you just walked right in. You didn't knock."

Jack said, "Why tip your hand? Why let them know who it is?"

"Maybe it's his mom. Maybe it's the Ghost of Christmas Past. He's going to play games with you, play games with him. He knows who the fuck it is. And how does he know what kind of game you bring in with you? He's got an Irish accent. Maybe you've got an Irish accent. Maybe you come up and say, you know, 'Mister Elijah, can I bring you a little hot water, sir?' Maybe, your objective . . ."

Jack said, "Oh, yeah, here we go, it's fucking Actors Studio horse-shit . You're going to give me all this fucking shit about that? What am I, an academic actor? Or am I somebody who knows how to fucking act without ever having been in the schoolroom?"

"Well, you don't have to do a schoolroom spot. It has to do with just moment-to-moment behavior."

"Oh, really. Now we're going to get the old Mr. twenty-one percent moment-to-moment behavior. "

I said, "You're pursuing him. What are you really after in the scene?"

He said, "I'm trying to get the drop on him."

I said "No. You're not after that. What are you really after in the scene?"

He said, "I really am after trying to get the drop on him."

I said, "No, you're after Jack Nicholson beating Marlon Brando in front of the cinematic world. That's what you're really after. So do that. Bury him."

Jack stopped, looked up, and said "Fucking Dernser. Going right for the jugular."

"Well, that's what it is."

He said, "What you tried to do to me on *Marvin Gardens* every fucking day, you fucking asshole."

"No no, I was pulling for you."

"You were never pulling for me. I doubted your every fucking move because that's what the character did."

And I said, "Were we good together?"

He reached across the table, grabbed my hands, and said, "When we wanted to be we were bigger than U.S. Steel."

Anyway, we talked about the scene and how we could do things. Every time we had a conversation about acting it was the most honest conversation I've ever had with anybody. I mean, he just gets it. To work with Jack is as exciting as it gets for me because his level of intellect, his ability, and his conceptual ideas are really terrific.

I was never lucky enough to work with Brando. I knew George Scott. I was lucky enough to work with Redford.

I regret the fact I haven't been able to work with Clint since Clint's been way up there. I was pleased I got to work with Edward Norton. But Sean Penn I've never worked with. I've never worked with Tim Robbins. I've never met them. Maybe they don't even know who I am. I hope they do. In the next few years I would like to work with those people. I've never worked with my own kid, for Christ's sake.

A critic went after Laura in *We Don't Live Here Anymore*, because the critic said she shouldn't be playing roles like that. "It's hard to accept Laura Dern as the wife of an academic and a mother. And look at her in the role in *Citizen Ruth*. I mean, it just doesn't make sense that she should be thought of for both roles." Oh, get fucked. Give me a break. It's like somebody once said about me: "*Silent Running* could have been a great film except for the crucial miscasting of Bruce Dern in the film's only role." How do you get over that? What do they want from me? "Loved *Gatsby*, hated Bruce Dern. Why can't they get somebody other than some psycho from the south to play Tom Buchanan? Somebody who tortures rats?" They have no idea what they're talking about. I thought I was rather well-cast in *Gatsby* if they want to know the truth.

The criteria for what makes a critic is far less severe today than it was years ago. I mean, Richard Schickel is now a historian. Robert Osborne is a TV star. Arthur Knight, Vincent Canby, are gone. Molly Haskell and her husband, Andrew Sarris, are still out there. Judith Crist, Miss Kael, the literary side and the film industry miss that viewpoint. Movie critics are not movie fans anymore. They're fans of being clever and being read and being popular, and particularly being quoted.

I like Roger Ebert. Roger is truly a one-of-a-kinder. He is an original champion of the small film. He, by himself, discovered *Silent Running* and fought for its right. He single-handedly made *Monster* what it was and helped Charlize enormously. But not because anyone twisted his arm; he loved the movie and put it over the top when Manohla

Dargis buried it. Her review on Christmas Day was the single most harshly negative review I've read in all the years I've been in the business. I mean, she buried Charlize. Miss Dargis should have checked her critical legitimacy before she thought she was omnipotent.

I've known during the making of a lot of movies that I had to raise the bar for the other actors and I enjoy the position much more than I did when I was the star of a movie like *Tattoo* or *Middle Age Crazy* where I had to pull the movie literally by myself. I'm not Kobe-izing here, I'm just telling you that it was up to me because I was in every shot of every scene. Nowadays when I'm hired, I feel one of my jobs is to help raise the bar, not just in front of the camera but on the set. The days I work, I'm on the set, not in my dressing room, so that the professional work ethic of everybody is up to a standard that I don't see enough on the sets today, not like I did thirty years ago. I see a different kind of attitude. I see cell phones everywhere. I see video cameras everywhere. I see guys sitting half a block away looking at the scene on a monitor. I'm talking about directors and producers. Nobody's right at the set watching. There's a camaraderie and a teamwork and a sense of family that has expanded way away from the heart of the set. There's a heartbeat that's not there anymore. That's one of my contributions. The second is to encourage the other actors.

On *Believe in Me*, Jeffrey Donovan came up to me after the second day of shooting. When we had done the master, then afterward we covered his close-up, and I stayed and did the scene off camera the same way I did it on the three or four takes we did of the master. He put his arm around me and thanked me. I was stunned.

He said, "Why do you seem so surprised?"

I said, "Why would you thank me?"

"Because I've never seen that before."

"What do you mean you've never seen that before? That's my job."

"No, that's not your job. Nobody ever does that."

"Are you kidding me? Where the fuck have you been?"

"Where have *you* been? All my career I've looked for people to do stuff like that."

"But when you sign your contract that's part of what you do."

"Not where I've worked. I've done a TV series and I've been in five movies and the other actor just goes home after he does his close-up."

That shocks me. It's such a lack of respect. A lack of history. A lack of understanding. A lack of caring. They don't give a shit.

I'm now being given unbridled emeritus status on movie sets, and I don't deserve it. I don't make a movie a better movie just because I'm in it, for Christ's sake. And if I do, it's a fucking shame. It's a shame that Bruce Dern makes a movie better. I'm a good actor. I'm not a great actor. But I can make a difference. And in those movies I made a difference. I raised the bar. But it shouldn't have to be that way. I mean, Jon Voight raises the bar. But I'm hoping it's because I'm seventy. I'm not hoping it's because I'm more gifted than the next one.

I don't know how I got this new role in *Big Love*. It's unusual subject matter to put on weekly TV in that it deals with the Mormons and polygamy. The producers called me in, and I started shooting the pilot four days later. I didn't want to do it. They talked me into it.

I said, "I don't know that I'll be good in a small format. It's a box. And my greatest fear is I'm free in people's living rooms. I never wanted to be that."

They said, "Yeah, but it's only for twelve weeks and then you've got forty weeks to go out and do movies and we want you to do that, encourage that, because that's what we need."

I said, "I've got a couple of things coming out but they were made back in the eighteenth century."

One of the tougher things you see as you get older in this business is the dropoff of actresses once they turn forty-five years old. It's not only sad and tragic, but it's shocking. There are just no roles for them. One nice thing about *Big Love* is that you see some older girls getting a chance to work. What's nice about movies for television is that girls get wonderful parts in them. You find actresses working who would never be working in films. Stockard Channing has a career. Christine Lahti has a career. The girls in my generation who are in their sixties would not have careers now if it were not for movies for television. I mean, Ann-Margret's always going to have a career. Miss Ladd will always have a career. Miss Burstyn will always have a career. Miss Rowlands has a career. Cloris has a career. The ones who never quite became full blown movie stars or Oscar nominees don't get that opportunity.

I don't have any regrets. I miss that Jack hasn't directed again and that I haven't been directed by Jack again. That I haven't worked with Jack again. That I never worked for Robert Altman. I've missed that a great deal in my career.

I never worked on a movie I didn't want to do. I did a couple of grim movies. *The Incredible Two-Headed Transplant*, that was a grim movie. *The Cycle Savages* was a grim movie. No money, no budget, no role, no script.

Am I a bona fide movie star? No. But I have starred in enough movies in the last thirty years that I'm bona fide in terms of the movies that I've starred in or that I've been one of the stars that are among the collection of movies that decade after decade get brought to the forefront when people talk about what the important movies are. So, I'm not Clint, I'm not Jack, I'm not Redford, I'm not Beatty. But I'm in with a bunch of guys and girls whose movies go on and on.

A lot of the guys I started with are out selling their movies now, partly because they're producing or directing them, and they have investments in them financially. They're not just actors. So they have a lot more on the line than they did originally. They have a greater responsibility. They have ownership.

It's like when Jack won the Oscar for *Cuckoo's Nest*, and I talked to him on the telephone the next day.

I said, "Well, you know, you're one for four." He didn't win for *Five Easy Pieces*, *Last Detail*, or *Chinatown*. "One for four doesn't get you in the Hall. That's .250."

And Jack said, "No Hall of Fame, but I got gross now."

Not being wanted as an actor scares me. The phone not ringing scares me. I'm not scared of not being remembered. I used to be scared of that until about five years ago. Laura's fantastic at reminding me of what I've done. She's my greatest fan. We'll just be talking and she'll look out the window and say, "Daddy, remember that scene where you put your hand on your chin when you looked out the window?"

It's so great because it'll be a total non sequitur to the day and she'll remember an image.

Laura came to me one day and said, "Daddy, you got the most wonderful compliment." A friend of hers who worked with me said that he'd been excited to go to work every day because he thought he was going to get to be in a scene where he might do something he'd never done before or be challenged to come up with something. He said, "Every day we're challenged because of the way he works. We have to dance along to hang in there." Well, that brought tears to my eyes. I really liked that. I thought that was neat. And that's what I try to do.

I would say that of the guys that are fifty-eight to seventy, which is my twelve-year age group, we've left some pretty incredible work out there and we've got a lot of incredible work yet to do. We're not retiring. What, I'm going to retire before Jimmy fucking Caan? Do you think he's going to quit before Jack? Do you think we're quitting? It's twenty-nine thousand dollars a seat to sit on the floor at the Lakers game. Jack's still going to have to work. If he wants to kick Shaq's ass, he's going to have to work at least a day to make fifty-eight thousand dollars.

Laura's husband, Ben Harper, and I went to a basketball game a couple years ago. Portland was playing the Lakers in the playoffs. And Ben booed Portland's Rasheed Wallace.

I said, "You know, I've never booed anyone in my life, and I never will."

He said, "Why is that?"

I said, "Because they're doing something I can't do."

And he said, "Good point." He's never booed anyone since.

I would like audiences to remember that I had game. Simply said, that's really it. I'm not here to make a statement. But while I'm here, I'd like to be allowed to do my thing. Until I go out, I would like to be able to go on doing what I do at the highest level. That, for me, would be to continue to star or costar in films or in plays on Broadway that are meaningful.

At some point, I'll just stop. But I'm not stopping until it's time, and I'm going for one hundred.

Acknowledgments

Without these acknowledged people and many who I'm sure I left out, this book simply would not exist.

Ashley Reed, Wendy Guerrero, and Mace Beckson.

Vera Hepworth, Charles Fulfer, Lennox, Joe Bradley, Neale Stearns, Alan Sex, Micky Fink, Buck Weber, John Madigan, Dick Segil, Jean Dern Segil, Rick Segil, Mr. Peterson (New Trier), Tom Cuniff, Pete Franzen, Jim McFadzen, Jerry Sprague, Gordon Phillips, Morgan Smedley, Charlie Dierkop, Lyle Kessler, Irv Kaye, Frank Mann, Salome Jens, Claire Griswald Pollack, Mark Rydell, John Frankenheimer, Doug Trumbull, Jack Nicholson, Harry Gittes, Bob Redford, Bob Rafelson, Steve Blauner, Tim Zinnemann, Dr. Beaty Ramsey, John Wayne, Mike Cimino, Jo Ann Corelli, David Tringham, Annette Tringham, Hambleton Hall, Buffy Birretella, Mia Farrow, Jane Fonda, Ben Harper, Marty Krofft, Sid Krofft, Mollie Mulligan, Richard

Mulligan, Ryan O'Connor, Nina Millin, Terry LaPina, Fred Specktor, Mick Sullivan, Stan Rosenfield, Edith Van Cleve, Elia Kazan, Lee Strasberg, Lee Remick, Jason Miller, Jason Patric, James Foley, Bill Robinson, Mike Gruskoff, Mark Hess, Mike Merrick, Ann-Margret, Gary Liddiard, Linda Geirerasich, Hal Ashby, David Picker, Mike Fenton, Lynn Stalmaster, Bob Rosen, Jerry Hellman, Nancy Ellison, Lee Rose, Tony Emerzian, Uncle John Nay, Burt Reynolds, Mr. Cardinal himself, Maud Adams, David Schneider, Annie Merrick, Michael Ritchie, Syd Pollack, Adam Roarke, Stacy Keach, Joseph Levine, Monte Diamond, Anthony Luchente, Chris Fryer, Bob Crane, Bob Crane's stepdaughter Meagan Hufnail, Dr. Daryl, Miss Diane, Sergei, Isis, Wolfy, Badger, Romeo & Gigilo, Papas, Barry Beckett, Jack Garfein, Juan Nayola, Carmen Pineda, John Cocks, Jay Cocks, Grant Wilkins, The Joker, Donna Hanley, David Savitski, Mojo, Joe Douglas, Tom Sturak, Bob Drake, Bob and Lyn Carman, The Nun, Walter Hill, Keith Larsen, Bobbi Jo Dummitt, Ronald P. Schneider, Ara Keshishian, Johnathan Ruiz, Lee Brillstein, Billy Graham, Lori K., Molly Becket, Jim Sparkman, Michel Rounet, Sherman Yellen, June Scott, Betty Graham, Alan Pfeiffer, Steve Nahigian, Rudi (Oliver Peoples), Bellina Logan, Charlene Ambrose, Sandy Simon, Carlos, Stuart Rosenberg, Benji Rosenberg, Bill Fraker, Conrad Hall, Jim Glennon, Martha Henderson, Randy Sugarman, Phil Kurschner, Jim Hitzman, Alan Chain, Ronnie Leif, Jere Hinshaw, Sean Dugan, Ellen Burstyn, Bette Davis, Barbara Stanwyck, James Whitmore, Teresa Wright, Bert Schneider, Grandma Mary, Jack & Lillian Abels, Tom Gries, Joe Miller, Judge Goodrich, Mary Goodrich, and Archibald MacLeish.

B. D.

Beyond the pages of any book there are a number of people without whose help and expertise many a manuscript would remain so much scrap paper. We would like to thank a few of those people who helped make this book a reality. First and foremost, thanks go to our editor, Eric Nelson, for all his hard work. Eric brought vision, enthusiasm, and a keen blue pencil. Thanks also to senior production editor John

Simko, senior editorial assistant Connie Santisteban, copy editor Alexa Selph, proofreader Ronnie Ambrose, media maven Mike Onorato, and everyone else at John Wiley & Sons, Inc., who had a hand in this book.

Our thanks go, too, to writer/editor, Pat McGilligan, who led us to Eric in the first place, and writer/actor, Joe Coyle, who started us down the road. For transcribing more tape than any one person should ever have to, Grace Kono-Wells at Keystrokes in Santa Monica gets our unending devotion, and to Trish Glick at the Copying Emporium in New Windsor, New York, our thanks for being both fast and perfect. Long-standing thanks to editor, John Rezek, who kept us solvent for years and taught us everything we know about interview technique, and to our one and only agent, Henry Morrison, for his sound advice and perseverance. To MaryEllen Strange and Susan Morettini at Henry Morrison, Inc., kudos for all the follow-up and for answering a million questions.

This book's genesis, development, and growth took place at the magnificent Ritz-Carlton Huntington Hotel and Spa in Pasadena, and we offer sincere appreciation to everyone there and to Kim Kessler, Director of Public Relations. An Oscar goes to the mayor of Colbath, Istvan Toth, for his fine Dern film clip package, and an Emmy goes to Mara Mikialian at HBO for helping with *Big Love* matters.

Personal thanks go to Desly Movius Fryer for always knowing what's important. Undying gratitude goes to Dr. Robert Dillon and Dr. Eugene Schreiner for their insight, intelligence, and skill, and for making this book possible in their own way.

To Leslie Bertram Crane for unending love and support, and Anne and Charles Sloan, *la última madre y padre*.

For their unconditional support, extra treats to Chloe, PJ, and Skunk.

And lastly, we'd like to thank Mr. Bruce Dern. We've been saying this since we first met in 1972, but we think this time you've really won the car.

C. F. and R. C.

Index